R

KIRKUS Reviews, August 2014:

Russell makes no claim to being a disinterested observer, and both his enthusiasm for working with his students and his frustration with the limitations of the public school system are evident as the driving forces of the book

Russell draws on his years teaching high school math, surveys of his students and colleagues, and news coverage of trends in education to indict many of the policies and assumptions that govern today's schools. He lays out what he sees as the most pressing challenges—lack of parental support, an incentive structure that rewards minimal student effort, the pressure of bureaucratic mandates, etc.

Russell uses his classroom experience and reasonable logic to explain why students benefit from being allowed to fail, or how problematic curriculum requirements demand that teachers fit 115 minutes of instruction into a 70-minute class.

An impassioned look at the shortcomings of public education, from the perspective of an inner-city high school teacher.

CLARION Reviews, July 2014:

"There is a crisis in public education in the United States. It's a familiar story—one that's in the news every day—and everyone has an opinion about how to fix it. Few news items, however, examine the crisis from the teacher's perspective. D. A. Russell does just that in this scathing critique of a particularly problematic part of the US public school system: urban high schools.

Russell offers a unique perspective as an urban high school teacher who has witnessed the rise of the inclusion classroom, content codification via Common Core standards, and the proliferation of standardized tests. In Lifting the Curtain: The disgrace we call urban high school education, the longtime math teacher calls on politicians and the media to stop blaming teachers for our educational woes and instead look at the inherent flaws in the system.

In Lifting the Curtain, Russell lends a passionate voice to the current conversation about the fate of our schools. It's sure to spark spirited debate and discussion among teachers, parents, and principals."

Women on Writing's Margo Dill wants to shout it from the mountain tops! -- 5 out of 5. Wow-WomenOnWriting.com, September 2014:

What's refreshing about *Lifting the Curtain* is Mr. Russell is an urban high school teacher. He is in the middle of the problem, and he has researched it. Even better, he's not just a whistle blower. In the first 2/3 of the book, Russell explains why he writes about this issue as well as a survey he created for urban educators and high school students (and the results) and then eight systemic failures in the schools. The last third of the book is the solutions--there's not just one as he points out. It's not JUST the teachers, or ONLY parents, or THE administrators.

His passion for getting to the root of the problem and helping teenagers is all over these pages. One of his main points is right now, this is what is going on in our schools, and we are failing our kids. Shouldn't we shake things up a bit, change things around, to reach more teens and bring them success? This book makes me want to shout from the mountaintop... Yes!

If you believe in education and want to help urban students succeed, *Lifting the Curtain* is a book for you to check out. All educators would benefit from reading it, regardless of where or whom they teach. Mr. Russell is brave to tackle this emotional and tough topic, and he does so with grace and passion.

Madeline Sharples, nationally acclaimed author of the exceptional book *Leaving the Hall Light On* -- 5 out of 5.

The recent convictions of high school teachers and administrators who changed students' test scores drew me to D.A. Russell's book, *Lifting the Current: the disgrace we call urban high school education*. And as I got into the book I found that changing test scores is just the tip of the iceberg. All involved – students, teachers/administrators, and parents cheat – just so the students will pass and the schools will continue to receive the funding they need to stay alive.

It is deplorable. And, according to Russell, it is easily solvable. He presents the symptoms, the causes, and the ways to solve our urban high school problems in his eye-opening book.

Russell, a long time high school math teacher, would not give in to 1) students requests for do-overs if they failed, 2) parents who believe education is only the teachers job and threaten law suits if they don't live up to their expectations, and 3) busy-work assignments from unqualified and inept bureaucrats. He holds the theory that if we let a student fail, that student will actually be inspired to get help and learn and eventually become more successful in the long run.

These kinds of problems in education did not exist twenty years ago. In those days students didn't copy homework from their buddies or be proud of their failing grades. Now they can get away with it. Parents will complain, teachers will cave, and they'll get a so-called passing that is as low as 20 to 29 percent anyway.

What bothers me the most is how these failing students will turn out as adults. How can people become our future leaders, business and technology experts, soldiers, police, and fire fighters? How will they ever be able to run anything or save anybody? As Russell says: "None of us saw the long-term negative impact of programs centered on the great-sounding, but completely destructive concept that a child can not be allowed to fail. We have ended up creating a culture of failure, where failure is expected, and failure is accepted. We fell into the circular logic trap of thinking today's children were too dumb to learn as we did, so we dumb down their education, so the children become dumb."

Lifting the Curtain (2d Edition)

The disgrace we call urban high school education

D. A. Russell

Illustrations by Jessica Fitzpatrick

Web: LiftingTheCurtain.com

Blog: LiftingTheCurtainOnEducation.wordpress.com

Huffington Post

Lifting the Curtain (2nd Edition)

Copyright © 2014 by D. A. Russell

All rights reserved. No part of this book may be used or reproduced by any means, graphic, electronic, or mechanical, including photocopying, recording, taping, or by any information storage and retrieval system without the written permission of the author, except in the case of brief quotation embedded in critical articles and reviews.

ISBN: 9781506015989   *(softcover)*
ISBN: 8-0-692-36394-2   *(self)*

Images used in the cover design were licensed from iStockPhoto.com
Help with cover design and editing by Emily A. Russell

Jim —

Please check out page 97! Thank you so much for believing in our school children, & for such an outstanding passage!

Don

*To all the great teachers I have been honored
to know, and to all the students who have been
such a joy to me*

About the Illustrator

Jess Fitzpatrick is a wonderful and talented art student studying graphic design at a Massachusetts vocational school. What better way could there be to illustrate all the promise that is hidden in today's educational system than to showcase a child who I am confident will be one of tomorrow's successful artists.

These illustrations were done when Jess was in 10th grade, and already show a remarkable ability to capture the essence of an idea. Somehow, she put up with my crude stick-figure sketches, and turned them into artwork that captured the heart of the message I was trying to convey. She is already a solid professional – even when having to work with a feisty math curmudgeon!

Before
My original artistic genius,
reminiscent of early Picasso

After
Some minor touch-ups and
trivial improvements by Jess

Great job, class! Billy's been absent for a couple days again, but his chair gets another "A" for the week. His parents think he might be at a Red Sox game this time.

Should you wish to employ her considerable talents, please shoot me an email at illustrator@LiftingTheCurtain.com. I will pass on your inquiries to Jess and her father.

About the author

D. A. Russell has spent the last ten years as a math teacher in one of the urban high schools that is the subject of *Lifting the Curtain*. He is an honors graduate of Dartmouth College, and has his master's degree from Simon School, where he was valedictorian of his class. Russell is a Vietnam veteran decorated for valor. He has two children that he treasures, and four grandchildren. His son is a police officer who served in the US Army in Afghanistan, earning a Bronze Star for valor. His daughter is a lawyer and his most passionate fan and honorary literary agent.

Russell has a passion for children that dominates his life. He has taught and coached children for decades. Few things are more important in Russell's view than to cherish the children who are our real treasures in this world.

Russell is a contributor for education matters to the Huffington Post, and runs a personal blog at: LiftingTheCurtainOnEducation.wordpress.com dedicated to letting teacher voices be heard in the *real* problems with education.

Website: LiftingTheCurtain.com
Blog: LiftingTheCurtainOnEducation.Wordpress.com

Foreword
By: M. Shannon Hernandez, M.Ed

Teachers across this nation have had enough. They are tired of remaining silent about the testing, the "reform", and the destructive practices forced upon them which are hurting our nation's youth. In fact, more and more teachers are using their voices and speaking out to fight for our public education system, and above all, bucking a system that has deprived our students of an education they not only deserve, but one which is engaging and authentic.

D. A. Russell has brought to light one of the most well-rounded and comprehensive books which highlights the crisis in U.S. public education. *Lifting the Curtain: The Disgrace We Call Urban High School Education* is not only the result of years of research, surveys, and data from students and teachers—it is the impassioned voice of an inner-city high school math teacher who had the courage to write a book that tells the truth about what is *really* happening in urban schools.

Through surveys, we hear the voices of students: *The worst thing about my education at this school is the class sizes*, and *The worst thing about education at my school is the limited availability of classes*. We also hear the voices of teachers: *On average, teachers receive merely 1.7 written emails or letters per year with positive comments from parents, only 4% of parents of struggling students attend parent-teacher nights*, and *32% of the instructional time allotted to teachers is spent on tasks that do not contribute to a student's education in a meaningful way*.

If there is just one thing the reader will take away from this book, it is this: If we are to find REAL solutions to the problems in education, then we must focus on the REAL issues.

What is refreshing about this book is that it reports on the failures and problems public schools are facing and also includes proposed solutions. These solutions are insightful, not only because they are practical solutions from teachers who are in the trenches of public education, fighting day in and day out for their students, but they address the plethora of issues many don't want to put in the public spotlight.

One of the biggest issues that must be addressed is the trust and integrity issues with which schools are managed and teachers are evaluated. A school can only be successful if its leadership is strong, fair, and compassionate. Too many principals have been assigned to schools across this nation without adequate management experience. When leadership doesn't have the experience to back the decisions they are making—decisions which affect the faculty, students, and parents—education continues to deteriorate. When teacher evaluations are based heavily on principal feedback, discounting peer feedback, student feedback, and parent feedback—evaluations are skewed. Quite simply, if the administration "likes" you as a person, you pass with flying colors. But if you are deemed as too vocal or too "out of the box" in your instructional techniques, the evaluations reflect that disgust.

As a public school teacher of 15 years, a professor, consultant, author, and student-centered education activist, I've seen, time and time again, the very flaws of the public school system D.A. Russell presents throughout this book. It can be a disturbing read, if you truly care about what is happening behind the curtain of public education—because you are left with the feeling that the task of making things better, for all involved, is one that is going to take loads of hard work, both at the very local level (individual schools) and on a very personal level. Real reform starts with teachers evaluating our own practices, fine-tuning our methodologies, asking for student feedback about what is and isn't working, and digging in to do the necessary work to make the classroom a better environment. Real reform also requires administrators to begin talking to their staff about what is and isn't working, and taking an open and honest look at school-wide policies. Administrators must begin asking *"How can we make this school a better environment for all?"* And after the feedback comes in, it's time to form leadership teams where teachers, students, parents, and administrators work together to create school-based decisions through conversation, diligent work, and innovative thinking.

Above all, real reform requires more voices from the field of education who will talk about the problems—with complete honesty. The teachers of this nation have the solutions, yet we are the very ones who continue to be silenced by bureaucrats, politicians, administrators, and school boards. We are the ones who know what is best for our students, and who understand the challenges we are facing day-in and day-out in our classrooms. Teachers must be able to speak openly, without repercussions from administration and school boards.

The education reform tables are turning, and it is time for the teacher narrative to be heard. D.A Russell has written a powerful book which does just that. Through the heart-breaking and raw accounts of teachers, to the data from years of Russell's research, this book chronicles the problems, suggests the solutions, and gives yet another chance for teachers and administrators to band together and do what's right for our nation's youth.

M. Shannon Hernandez M. Ed., is a nationally acclaimed education activist.
She is author of "Breaking the Silence: My Final Forty Days as a Public
School Teacher." Shannon blogs about education for the Huffington Post,
and for her personal website at MyFinal40Days.com.
Brooklyn, New York
February 2015

Table of Contents

(Chapter 1) Caveat – Some Truth in Advertising 1
(Chapter 2) False Introduction *(Teachers as seen in the media)* 2
(Chapter 3) The Real Introduction *(The one that no one wants to hear)* 5

The Challenge 7

(Chapter 4) Intentional Misdirection by Career DoE Bureaucrats and
    School Admins 8
(Chapter 5) Teachers Bullyied by School Administrators – The Silence
    of the Lambs 13

Clear Signs of Educational Failure 24

(Chapter 6) Failure – Readiness for college 25
(Chapter 7) Failure – Rapid loss of good teachers 29
(Chapter 8) Failure – Charter school failures 36
(Chapter 9) Failure – Loss of music, arts, and electives 39
(Chapter 10) Failure – The increase in homeschooling 44
(Chapter 11) Failure – Cheating and rampant cronyism in schools 50
(Chapter 12) Failure – Resistance to Common Core and standardized
    testing 51

An Original Survey of Teachers and Students 60

(Chapter 13) Setting the table – Teacher and Student Views 61
(Chapter 14) The Student and Teacher Survey Results 64

Three Myths We Must Debunk 91

(Chapter 15) Myth #1 – Children don't want to learn anymore 92
(Chapter 16) Myth #2 – The main problem with education is too many
    bad teachers 98
(Chapter 17) Myth #3 – All we need to fix education is more funding 101

The Eight Systemic Causes of Education Failure 104

(Chapter 18) The symptoms of failure are not the causes of failure 105
(Chapter 19) Systemic Failure #1: Unintended Consequences – good
    intentions gone horribly wrong 107

(Chapter 20) Systemic Failure #2: Unqualified Administrators and rampant cronyism 144

(Chapter 21) Systemic Failure #3: Inclusion classes – Everyone loses 165

(Chapter 22) Systemic Failure #4: Special Education – Hijacked by parents 175

(Chapter 23) Systemic Failure #5: "Bureaucrat" – Our newest four-letter word 183

(Chapter 24) Systemic Failure #6: Burned out teachers 208

(Chapter 25) Systemic Failure #7: The Untouchables – Parents, and Teacher Unions 229

(Chapter 26) Systemic Failure #8: Rewards unrelated to performance 237

Practical Solutions 243

(Chapter 27) The solution – Surprise! There is one, and it's not more money! 244

(Chapter 28) Concluding Remarks 258

(Chapter 1)
Caveats – Some Truth in Advertising

Two very important caveat for readers:

- this book is heavily focused only on **metropolitan and urban high schools**
- while I frequently refer to a "minority" of students or parents, I am always referring to a **numerical minority**, not a demographic minority

Such urban high schools comprise a large minority (38.7%)[1] of our nation's students – yet they also contain the vast majority of reported issues with graduation rates, drop outs, cheating scandals, and poor standardized test scores. Very little of this book's analysis was based upon research or experience in suburban or rural schools, and <u>none</u> was based upon middle schools or elementary schools.

Some of the key findings are less relevant to non-urban high schools, and might have much less relevance to elementary schools. The problems center on a numerical minority (a mathematical minority, not a demographic minority) of students and parents in these schools – education for all the great students in urban high schools is being held hostage to make sure a numerical minority of children pass.

There are exceptions, of course, to the bleak picture drawn by this analysis. I have been excited to find a handful of city schools that seem to defy the trends and conditions faced by all their peers. Invariably in those cases I have found a single, critical common denominator – teachers, parents, and students still share the powerful sense of co-responsibility for educational success.

---

[1] Enrollment, US Census Bureau, 2008

(Chapter 2)
False Introduction
(*Teachers as seen in the media*)

(Author's note: I couldn't help putting "tongue in cheek" to write the introduction that so many would like to read. I should dedicate this to talk show hosts, newspaper writers, a minority of parents, and news commentators everywhere – who simplistically think the only problems with education could be solved by more funding and eliminating a few bad teachers.)

All of us should have realized that we had it completely wrong. Money is not the root of all evil. It turns out that the real evil among us is teachers.

My son skipped school six days last month to go play video games. After all, with all we pay these teachers, if they won't ensure my son goes to school each morning, who will?

The signs were all there at least 15 years ago had I just paid more attention to parents sitting in front of me at a school play. The two moms, with husbands next to them in full agreement, were years ahead of the rest of us in understanding that all of the world's ills can be solved if teachers would just start to do a competent job of raising their children. The two were irate because the teachers had failed them yet again – letting their children skip school and go to a newly opened video parlor in town. (Back in the "old days" before Xbox and PS3 when video arcades became the hottest new craze.) Even more irritating was that they only discovered the absences months later, after it had occurred many times.

The issue was simple to them. If they had not happened to notice the number of absences in their children's report cards, they never would have noticed that their children were cutting school. With their difficult work and life schedules – work, shopping, PTA meetings, and social commitments – everything combined to make it impossible for them to notice the teachers' failure to get their children onto the bus each morning.

Look at this! These kids dress like slobs, use horrible language, and eat like pigs! A dozen teachers watching, yet these children don't even know how to use a fork properly!

One of the parents summarized the problem perfectly. "After all, if the teachers won't ensure my children go to school, who will?"

Today the rest of the world has finally discovered that all major problems are caused by teachers. The right-wing talk show hosts correctly identify the problem as a bunch of left-wing communist liberal teachers who are more interested in union perks and in brainwashing their children to vote

Democratic than in teaching. The left wingers correctly see that the problem is old-time, overly-conservative Republican teachers clinging to 1950's ideas of learning, and too cheap to spend what is needed to fund education. The legislators correctly see that the issue is more money to reward their largest donor and voting constituency – and to gain the approval of parent voters by punishing teachers for bad grades whether or not the child attends, studies, tries, or passes high school. And the parents correctly see that the problem is teachers who don't care enough to teach children basic table manners and social responsibility, or see that they do their homework. Meanwhile, the teachers spend so much time complaining about the problems they are forced to deal with every day that they never look at themselves, and never see how burned out and inadequate their teaching has become.

As I walked out of the auditorium that night, I missed the significance of the final comment from the two parents. The teacher problem was far more pervasive than I ever realized – it even extended to a total failure to teach basic language and manners. "And have you ever seen what happens in the cafeteria?" one asked. "Pigs and slobs … that's all you will see. A dozen teachers are supposedly monitoring the lunchroom, and yet the children don't even know how to use a fork properly!"

Thankfully, there is an easy solution. No need for heavy lifting, or thinking through anything very complex – just fire all the teachers.

(Chapter 3)
The Real Introduction
(*The one that no one wants to hear*)

Now the bad news. It isn't that easy. Fire all the teachers and 90% of the problems still remain. The system will ensure that the new replacement teachers will all become exactly like the old teachers within five or six years.

The sad part of the preceding "false" introduction is that it is "truth," as seen through the eyes of most people looking at today's education issues. Yes – there are major, obvious problems with America's urban high schools. Yes – there are problems with some urban high school teachers. Yes – the education problem is worsening. And yes – there are exceptions where all *appears* good. But unless we address the real issues, and address them fast, these issues can only get worse than they already are.

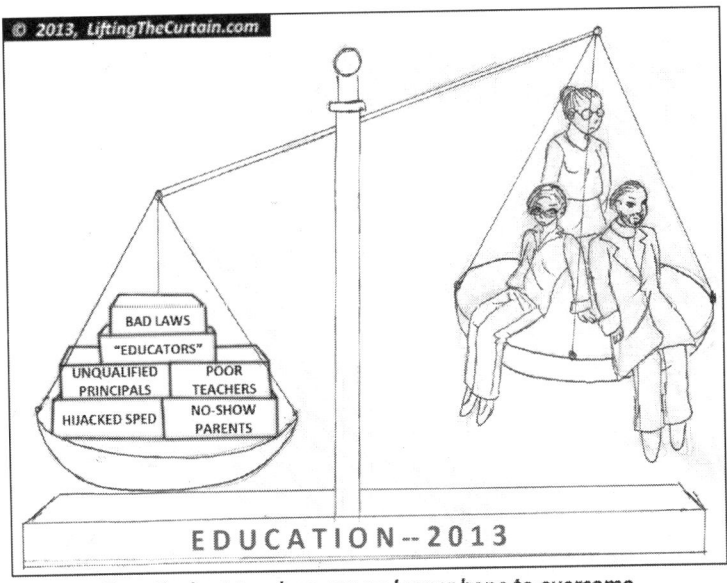

Even the best teachers can no longer hope to overcome all the major problems in the educational system

The real problem in education today is that we look to our teachers to resolve huge societal and parental issues, and systemic educational issues, that extend far beyond the boundaries of the school, and far beyond the capabilities of even our best teachers. Some of these are as ludicrous as the parents sitting in front of me at that play expecting the cafeteria monitors to do a better job of teaching children table manners.

To understand problems that pervade a _system_, you have to look at the _system_, not the parts.

Major organizations do not "fail" because of just a handful of bad employees. A couple "bad" teachers out of hundreds at a high school does not explain why education is failing across the USA. The problem is the system itself.

There are exceptions – thankfully! I have had the privilege of hearing about a few principals (who stand out amidst a lot of very bad ones) who are qualified to lead any school in the state. I have been blessed by *most* parents who care and support their children. My best moments in teaching are from students who decide to challenge themselves and succeed *despite* their home background. Even in the most under-performing schools, many children work hard and want to succeed. Those are the children who cause a teacher to head home after a rough week and feel good about their profession.

But please do not be fooled by the exceptions. These same problems lie under the surface of even those schools that appear to be performing at the "highest" levels.

But there is good news. Large parts of this systemic collapse can be remedied quickly. It will not occur without courage, without pain, and without ruffling a *lot* of feathers. Expect strong opposition from legislators, a small number of teachers (especially the "clique"), school administrations, career bureaucrats, and a numerical minority of parents.

But you also will see strong and enthusiastic support from the overwhelming majority of parents, students and teachers.

The bottom line – the changes detailed in the final chapter address the real, systemic factors causing our schools to underperform. Like any major change, there will be a lot of resistance. But the changes will work, and all of our children will benefit.

The Challenge

How do we disclose the *real* problems that are carefully and intentionally hidden by career DoE bureaucrats and school administrators to hide their failures

(Chapter 4)
Intentional Misdirection by Career DoE Bureaucrats and School Admins

Education is broken. Badly broken. Our children are being taught by methods guaranteed to fail. A large portion of high school graduates now graduate lacking even basic high school skills. More than half of college applicants who take the SAT and ACT tests are considered unprepared for college by those two services. Even Massachusetts, which loves to brag about its number-one national ranking on standardized testing, has only achieved this "distinction" via an openly dumbed-down test, salted with many middle-school problems, that requires a score of just 29% correct to "pass."

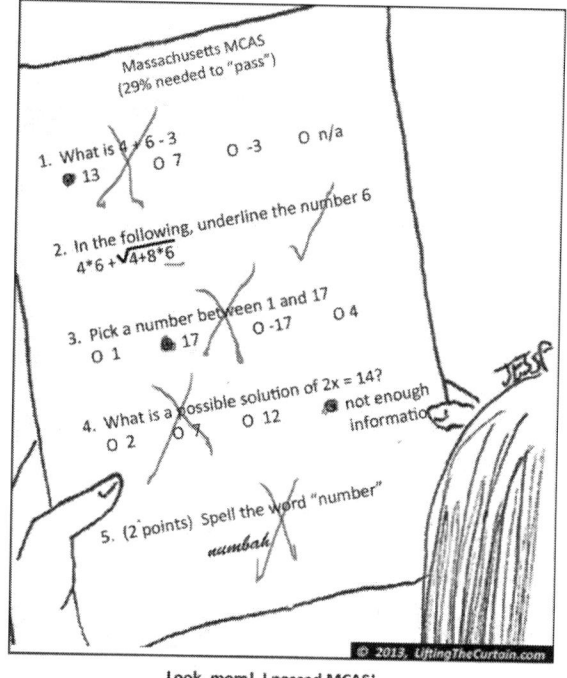

Look, mom! I passed MCAS!

A "Number One" ranking, with the bar intentionally and openly set that low, is a disgrace to the educational system.

And yet, despite all the agreement that education must be fixed, we have undergone years of increasing funding, and have seen countless new curricula approaches, with no improvement. It just keeps getting worse.

Why? It's because parents and legislators <u>never see the real issues</u>! Parents are the very people who teachers most need to help us tell legislators and career DoE bureaucrats to fix the real issues with education, yet parents have no chance of seeing what is actually causing the problems. The real problems are carefully and intentionally hidden from view by career DoE bureaucrats and school administrators focused on hiding the abject failure of their policies.

If we ask the typical parent what is wrong with education, they will reply with the usual four issues – the only ones the administrators and career DoE bureaucrats allow to be seen.

The intentional red herrings – the false claim that all education problems are caused by:

- Bad teachers
- Lack of Funding
- Teacher Unions
- Students who don't want to learn

Even though these four issues don't even make the top five of the eight systemic failures destroying education, and even though the perception is completely wrong that "….students don't want to learn," it is understandable that parents only see these four items as possible reasons. For one, parents look at *today's* education through the lens of their education twenty years earlier – *before* inclusion classes, standardized testing, abuse of SPED, bullying, lockdown drills, forced promotion of failing students, and a host of destructive mandates by career DoE bureaucrats.

The *real* causes of the abject failure in education are carefully hidden:

- The destructive unintended consequences of well-meaning legislation
- Unqualified administrators and rampant cronyism
- Inclusion classes where everyone loses
- Special Education hijacked by a numerical minority of parents
- A yearly flood of inept mandates created by unqualified career DoE bureaucrats
- Burned-out teachers
- The untouchables – teacher unions and parents
- Rewards and punishments unrelated to performance

You rarely or never see these real causes!

Even the most caring and involved parents who genuinely try to understand what is happening don't have a chance to see what we really need to fix. The inept career DoE bureaucrats have become masters at hiding the real problems DoE caused that prevent us from teaching. In Massachusetts, career DoE bureaucrats are certain to tout, in *every* education press release, that the state is "...first in the nation" in standardized testing. Of course, these same career bureaucrats are careful to hide that the "passing" grade on the state test is just 29%, that they salt the test with many easy middle school problems, and that they routinely reduce that to as low as 25% in years when the students do worse.

The Massachusetts standardized test long has been a way for career DoE bureaucrats to hide their DoE policy failures, and has little to do with helping children learn.

Meanwhile, unqualified school administrators focus first on taking care of their friends, and second on bullying teachers who speak out about the real problems in schools, with a culture of intimidation that dominates almost all schools. (See chapter 5 – teacher bullying by school administrators.) The one potential objective view of classroom issues that the parents might hear, teachers, has been effectively silenced.

With teacher views about the *real* problems effectively silenced, school administrators use intentional misdirection to plea for more funding. Later in this book you will see examples of music and arts being cancelled "...because of lack of funding" (Chapter 9) when the *real* reason is that all the available course slots are tied up in standardized test preparation classes. You will see examples (Chapter 20) where the parts of the school parents see – entryways and administrative offices – are decorated and furnished well, while back in the student areas the bathrooms, water fountains, and heating systems haven't worked for years. You will see school administrators spending hundreds of thousands of dollars on special assignments for their friends while classrooms go without books and with broken computer equipment.

The shell game is pervasive, and extends to nearly every urban high school.

Given this, even the most caring parent cannot see beyond the four red herrings listed above. Enlisting their help in fixing education is monumentally more difficult for us. And that is why a growing number of writers, blogs, and reporters try, day after day, to get the message out about the *real* problems with our children's education.

The heart of the problem is simple – a series of systemic failures resulted in two conditions that undermine any chance at an effective education for all our children.

- First of all, we have taken away from children the possibility of failure – ensuring their "success" to the point where a rapidly increasing percentage of students know they do not have to try in order to graduate from high school – the "system" now <u>forces</u> teachers to find a way to pass them regardless of effort.

- Second, the ages-old education partnership of teacher, student, and parents has been eroded to the point where teachers are often held <u>solely</u> responsible for the performance of a student, while the student and a growing minority of parents often take no co-responsibility.

These two conditions are destroying education in the United States.

- We have fallen into the deadly trap that children cannot be allowed to fail. The truth is exactly the opposite. In order for children to want to succeed, they must know they <u>can</u> fail!

- The unintended consequences of well-meaning laws end up destroying the very thing they are trying to help. Those laws guarantee poor performance, failure, cheating, and abuse.

- Superintendents, principals, and administrators are promoted by a system that does not prepare them for the high complexity of their new positions, and ensures that *most* (thankfully, not all) are completely unqualified for the duties they assume.

- Cronyism is rampant in assignments and promotions within schools – often rising to the level of corruption, and severely undermining teacher faith in the system.

- A rapidly growing numerical minority of parents looks for anyone other than themselves to take responsibility for the actions and efforts of their children.

- Teachers are under fire from so many directions that *most* have developed a "bunker mentality." Their dissatisfaction is reflected in their tone, attitude, and teaching effectiveness. They are forced to dumb down their teaching, are forced by administrators to "pass" children who have failed, and are forced to and follow the minimum acceptable path. The parallels between today's teachers, and yesterday's Vietnam Veterans, is uncanny.

- Special Education has been hijacked by many parents as a way to get their child through school without working, rather than as the vital tool SPED was meant to be.

- "Rules-based" teaching has sadly become the norm in many schools. Rather than explain concepts and help children understand the material, the focus is on getting the child to memorize a series of steps (or dates, or facts) for a week, pass the test, and then move on. It is a teaching methodology that cannot, and does not, succeed. It sends a constant message to the child that he or she is stupid, and saps any hope the child will develop earned pride in what they do.

- Children have been programmed by parents and teachers to have low expectations about their abilities, and to do minimal work. One of the most deadly unintended consequences of well-meaning legislation is that children know the school <u>must</u> graduate them – so there are always do-overs, extra credit opportunities, "the curve" to make sure they pass, or principal-forced grade changes – *regardless of their effort, and regardless of their understanding of the material*

And that is why this book was written – to let parents and legislators start to see the real problems destroying the education and futures of our children. We must fix this.

(Chapter 5)
Teachers Bullied by School Administrators – The Silence of the Lambs

The most difficult and frustrating part of making visible the real problems undermining the education of our children, is that most people have never heard a teacher's perspective before. Even Kirkus and Clarion, in their reviews of *Lifting the Curtain*, were surprised to see "…the unique perspective of a classroom teacher." That gives you some idea of how rarely the teacher's views and insights are heard. I cannot tell you how many times, even in real-world one-on-one conversations with parents about the problems in today's classrooms, that I see a look of skepticism on their faces.

Normally, there is only one thing they *do* see – the teachers, an easy scapegoat for the other seven systemic failures that have so terribly hurt urban high school education. Yes, there certainly are teacher problems, and burned-out teachers have earned their #6 placement on our list of systemic failures. But the top five causes of failure in urban high school education are completely (and carefully!) hidden to almost all parents and legislators.

And this denial is not limited to parents. My incentive to write *Lifting the Curtain* was an off-hand joke by a Boston talk show host (Margery Eagan[2] – sadly her show was discontinued a year ago). Here was a person whose views I very much enjoyed, and who had such good insights that I listened and respected her point of view even on those issues where we were far apart. Yet, even she had a huge blind spot when it came to the real problems with education – every educational problem she saw was laid at the feet of the teachers or the teacher unions. She had no idea the other issues that are far more destructive. So when four years ago she said the answer to fixing education was to "…just shoot all the teachers," (it was a joke — she was not at all serious!) I started writing *Lifting the Curtain* that very night.

Why? *I realized that if someone of her caliber and insight didn't know what was really happening, we were doomed to never fix this for our children.*

So why are teachers the scapegoat while the other seven systemic failures are invisible to almost everyone outside the curtain of the school entryway? There are four reasons.

---

[2] Margery Eagan, Boston talk show host, WTKK-FM Boston, show discontinued 2012

- Teachers, the one group who could help people see what is really happening, have been silenced. The culture of cronyism and intimidation that was in *every* single one (I should repeat that in bright red, bold, italic and larger font! "...every single one") of the urban high schools I visited in three years of research leading up to *Lifting the Curtain*, quickly and effectively slams down any teacher attempt at whistleblowing.

- School administrators and career bureaucrats at DoE are remarkably good at hiding the failure of their policies. As one example, Massachusetts DoE career bureaucrats, in order to hide how badly high school students are doing under their watch and policies, rigged the state standardized test (MCAS) for high school math with many dumbed-down middle school topics and a carefully hidden "passing" grade of just 29% correct. Parents only hear the message "...we are #1 in the nation in standardized testing." They never, of course, realize that the passing grade is a shameful one, so low that would have caused a student back when today's parents were in school, to fail and have to repeat the year! Ironically, in Massachusetts 29% on MCAS is passing, yet any class grade below 55% means you *do* have to repeat the year and do not even qualify for summer school.

- Parents see today's schools through the lens of their experiences 20 years earlier when they were in school. Yet, most of the real damage to urban high school education has occurred in just the last 10 years, especially concentrated in the last five. The abuse of SPED by a numerical minority of SPED parents, severe difficulties with inclusion classes, bullying assemblies, lockdown drills, peanut allergies, endless inept DoE mandates and micromanagement, and a host of other issues were things that did not yet exist when my children were in school.

- Commentators and news sources concentrate on the on the sensationalism in a story about some creep teacher 500 miles away, and ignore the other 150 good teachers in that same school who are as repulsed as I am at his/her conduct. A couple highly-visible teachers each year color the view of the remaining 7,200,000 teachers across the USA. Teachers nationwide get painted with that simple brush, are seen as "the problem," *and it diverts all attention away from the real failings*!

Overt intimidation of teachers and a "...culture of cronyism at the very heart of education"

The culture of intimidating teachers impacts nearly every urban high school, and effectively silences any possible visible pushback by teachers against the real failings in education. In short, school administrators routinely use the control of assignments, coaching positions, club leadership, and the threat of citing a teacher for "inappropriate action," as weapons to silence teachers. Speaking out against failed DoE policies or administration shortcomings is the fastest way for a teacher to lose any chance at coaching a volleyball team or being senior class advisor, being assigned to the best classes and classrooms, or being selected for paid conferences and training. And it is also the fastest way to get a memo placed into your personnel file for "inappropriate actions" or "insubordination" – both having the tangible threat of justifying potential termination if the "problem" continues.

Teachers learn quickly – unless you are one of the principal's cronies, be sure to keep quiet, do your job, and don't rock the boat.

In the three years of research, 760 surveys, and hundreds of interviews preparing for writing *Lifting the Curtain*, this air of intimidation was tangible in *every* school I visited. There was no finding more disturbing to me, and more discouraging, than to see how well the system hides failed polices by silencing the teachers. Just today, as I write this paragraph, I found a blog (http://cityneighborsfoundationblog.org/) that also clearly recognizes what is happening in classrooms:

> *"In schools where that teacher voice is suppressed, dismissed, or disregarded by systems, leaders, or practices, the [teacher's] voice does not disappear – it just sounds different and its possibility is muted."* [3]

And in an excellent book researched more than five years ago, author Laurie Rogers saw the same thing when she was interviewing teachers, and put it very bluntly:

> *"But many teachers are afraid to speak frankly lest they be disciplined or fired. Those who spoke with this author spoke carefully, as if the walls had ears. Some agreed to talk if they could meet outside of school. Several said they had been disciplined, with letters in their files, for talking with parents. One spoke with his lawyer before agreeing to meet. Almost all spoke on the condition of anonymity. Three began to talk, then decided the risks were too great. A frequent explanation: I have just a few years to go to retirement. I can't afford to get into trouble."* [4]

---

[3] (http://cityneighborsfoundationblog.org/)

What saddens me deeply, and still angers me, is that I could have used the exact same words as Ms. Rogers five years later when I wrote *Lifting the Curtain* – nothing had changed. This is just wrong!

Intimidation method #1: The "cookie jar" and the cronies

Cronyism is rampant in high schools – often reaching a level that would be called corruption anywhere else but in a bureaucracy that has no effective accountability. A school is simply another example of an unaccountable bureaucracy, and the same problems we see today – in IRS (70% of employing get performance bonuses), GSA (spending $750,000 on an employee hot tub conference in Vegas), HHS (healthcare rollout mess with no single person in charge), NSA, VA (faking records to qualify for bonuses), and many more – exist in *every* urban high school.

One US Inspector General report about cronyism abuses in the Department of Energy summed up the same attitude seen in all these examples, and in every one of our urban high schools:

> *"....the report found the senior staffer didn't think he had done anything wrong and defended his actions to investigators, saying doling out favors for family members is a common practice in the department."* [5]

A British report from the UK Daily Standard is a good précis of the dozens of examples and reports of blatant cronyism in USA schools that I included in *Lifting the Curtain*:

> *"A culture of cronyism is at the very heart of education."* [6]

The principal (in some schools, the superintendent) has unquestioned authority on almost all internal decisions – hires, fires, promotions, assignments, etc. – all with no effective accountability of his/her decisions. School boards take a pass on questioning any such decision. The principal's statement that "...it's an internal matter. I made the decision I felt was best for the school" is all that is needed to end any discussion. Even grievances and arbitration hearings triggered

---

[4] *Betrayed: How the education establishment has betrayed America and what you can do about it*, Laurie Rogers
[5] *Alleged Nepotism and Wasteful Spending in the Office of Energy Efficiency and Renewable Energy*, US Inspector General, June 2013
[6] UK Daily Standard, Jun 2007

by a local teacher's union inevitably fail when they come up against the brick wall of "…principal's best decision on internal matters."

Nowhere is this more visible than when the principal assigns the "cookie jar" positions. These are the 30-50 positions in every urban high school that are handed out each year. Each typically has a stipend of $2,000 to $6,000 (some $20,000-plus) and total up to between $250,000 and $400,000 each year for a typical high school. Here is a <u>partial</u> list of such positions (provided for any non-teachers reading this article).

    Equipment Manager
    Head Baseball Coach
    Coordinator Intramural Fall (2)
    Assistant Baseball Coaches
    Coordinator Intramural Spring (2)
    Head Softball Coach
    Head Football Coach
    Assistant Softball Coaches
    Assistant Football Coach (4)
    Head Outdoor Track & Field Coach
    Head Cross Country
    Assistant Outdoor Track & Field Coach
    Head Boys Soccer
    Head Lacrosse Coach
    Assistant Boys Soccer
    Assistant Lacrosse Coach
    Head Girls Soccer
    SADD Advisor
    Assistant Girls Soccer
    Freshman Class Advisor
    Head Volleyball Coach
    Sophomore Class Advisor
    Assistant Volleyball Coach
    Junior Class Advisor
    Head Golf Coach
    Senior Class Advisor
    Head Boys Basketball Coach
    Gay Straight Alliance
    Assistant Boys Basketball Coach (2)
    Cheerleader Advisor (Fall & Winter)
    Head Girls Basketball Coach
    Honor Societies Advisor
    Assistant Girls Basketball Coach

Scholarship Committee Advisor
Head Hockey Coach
Student Activity Chairperson
Assistant Hockey Coach
Student Council Advisor
Head Swimming Coach
Skills USA Advisor
Assistant Swimming Coach
Skills USA Advisor
Peer Mentoring
Yearbook Advisor
Equipment Manager
Co-op Director
Safety Coordinator
STEM Coordinator
Athletic Director

The way these are handed out is simple. First they go to the principal's friends and cronies, then leftovers to anyone else who is considered an "okay" person, and <u>never</u> to someone who is a "troublemaker." I found examples of a superintendent hiring his daughter's town coach for a school varsity position, a superintendent's nanny being hired as a paraprofessional, and countless family members being hired — and all were perfectly "legal," of course, as it was an "internal decision."

Cronyism is the perfect intimidation tool. Just think about a new teacher at a starting salary who quickly learns that a job they are passionate about (they love to coach baseball, or have a real heart for LGBT issues…) and the added income from it are dependent almost entirely upon whether or not the principal likes you.

In my research[7], 60% of teachers felt all such decisions were either totally or strongly based upon cronyism. Only 34% felt the principal was qualified for their position. An NEA survey[8] two years ago found 81% of teacher expect the principal (or superintendent) to abuse the power of his/her position. This distrust trickles down into all areas of a school – just 30% of teachers felt they got full or strong support from the principal when there was a conflict with a parent.

And the most reprehensible impact of all is when good teachers start to burn out. The most disheartening phrase I have repeatedly heard

---

[7] Original survey of teachers and children 2012-2013
[8] *NEA membership decline heralds loss of power and influence*, Education News, July 2012

the past two years is from once very good teachers who become mediocre teachers when they finally say:

"I give up. I will just do it their way."

I know. I'm as strong-willed (my friends would say downright feisty!) as they come, but I have been on the edge of making that same statement many times over the past couple years.

Intimidation method #2: It's "inappropriate"

Another deadly impact of the deadly mix of a bureaucracy with no accountability is the ugly new weapon used by principals and superintendents – the word "inappropriate." In the last few years the use of the word has taken an alarming twist. Now it is a way for a principal who does not like your point of view to justify putting a letter in your personnel file that potentially could mean the end of your career. It's the letter claiming "inappropriate conduct" with no need to justify why the alleged conduct was "inappropriate," and with the principal getting to define for his/her own purposes what is inappropriate and what is not.

Being fired for "inappropriate conduct or contact" does not mean you have to look for a new school. The deadly threat is that it means you will be on the CORI list as an offender from that day forward, and will never teach again. Few teachers can ignore a threat that would take away what they care for most – the joy of teaching our children.

The most effective use of the "inappropriate weapon" is when it can be loosely tied to a child or parent. "Mr. Smith made inappropriate comments to a parent during a parent-teacher conference…" or "Ms. Jones' actions at the student assembly were inappropriate for a teacher." In the file letter, you don't even have to say what the comment was, or why it was inappropriate. And the most repugnant use of inappropriate is when the principal wants to send a very serious shot across the bow of a teacher who speaks out – using the deadly "inappropriate conduct with students" or "inappropriate contact with a student" charge.

That last statement is likely to be met with strong skepticism by any non-teacher reading this who will not believe this can ever occur, or must be a very rare occurrence. Yet, in the hundreds of interviews that were part of my research, it was disquieting how often teachers brought up examples of exactly this. I had no problem believing them

– for I have three examples over the past 10 years where my outspoken criticism resulted in me being the target of an "inappropriate conduct" charge.

The worst was a claim that I had "...inappropriately touched a female student." Just those words will have some reading this chapter feeling a bit squeamish and start to wonder about me. <u>*That is their purpose*</u> *– if that can be placed in my personnel file then I am "on notice" that the groundwork has been laid to terminate me if I continue to be a problem with my outspoken views.*

But what was the "real" story? I was coach of a girls soccer team, and a player went down in great pain with a twisted ankle during the game. Some 40 players, coaches and referees, and 100 people in the stands were watching a very hurting young lady. After 5 minutes of her lying in the mud of a cold, wet New England field, I carried her to the sidelines where we could put her on a bench and cover her with jackets. End of story.

In case you blinked and missed it – the evil "...inappropriate touching of a female student" just happened. When carrying her off the field, my left arm was under her back, and my right under her "bare legs." The inappropriate part was that my forearm supported her legs in the traditional invalid-carry posture – that was the "touching." The claimed "inappropriate" choice was that I should have left her in pain on the cold, wet field until the ambulance got there, or gotten women in the stands down to the field to support her while she walked off the field. It took strong legal action and significant expense to get that potential letter debunked and stopped in its tracks.

The "inappropriate" label can very easily be used with language (when the target is not one of the principal's cronies) and the principal wants to put another warning letter in the teacher's file. "Mrs. Smith used inappropriate language in her class..." which is short hand for one of the cronies reporting to their friend, the principal, that he overheard a comment of "Sh*t, where the hell did I put my glasses." The letter might claim "inappropriate touching" (a deadly charge) where the real story was that "Susie was sobbing in the cafeteria, and Mr. Jones put an arm on her shoulder while comforting her in front of 200 other students." Yet, since in restraint training we are told we must never touch a child, even for comforting, this can "legally" be labeled "inappropriate" and have the desired intimidation effect.

Last year an outstanding book was published by M. Shannon Hernandez that provides a far more powerful look at rampant bullying by a principal than I could ever write. It is so powerful that I asked her to provide an extended summary of that part of her book for inclusion in this 2nd edition of Lifting the Curtain.

> *Shannon Hernandez was a public school teacher for 15 years. She is now a college professor, consultant, and author of an outstanding book about teaching* – Breaking the Silence: My Final Forty Days as a Public School Teacher. *Shannon blogs passionately about student-centered public education reform at her website and at* The Huffington Post. *She calls herself (a title I love and plan to steal!) an "education activist." You are strongly encouraged to visit her website and blog.* [9]

(M. Shannon Hernandez) Judgment Day

For the past two weeks, I have been sick to my stomach over the misconduct investigation, which I learned of 14 days ago from my principal. He informed me that I was under investigation for something a parent had reported last school year, but he could not tell me what had been said. I can't eat. Last night I didn't sleep. Today is the day I travel into downtown Brooklyn for my misconduct hearing.

I arrive at 10:45 a.m. and meet Linda, my union representative. She welcomes me with a smile and I burst into tears. She sits next to me in the waiting room, completely sympathetic, and hands me a tissue. We spend a few minutes trying to pull me together before we are called back into the cold cubicle with the bare walls and icy white paint.

The investigator strides into the tiny room and takes a seat, looking pleasant enough. She has long red hair and a kind smile. She sits across from us at the round table, opens the folder, and begins.

"Ms. Hernandez, you are here because of a report we received from your principal last year," she states. "Your principal witnessed you inappropriately touching a group of girls. He states that he walked into the classroom where several of you

---

[9] *Breaking the Silence: My Final Forty Days as a Public School Teacher*, M. Shannon Hernandez.
Web: http://myfinal40days.com.
Blog: http://www.thewritingwhisperer.com/

were in a circle, embracing in a hug." The investigator looks up and her gaze meets mine.

I remember like it was yesterday—that day a year ago was a special day. I had finished administering a high-stakes state exam to my wonderful group of special education students. They finished the test, so proud they hadn't run out of time and completely ecstatic because they were well-prepared to write the essay. They were so proud of the work they had just completed and had struggled with all year long. And at the end of the test and after all the materials had been collected, one of my students said, "Can we have a group hug? We did awesome!"

And so we embraced—there were about seven of us in the huddle. I gave them a pep talk about hard work and we circled up, much like a sports team does when strategizing. And in that moment—I remember it clearly—the principal walked through the door. He smiled, did what he had come to do, and left.

"Why has it taken you so long to investigate this case?" I ask. I assume there are thousands of other bogus cases clogging this screwed-up system, but I want to hear her answer. She tells me that for the last year, she has been chasing my former students—to obtain their statements. She has visited their houses and their cousins' houses. And with the next piece of information she shares with me, I know that everything I have ever stood for, as a human being and a public school teacher, matters.

"And Ms. Hernandez, not one student or their family would speak against you. Time and again, each one said, '"Leave her alone. She's the best teacher I ever had.'"

I weep tears of relief, gratitude, and joy. My anxiety is gone and the shame has dissolved.

The investigator tells me the case will be closed because the allegation was unfounded. Linda and I are dismissed and we take a seat in the lobby. I am still sobbing tears of relief. And while I know this could be the end of the saga, I decide I'm not going to let it be. You see, I also discovered in this

> meeting that it wasn't a parent who had reported me at all, but it was the principal.
>
> This is adult bullying at its best and I won't stand for it: My principal will know exactly how I feel about him within the week. I plan on standing up to my boss—the silent bully.

The result of cronyism and intimidation is deadly to a school in two ways. First, the one potential source of what is really happening in schools is effectively silenced. But even worse, teachers are soon burned out when they have to face this environment day after day. I have seen too many great teachers become mediocre teachers in the process, and many very good teachers, like Shannon, finally give up and leave teaching.

Combine an atmosphere of cronyism, an unaccountable bureaucracy, and inept DoE mandates that prevent teaching, and today's urban high school teacher can only hope to succeed with children if they ignore portions of system mandates that undermine our teaching efforts. But that's Hobson's choice — for by ignoring the system they set themselves up for more letters to their personnel file, yet by not ignoring it they fail in what they want to do most — teach our children.

We need to fix this.

Clear Signs of Educational Failure

(Chapter 6)
Failure – Readiness for college

Most children graduating from urban high schools are not qualified to enter college. That staggering fact is becoming more and more visible. When both the ACT[10] and SAT[11] testing services report that less than half of 2013 students tested were ready for college, it is as strong an indication possible that something serious is wrong with the education system. Routinely today, students have to take a remedial side trips to community colleges, or take developmental make-up courses of high school material in their freshman year of a 4-year college, just to be able to later start the "college-level" courses.

> *Monique Anair is an assistant professor and academic chair at a community college in New Mexico. Her view of incoming math students demonstrates how much we cheat our children by sending them to college unprepared to succeed. In the process she describes an approach to help fix this issue – ironically, one that is rare in traditional urban high schools but is common in most vocational schools today.*

(Monique Anair) A call to change preparation for college math

By continuing to separate math from applied science, we put our students at a disadvantage. Integrating math into arts and sciences allows students to achieve success in advanced high technology careers. Engineers and computer science majors with integrated skills will make better decisions – decisions that profoundly affect our world.

Yet, more than 70% of students entering community colleges test at or below Algebra I, and need to complete three semesters of math classes to "catch up" to their university peers. A student who is expecting to graduate from a two-year college in four semesters will find they start three semesters behind.

Few students will take on the challenge of additional semesters of mathematics to catch up. Community college students often opt to switch their bachelor's degree ambitions to an associate's degree which requires lower math proficiency. Students often can achieve success in technology-based entry-level positions if they choose a two-year degree. However, those same associate degree graduates find that

---

[10] Huffington Post, 16 Sep 13
[11] ACT, *The Condition of Career and College Readiness*, September 2013

> without a bachelor's degree they eventually "top out" in job markets that are flooded with university graduates. Employers expect that two-year degree students lack needed higher mathematical theory and application skills for advanced positions.
>
> The answer is to integrate math with the arts and sciences at the high school level. That prepares students for a traditional technology-based bachelor's degree requiring both math and science, and gives students much greater likelihood of a technology career in engineering or computer science. Those with such bachelor degrees have the language and vocabulary of science and mathematics that is crucial to invention and endeavor.

Why are students so unprepared for college? Of course the easy answer is "bad teachers" for those outside the actual classrooms. But, as with many of the system failures in urban high school education, the real reasons are hidden behind the curtain of the school entryway. Few see that the real culprits here are teachers *ordered* to promote failing students, and mandates that *force* teachers to dumb-down instruction and to teach-to-the-standardized-test regardless of student ability.

One of the hardest concepts for many well-meaning parents and legislators is understanding that giving a child a free ride through high school is not *an act of love. It is a destructive choice by an uncaring administrator that serves just one purpose — it protects the administrator's position by preventing the school from recording a low passing rate that would risk state sanctions. It has nothing to do with "helping" the child.*

Ironically, that same principal, or head of guidance, or dean, who forced a teacher to change that failure to a D-minus, ends up shooting themselves in the foot — for it makes the school's position steadily get even worse. The child "passes" one grade, but comes back the next year with an even more serious education deficit.

And for the child, forced promotions take away the one chance that student had to turn things around and begin to earn good results. You see — the cynical view of that administrator who changes a teacher grade is paramount to saying a phrase all teachers would abhor — "…this one's too dumb to pass on her own, so let's just move her along each year until we can get rid of her after graduation."

In so doing, the child has been put on a cycle of failure that will dominate their entire life. And at the same time, the teacher is crushed by being prevented from doing what we have spent our lives trying to do — teach and help children.

Anonymous, a past college professor who is now a high school English teacher in Illinois, describes how the dumbed-down approaches forced upon teachers ensures the child will fail. Like most teachers, she prefers to not reveal her name in order to avoid retribution from school administrators for speaking out.

(Anonymous) Readiness for college – English writing skills

After years of teaching developmental English to college students whose literacy skills were appalling and unready for college, I acquired certification in secondary education to teach these children when they were still in high school. In the process, I saw for myself why so many inner-city students can barely read.

Juniors and seniors were reading out loud in class as children do in the primary grades. It was clear from their lack of word recognition and mispronunciation that the literature was far beyond their comprehension. Nevertheless, teachers pressed on and found ways to impart the stories to students who couldn't actually read the stories. There were audio versions, movie versions, class discussion of the issues raised in the play or novel, chalk-talks, graphic organizers, the drawing of pictures, and simply telling them what they read as they stumbled over words in the text.

When I questioned the appropriateness of using such sophisticated literature with students who are obviously struggling with basic literacy, the response was that *The Crucible* and *The Great Gatsby* were pretty standard for high school. The fact that they were not dealing with high school students who could read anywhere near the standard for their grade level didn't seem to enter into the decision on curriculum.

Just as Chopin and Liszt are not for piano students in the early stages of playing, Miller and Fitzgerald are not for language-arts students in the early stages of reading. These teenagers ended the semester where they started—unable to read beyond a most elementary level— apparently because of a "one-size-fits-all" philosophy of education.

And it doesn't have to be this way! I know – been there, done that, and watched "dumb" children *earn* (repeat: *earn*) Bs and As at the CP level after failing the first term of a tough math course. I've seen the pattern again and again, in my classes and in the classes of many good teachers. The child would fail term one *expecting* an "extra credit pack" to pull up their grade to passing, but I would give none. They *expected* help during tests to answer questions, only to hear my stock reply "That's what I'm testing to see if *you* know." They *expected* do-overs on tests or outright grade changes.

Notice a theme here? It's the word "*expect*!" Kids are smart! They quickly learn the game, and that the school will pass them. They all *expect* it! So we have another unintended consequence that leads to a cycle of failure. The principal forces a promotion, children learn about it, children now expect a forced grade change, the minority of children without supportive parents stop working in class, they fail – and guess what – their grade is changed as *expected*.

But in my classes, when they still failed after all I would do to help them in class, assigning a student to team with them during class, and meeting them before or after school, I would let them fail! I refused to let administrators change their grade (and, of course, paid the price for that by being labeled a "troublemaker"). The child who failed would run to guidance asking to be moved out of my class. Guidance would refuse because they knew what always happened in my classes.

Then the miracle happens – time after time after time. In term two the child started to work. By term three they were earning Bs and As and prouder than ever in their school lives. In term 4 they were down in guidance asking to be in my class again next year.

A free ride through high school is not an act of love.

(Chapter 7)
Failure – Rapid loss of good teachers

As our legislators and career DoE bureaucrats continue to ignore the real systemic failures in education, in their endless search for more funding and unlimited freedom to create ever more inept mandates, they are doing far more harm than just destroying the education of our *current* generation of children. They are also condemning *future* classes to an even worse set of conditions by driving good new teachers out of the system.

The number of "early retirements" is staggering in urban high schools. Nearly 20% of urban high school teachers leave every year – either to quit the profession, retire (often early retirement when they give up on the system), or to move to suburban, rural, or private schools. And the one potential counter to these losses, an influx of new teachers, is being so discouraged when they see the realities of today's urban high schools that they soon quit. An estimated one-third quit by their 3rd year of teaching, and nearly half (estimated 40-50%)[12] are lost to the profession within the first five years.

The unintended destructive consequences of well-meaning legislation, combined with the inept and conflicting mandates by career DoE bureaucrats with little understanding of our classrooms, prevent our teachers from teaching *today*, and drive away the teachers we need to solve this crisis *tomorrow*. It is a self-fulfilling cycle of increasing failure for our children.

> *Below is a remarkable and devastating journal by a teacher driven out of the profession by all the inept mandates created by career DoE bureaucrats, and the culture of today's urban high schools. It is the second of the two teacher submissions that were so well done and insightful that I am including a much longer "uncut" version. "Anonymous" resigned as a high school teacher in Colorado this past summer after just two years in the system. Her story was far too long for inclusion in the book, as is, but was so outstanding an insight into what new teachers face that I asked her for permission to make the following shorter version. Like most teachers, she prefers to not reveal her name in order to avoid retribution from school administrators for speaking out.*

(Anonymous) What I learned in my two years as a teacher

---

[12] *Beginning Teacher Induction: What the Data Tell Us*, Education Week, December 2014

Like any baby teacher, I entered the field 2 years ago completely naïve, optimistic and enthusiastic, convinced I would model myself after every teacher who ever inspired me, determined to make a difference. I attended the New Teacher Orientation and came home so confused as to why so many people responded overly nicely when they heard I was a brand new teacher "Wow! Congratulations! It gets easier by year 3!" or "Welcome, I love your enthusiasm...let me know what I can do to support you!" I couldn't help but wonder if everyone knew something I didn't behind the kind and contrived smiles. Then I started noticing this strange negative attitude coming from "seasoned teachers" who seemed to have lost the spark that inspires teaching. So many comments about "hands being tied in the system", relentless "mandatory Professional Development," new policies and procedures that time will be wasted on – just to have them all change in another year or so, etc.

Little did I know what I was getting into.

After my first 2 weeks of teaching, I felt completely alone. There were some highs, and there were many lows. I found websites dedicated to helping 1st year teachers survive and realized – I WAS NOT ALONE. I read about how 49% of new teachers leave the profession within the first 5 years of teaching and thought "Hmm...maybe if I can just make it until year 3 I will be okay."

Since them I have attended countless hours of Professional Development and submitted many required justifications to my supervisors and the New Teacher Induction program proving my worth as an instructor. I have been subjected to both inspiring compliments and heinous student feedback on an anonymous student survey via Survey Monkey, as well as the anonymous 'Make Your Voice Heard' surveys. I have received threats from parents last year (reporting me to the Department of Education, suing, etc. for holding their student accountable) to singing my praises as the teacher who changed their son/daughter's lives this year. I often worked 60-70 hours per week developing curriculum and the ever-elusive "perfect assessment", trying to find that perfect balance between challenging students, keeping students engaged and inspired.

How "effective" have I been as an instructor? My students have A's, B's, and C's, except for the students who do not turn in assignments – they are failing. I had 10 students drop my class in the final three months of 2013 due to my program "...being too rigorous." When I tried to address the amount of "rigorous" curriculum I am mandated to squeeze into a *very* short amount of time, I received comments like:

"Well if you think it's rigorous now, you should have seen what the students had to do 3-plus years ago...this is nothing! *We have already taken so much out of the curriculum.*"

So does this measure my effectiveness as a teacher? If so, I should quit.

In an email I received just last week from a student, "I just wanted to say thank you for everything you have done for us. I know that sometimes we take advantage of how much you have helped us and we never say thank you because we expect for you to help us. I have never felt so good about my work and how I am as a student until I came into your class. You never set us up to fail and you are always there when we need help."

Or from another student who apparently nominated me for HOSA Advisor of the Year 2 weeks ago, "She cares about her students & always goes the extra mile to make sure that we understand what we are learning. Even after she is no longer on the clock, she is doing things to help us succeed. She inspires her students daily, & helps her students see things from different perspectives. She pushes us out of our comfort zone, helps us grow, & helps us succeed. She gets us out of our comfort zones by showing us that we are capable of much more than we think."

So does this measure my effectiveness as a teacher? If so, I should stay.

What I have learned is that the educational system is beyond repair and no amount of mandatory Professional Development will fix a broken system. I have learned that teachers can be heroes or punching bags. That students love you until you hold them accountable – and as a teacher it is much easier not to. I have learned that any incentive to being a "good teacher" – the kind that challenges students and holds them accountable – is being squashed by sue-happy parents and SB191 which rewards teachers for ensuring their students pass (wink wink). I have learned that teachers need to be robots without feelings, willing to work countless hours while sacrificing all manner of health and sanity – without complaint, be willing to constantly justify their existence with ridiculous tools such as the one I am using right now to "prove" we are "good enough" and worth our meager paycheck or tiny "bonus" check for complying with countless hours of Professional Development on top of all of our "…other duties as assigned".

I now realize why I received so many overly nice comments of support when I first started teaching, why the "seasoned teachers" have that negative attitude about everything, and I now understand why the system is failing. I know that the culture of teaching is ripe with "not good-enoughness" due to a myriad of subjective factors that the system tries to fix with unrealistic objective measures and comical catch 22's. I have learned that it is a system that sets teachers and students up to fail with impossible and contradicting expectations.

I now understand why 49% of new teachers leave the profession within the first 5 years of teaching. And on May 29th, 2014, I joined that terrible statistic.

The reasons for teachers burning out and leaving the profession come from many sources. But three stand at the top of the list.

- Inept mandates from career DoE bureaucrats (Chapters 19 and 23)
- Rampant cronyism and bullying of teachers (Chapters 5 and 20)
- A minority (a mathematical minority, not demographic) of parents

In my survey and interviews of teachers, it became very clear how much a numerical minority of parents could deeply undermine all the great and supportive parents out there. These were the parents who threatened to sue if their child was not passed, or forced the child to get a Special Education set of accommodations that were unneeded just so the child would "pass and graduate." The most disturbing were the minority of parents who just didn't seem to care. In the survey and three years of research leading up to this book, teachers averaged 3.1 "difficult or nasty" parent conflicts per *month*, compared to 1.7 positive written comments per *year*. Just 4% of the parents of struggling parents attended parent-teacher nights. A staggering 71% of parents requested to attend a conference about their child refused to come or ignored the request.

One of the most common observations I received from non-teachers who reviewed the 1st edition of *Lifting the Curtain:* was that my narrative about "Myrtle" had to be an exaggeration, or a rare thing to occur. (I invited Myrtle's mom in for a conference because Myrtle was a past failing student who was now doing exceptionally well, and I wanted to share the pride with her parents. Myrtle's mom entered the classroom on parent-teacher night, staggering, and announcing loudly "What has the little shit done now?" That was the closest I ever got to losing it with a parent.)

But this is *not at all rare* for the urban high school teachers I interviewed and surveyed in the three years of research preparing for the book. And the situation gets even worse when urban high school teachers have to rely upon their principal to support and help when a parent gets this confrontational. Just 30% of those surveyed and interviewed said they got strong support when needed. Many teachers related incidents like one of mine, where the principal, over his head, completely unqualified for such a complex "management position" at the level required of today's principals, and unable to handle conflict, actually skulked out of the conference room announcing "…you take care of this, I will go cover your class for you."

> *And in urban high schools, all too often the conflict is about a far more serious issue than just "grades." We expect our teachers to be fully qualified to handle the most difficult of societal and family issues. Louise K is a retired high school ESL teacher in California. She recreated these two conversations from memory to share with other teachers, and to give those outside the classroom a look at what really happens in our schools. Interactions like this are not rare – all of us in the classroom have lived through them. Thankfully, they are still the minority of parent interactions.*
>
> ### (Louise K) Cold Call
>
> "Mr. Johnson, please?"
>
> "Just a sec. Da-a-a-d! It's for you," then softly, "Somebody selling something."
>
> "Well, why'n't ya just hang up? Dammit, girl, there's a game on."
>
> "Mr. Johnson?"
>
> "Is this one of them sales calls?"
>
> "No, this is Patty's English teacher. You left a message for me to call."
>
> "Oh. Patty, get in here right now. It's your teacher."
>
> "Mr. Johnson?"

"Yeah, what I wanna know is why Patty's got three F's."

"I can't speak for the other teachers, but Patty hasn't turned in any of her English homework."

"Patty, look at me. Why the f*** aren't you doing your homework?"

"Mr. Johnson! I assume you want to figure out how to help your daughter get back on track."

"Dammit, girl! You need to do your work."

"Mr. Johnson," I say, speaking to this grown man as if he were one of my ninth graders. "Why don't you have her pick up a grade check form in the office to take to her teachers every Friday?"

"Patty, your teacher says you need to get a grade check form."

"One more thing." I hesitate. "Might Patty's low grades be a symptom of something else?"

"Patty's not allowed to have a boyfriend."

Pause. Struck a nerve?

"Get those earphones out!" he yells at Patty. "Are you seeing somebody?"

"Goodbye, Mr. Johnson," I say, hanging up quickly.

So much for No Child Left Behind – or Reach for the Top.

(Louise K) Powder Keg

Dave, my dean, slumped over his desk, looked up when I entered his office." Hey," he said, raising his head, "I hope you're right that Billy is probably not in a gang," he said, referring to a student who had been shot after a game. He sounded doubtful, but he was the dean of discipline and dealt with the trouble-makers.

"Got a question," I said. "I went to turn in a five-day absence form for Allison and was told the transfer came from this office, not attendance. Is Allison in trouble?"

"She's being transferred for her own protection. The nineteen-year-old who's the primary suspect in Billy's shooting is her brother – well, her half-brother."

"Isn't he from the Bay Area?"

"Somebody might find out they're related."

"Allison is – was – in my sixth period class," I said. "*The same class as Billy.* And I had a big talk with the class after the shooting."

"Clearly, for her safety we had to get her into another school."

Something began to rumble inside me. "Do you think I could have been told a week ago?"

"I meant to," Dave said. "I'm sorry. It's been so crazy and – well, I just forgot. You should have been kept in the loop."

Okay. An apology. Still, without knowing it, I had been sitting on a powder keg.

And at the last faculty meeting, before the shooting, the principal had stressed the importance of communication.

Nearly half of all new teachers quit the profession within the first five years of teaching. Given the impact of inept mandates by career DoE bureaucrats with little understanding of today's classrooms, bullying and cronyism by school administrators, and the attitude of a minority of parents – it is no surprise.

(Chapter 8)
Failure – Charter school failures

Few educational initiatives have had the degree of hype and false promise we see every time a new charter school is launched. Career DoE bureaucrats tout the success "…certain to follow" by allowing teachers the freedom to teach differently, and schools to operate under conditions that foster learning better than public schools. Caring parents, especially those struggling with private school bills, rush to apply and move their child to the new school. Hope and promise are in the air. Every teacher I know has been hopeful that charter schools would be the trigger to show how *real* changes could help us be able to teach again, despite all the destructive mandates that prevent effective teaching.

But reality is starting to hit across the nation. Charter schools are just another failed bureaucratic shell game.

Those "big changes" never happened. The rush to charter schools has ignored one predictable unintended consequence – since all those "…changes and mandate exemptions" to <u>state</u> mandates turned out to be mainly cosmetic, with little of substance actually changing, and since <u>every</u> one of the destructive unintended consequences of <u>federal</u> mandates stayed in place – nothing happened to fix the underlying systemic failures in all urban high schools, including in the new charter schools.

In 2013 alone[13], while 642 new charter schools were being launched as "…the next big thing for education," another 206 failed and were closed. And literally hundreds more (perhaps one third of the 6000-plus in place today) across the nation are reported to be in the process of failing. In Indiana alone, more than half of the current charter schools are "…doing poorly or failing" according to the state accountability data.[14] And a Stanford University study in 2013 found that the quality of education in charter schools was far from the levels promised:

> *That is the clear message of continuing analysis from the Center for Research on Education Outcomes at Stanford University, which tracks student performance in 25 states. In 2009, its large-scale study showed that only 17 percent of charter schools provided a better education than traditional schools, and 37 percent actually offered children a worse education.* [15]

---

[13] National Alliance for Public Charter Schools, publiccharters.org
[14] *Nearly half of Indiana's charter schools doing poorly or failing*, WTHR Columbus
[15] NY Times, 1 February 2913

The false hype from career DoE bureaucrats and legislators no longer hides all the failures – and can't hide the exact same underlying problems as traditional public schools Yet, no one seems to be able to see the huge disconnect here – if all these special changes need to be made to enable a better education in charter schools, why are the old rules still right for traditional public schools? And if the underlying conditions in the charter schools don't change, is there any *real* possibility of long term success?

Why such a high incidence of charter school failure? The answer is simple – none of the federal mandates of NCLB or RttT are waived with charter schools, and many of the states either did not waive state mandates, or only made cosmetic changes.[16] The underlying systemic failures remain.

So why the success in *some* of the new charter schools? Again, it is a simple answer. It has nothing to do with the structure of the schools, mandates, or policies.

It is 100% about expectations. Parents and students coming to the school are those who already have high expectations and motivation. According to Census and National Center for Educational Statistics[17], the <u>overwhelming bulk</u> of the growth in charter schools has come from students transferring from private schools. And it is clear to any classroom teacher that most of the remaining transfers have come from children of the most motivated and supportive parents in the public school system.

Fill a school with the most motivated students of supportive parents, and teachers have a chance to succeed in helping these children learn, *despite* all the educational system does to prevent teachers from teaching. We cannot "fix" education with cosmetic changes by career DoE bureaucrats and legislators – we will only succeed for our children when we fix the real systemic failures in urban high school education.

> *Sarah B is a middle school social studies and language arts teacher in Colorado. She provides an insightful look at charter schools from inside the classroom:*

> **(Sarah B) Charter schools – same old, same old?**
>
> I teach in a K-8 charter school founded on the idea that children will learn if they're given choice in learning that is experiential and relevant. Last year, I took a job teaching social studies at this school because I was tired. For eleven years, I'd watched public education

---

[16] NAPCS database, Automatic exemptions from state and district laws and regulations
[17] National Center for Education Statistics, NCES.ed.org

turn teenagers apathetic or angry, I'd fought administrators obsessed with data, and I'd taught beside colleagues so burned out they'd begun to resort to formulaic lesson plans and disconnection from their students.

I knew I needed to quit teaching or find a different world. In some ways, I have found a different world. But in many others I have not. The challenges I experienced in standard schools exist in charter schools, too. As just one example, no charter school in today's education system can escape testing. *[Author's note: testing is a federal mandate – none of the federal education mandates are ever waived for charter schools.]* For four weeks this spring, the students in my school will stop their project-based, meaningful learning to sit for state tests.

Is it a coincidence that the middle school students in this alternative school are just as apathetic as teenagers in any school where I've taught? Like their peers at other schools, these kids have short attention spans and a closely held belief that school is irrelevant in a world connected by Instagram and YouTube. At conferences, their parents say they're grateful their kids are at a school like ours, and I nod and smile – but I worry, secretly, that this isn't the solution either, and that what is wrong is much deeper than an educational approach.

I think we would all find more answers if we'd look more directly into the increasing emptiness in an American teenager's eyes.

The bottom line is that little of substance has changed for charter schools other than the success from attracting students who are *already* highly motivated and performing at the top of their existing public or private schools. The evidence strongly shows that without the bulk of their enrollment coming from parents who look to save significantly over private school tuitions, they would do no better than our existing failing urban high schools.

(Chapter 9)
Failure – Loss of music, arts, and electives

The decline in music and arts courses in our schools is shocking. Even the most stressed-out classroom teacher will admit music and arts teachers have it worse than the rest of us. And the worst part is the intentional lie that is almost always used as the false "reason" music and arts are cancelled.

> *One of the most powerful insights into today's teaching environment for music and the arts came from an anonymous spouse of a high school band teacher in Florida.*

> **(Anonymous) The despair of being today's music and arts teacher**
>
> From a spouse's point of view, I can clearly look outside the box, yet it breaks my heart to see all the changes in our schools. Being a band director makes the difficulties of my husband's teaching career even worse. Budget cuts and talk of cutting art and music out of the schools is an added worry to the everyday problems. He has to all but donate his free time for extra rehearsals and the three weeks of must-have summer band camp he needs to provide to have a superior band program.
>
> Students have to be held accountable for their grades, and after-school marching/concert rehearsals are equal to homework assignments in other classes. When the end of semester arrives and a student is almost failing, the parents hit the roof – not caring that "Billy" skipped six after school rehearsals, and that all the times the parents pulled him early from rehearsals because of other family obligations or an inconvenient time schedule lowered their child's grade.
> A teacher is always under scrutiny for every action, has all the added pressure from parents, and not all administrators back their teachers up. It's each teacher for him or herself.
>
> When not teaching a class they have him running from room to room subbing for absent teachers. Factor into that the useless workshops, Professional Development, faculty meetings, teacher workdays, unhappy parent meetings, and numerous half-day schedules – and all of these combine to prohibit holding rehearsals. This hectic schedule has left him no time in his office to get paperwork done for his band program and mandatory football games, marching contests, concerts,

etc. With all this chaos, he's still expected by the administrators to have a superior band and bring home the trophies.

I know how much he loves his job, but with all the changes that have occurred in the past few years it makes his teaching a hardship now instead of the joy it once was. With his retirement in the near future, he just keeps teaching, smiling, and plugging along trying not to let it all get the best of him, but I can see the pressure rising.

The big lie – cancellation is a school funding issue

In the urban high schools I researched over three years before writing *Lifting the Curtain*, almost all of them had eliminated arts and music electives. In each case it was under the patently false pretense that it is due to a lack of funding. The truth was, in each case that additional funding, if given, would always be applied to programs *other* than arts and music – because no matter what the funding level, there was no room in the curricula for these courses anymore. The elective class periods had all been preempted for standardized test prep. And non-teaching mandates take up so much urban high school classroom time that teachers are prevented from the level of teaching that would make prep classes for standardized tests totally unnecessary.

Look at a typical 5-course freshman or sophomore day in school 20 years ago when today's parents were in school:

- Math
- English
- Science
- History
- **Electives**

The electives slot was the joy for children. Here is where we painted, crafted, and learned about music (other than Elvis and the Beatles!). Here were study halls and gym (more than just one day per week). But look at the same 5 course schedule today:

- Math
- English
- Science
- History
- **Standardized test preparation**

The real reason for cancelling arts and music now becomes clear. Disingenuous administrators claim it is a "budget" issue. But their real reason has nothing to do with budgets – it's that there are no open freshman or sophomore open course slots for electives, because all are being used for test prep

The little lie – music and arts are too expensive

The second lie is one that sounds reasonable – music and arts are far too expensive for today's school budgets. After all, it is true that equipping a large band or orchestra is expensive. But school administrators intentionally leave out an important factor in their effort to hide the need for test preparation classes. The cost issue is superbly addressed in the Regina Paul submission, below – today's children dearly want low-budget music appreciation courses, not the high cost performance courses administrators use as a false red herring.

Regina Paul is the President of the highly respected Policy Studies in Education, a non-profit organization that has created K–12 curricula in all subjects, assessments for school districts and states, parent materials, and policies for school boards, working with over 400 school districts and 150 colleges. She co-hosts NYCollegeChat, a free podcast for families about choosing a college.

(Regina Paul) For some students, music or art is the only reason to come to school.

When my nonprofit organization conducted educational goals surveys (in cooperation with the National School Boards Association) in communities across the U.S., we gave citizens, school staff, high school students, and recent graduates an imaginary $1,000 and told them to spend it as they pleased across a dozen school subjects to show their educational priorities. Every time, some respondents spent their entire $1,000 on music or art.

When given a dozen fine arts goals and asked to rate how important each of them was to teach, respondents voted every time for "spectator art and music," not "varsity art and music." In other words, making students into appreciative and knowledgeable consumers of the fine arts was far more important to children than making them into performers. The public knows that relatively few individuals can make a living

> as performing musicians and artists, but everyone can enjoy the arts as a spectator in the audience.
>
> Schools that do not offer music and art—both performance courses as well as history and appreciation—are shortchanging students now and in their futures. I understand that the great Quincy Jones said that, sadly, no country thinks as little of its music heritage as we do of ours. What a crying shame, given all that we have created in music—and in art and dance. Far too few public schools require the study of fine arts history and appreciation.
>
> It is time to change that.

So, we have hit upon yet another unintended consequence of mandates (standardized testing and penalties to schools with low results, and non-teaching mandates in the classroom) that shortchange our children. In every urban high school I researched, the freshman and sophomore children had at least one class each term dedicated to helping pass standardized testing – often one for both English and one for Math. All but two had no freshman or sophomore courses for amy electives such as art and music. Dozens of emails and Facebook posts I have received confirm the same situation in schools nationwide. Many schools are even starting to look at adding more such "test preparation" classes for bio, chemistry, and history as those topics become part of standardized testing. After all, the sanctions on a school that does not meet mandated test results can be very severe.

And reprehensibly, many of the schools that still claim to have music and arts programs treat them as second class citizens with little support.

> *Gregory Pavliv is a former public school music education teachers from New Jersey. He has earned a national reputation as one of the country's foremost music education advocates. He created, maintained and enhanced programs in dozens of school districts, including New York City, Los Angeles, Dallas, San Francisco, Chicago, and Tamp. He has delivered presentations and implemented curriculum in 26 cities across 14 states and was elected as a State Delegate to the NEA in 2008 where he authored legislation protecting performing arts in the public schools.*
>
> ### (Gregory Pavliv) Music and Arts courses – Second-hand citizens
>
> I was given the opportunity to create a music education program in a school with 100% free lunch, which also became a magnet for autistic children in the district due to the way standardized testing was being averaged. Having one school wildly fail wouldn't throw the district

average off – instead the data would be discarded. Despite that, when the opportunity came up I wanted to take the challenge of teaching music to an almost entirely special-needs community of learners.

The school gave me a room, a desk, a chair – and that was it.

There was no furniture, no carpeting, no chairs for the students. And of course there were no instruments, no books, no materials or supplies. So yes, the board of education wanted to give these special needs children access to music education, but no, they weren't willing to invest in it. I worked hard to partner with colleagues and third party organizations to outfit my classroom with everything from a piano to a full range of modern instruments to carpeting, furniture and a full stock of supplies.

And after we fought through the budget, something magical happened. Those children, who were marked as being so severely 'special' that the district thought it a good idea to separate them from the population, all of a sudden integrated, relaxed and embraced the music class. Somehow they connected to the music, and felt appreciated and accepted when they were taught the same instruments in the same way as those students who were there under different circumstances. It was like a series of clouds being lifted from all those little faces!

In every one of the urban high schools I studied, I found administrators focused only on protecting their positions and the school's status by concentrating curricula on passing the tests, rather than helping teachers be freed up from micromanaging mandates so those same teachers could teach again in their classrooms, making test prep classes unnecessary.

So do the math – who loses when one or two classes each day are tied up with remedial test prep training? A typical school has just 5-6 classes per day. If two (and soon to be more than two) are for additional Math and English training to help with passing standardized tests, where is there room for electives anymore? Where is there a space for creative writing? For law? For small business issues? For psychology? For that matter, where is there a slot for band, art, home economics, study hall, or carpentry?

Once again, the real reason for the loss of arts and music in our schools is simple – too many mandates trying to compete for too little time. The career bureaucrats, year after year, do not understand something as obvious as that 7-8 classes cannot fit into a 5-6 class day – and our children are the losers.

(Chapter 10)
Failure – The increase in homeschooling

I have started to significantly revisit my long-standing negative views on homeschooling. The frame of reference is changing for me – from my prior question of "…is homeschooling equivalent to a top public school education?" to "…is homeschooling a better alternative to a attending a failed local urban high school?"

The growth in homeschooling has been dramatic, rising from 2.9% in 2007 to 3.4% in 2012. According to the latest (2012) NCES[18] survey, the number of students being homeschooled now equals the number of students in charter schools. The NCES estimates that almost two million (1,770,000) students are now homeschooled, although there are other estimates placing the total at over 2,500,000. Urban schools have a lower percent (3.2%) of students being homeschooled than rural areas (4.5%).

The growth in homeschooling is concentrated at the high school level – with 3.7% of grade 9-12 students now being homeschooled. And in 74% of the cases, strong dissatisfaction with the quality of public school education was a primary reason. The widespread view that homeschooling is based upon religious or social views is rapidly becoming a major misconception.

Such a strong movement towards homeschooling surprised me as I researched the topic. I have always had such serious reservations about homeschooling that almost always I felt it was a *very* serious mistake by parents. The reasons for those reservations have not changed. I was not swayed by two of the common arguments I had heard for homeschooling – too many homeschool advocates focus only on the financial aspects (to many a boring, highly disputed can of worms — people don't even understand the disaster of huge national deficits despite tons of press about them) or on the religious or environmental/attitude issues (a valid personal choice, but one that sometimes seems to ignore whether the perceived gains in environment offset the loss of educational quality if a good public school is available.)

---

[18] NCES.org, 2012

No, my one major issue was that no matter how diligent a parent, I know no single person who could to a competent job of teaching such a wide range of high school courses as English, Chemistry, Algebra II, Physics, history, music, etc. In high school, a student receives the entire curricula from 15-20 teachers who specialize in each topic and level. Expecting one person to match that level of competence and expertise seemed impossible.

To me, that always cancelled out any perceived positives I read about. *Now – truth in advertising* – I am NOT a person qualified to speak more than anecdotally about home schooling. Unlike the three years of research, surveys, and interviews that went into writing *Lifting the Curtain*, I only recently started to revisit some of my perceptions on the subject to understand why there is such an upsurge in homeschooling.

Please don't get me wrong – as a teacher, I still have very serious reservations, and am personally against homeschooling if there is a good public school nearby. But there are two words ibn the prior sentence that I used to take too lightly – "if" and "good." I am now starting to understand the urgency of an estimated 1,700,000-2,500,000 homeschooler parents when the only available nearby public school is yet another failing urban high school.

As I researched homeschooling, I discovered two major changes that have me now starting to seriously look into the evolution of the 2014 version of homeschooling. One is that homeschoolers see today's urban high schools (and apparently some suburban and rural high schools) as having had a major drop in the quality of education compared to the schools parents attended 20 years ago. And the second is a cottage industry for homeschooling materials a decade ago that has evolved into a major industry providing some strong support, materials, and services — current homeschoolers have to "wing it" in difficult topics much less than just a decade earlier.

And the result? The quality of homeschool education has increased dramatically over the past few years. Many reputable studies have shown that homeschooled children are often *outperforming* their public school counterparts. I still am adamant that homeschooling is a much weaker education than if a good public school is available, but can no longer deny that homeschooling can be a better educational alternative to urban high schools that have been undermined by inept mandates forced upon teachers by career DoE bureaucrats.

Education Week in May 2012[19] published a powerful summary of the growth in homeschooling. Here is a précis of their report:

---

[19] *Number of Homeschoolers Growing Nationwide*, Education Week, 21 May 12

As the dissatisfaction among parents with the U.S. education system grows, so too does the number of homeschoolers in America. …the number of primary school kids whose parents choose to forgo traditional education is growing seven times faster than the number of kids enrolling in K-12 every year.

Homeschooling statistics show that those who are independently educated typically score between the 65th and 89th percentile on such [standardized state] exams, while those attending traditional schools average on the 50th percentile. Furthermore, the achievement gaps, long plaguing school systems around the country, aren't present in the homeschooling environment. There's no difference in achievement between sexes, income levels, or race/ethnicity.

Recent studies laud homeschoolers' academic success, noting their significantly higher ACT-Composite scores as high schoolers and higher grade point averages as college students.

College recruiters from the best schools in the United States aren't slow to recognize homeschoolers' achievements. Those from non-traditional education environments matriculate in colleges and attain a four-year degree at much higher rates than their counterparts from public and even private schools. Homeschoolers are actively recruited by schools like the Massachusetts Institute of Technology, Harvard University, Stanford University, and Duke.

So, given how bad urban high school education has become, I am now starting to understand why it looks much better than just the "…lesser of two evils" to some parents. They look at their local urban high school and see one that deserves an "F" for education – with teachers being forced to dumb-down lessons, administrations passing children to set them up for failure, a blind focus forced upon teachers to teach to standardized tests, teacher hands tied by micromanaging mandates that prevent teaching, music and arts electives vanishing, and only 25% of high school "graduates" seen as ready for college by the ACT testing service.

Compared to that scenario, even a "C-minus" homeschooled education is a huge improvement.

Most homeschoolers I have read about will not like my "C-minus" designation at all, but regardless of what grade we apply, they feel homeschooling is a significant step up from the local urban high school. And the recent data on test scores and college admissions supports that the homeschoolers often are right, and I was wrong, in my assessment of homeschooling quality.

Parents today look to homeschooling far more than for the stereotypical "school environment" or "religious" reasons. Their goal is a better education than they see as available via the local public school. Here is a very insightful view on homeschooling by Ashley Kimler. She is a parent and writer in Oregon who actively homeschools her three children.

> **(Ashley Kimler) Why Homeschool? A Mother's Perspective on the Public School System**
>
> "Stand up, put your hand over your heart, and say the pledge of allegiance. Get in line and eat your GMO's. Take this toothpaste home for Crest's marketing campaign. Tell your friends and family to buy this imported plastic junk. You can do this. You *can't* do that. You stood up to a bully? Good for you, but you need to stay home for a week now," they said.
>
> Well, at least that's all *I* heard from the public school system. I've asked myself questions like, 'did we really *vote* to do away with music and art?' and, 'If my son is testing at a 7th grade level, why is he bringing home 4th grade work?' Like all other great American institutions, the public school system has been strategically replaced by a one-size-fits-all approach, implemented by those in power. No longer are our children's educations the top priority. Backed into a corner with three kids who have extremely unique personalities and needs, I realized that if I want it done right, I have to try to do it myself.
>
> Home schooling for high school takes 4-plus dedicated quality hours per day compared to the 8-10 they are at bus stops, on the bus, or lost in 25-30 person classes at public school. By joining local homeschooler groups and playing sports, children outside the mainstream system can have just as much quality social interaction.
>
> These days, it just makes sense.

Ashley presents a view that is provocative and controversial, but an excellent insight into how so many homeschoolers view today's urban high school education. And it is a clear pointer to the failure of public schools to meet the educational needs of many children.

The pinnacle of the "passionate teacher" and the "small class size" concepts?

> The potential of homeschooling also benefits from something that is disappearing from public schools because of the micromanagement and dumbed-down curricula being forced on teachers by school

administrators and career DoE bureaucrats – excitement and passion in the classroom. Today's teachers are burned out (much more on this topic in chapter 24). And in today's classroom, nothing is more important to unleashing the potential of a child than having a teacher who is engaged and excited about teaching. Nothing!

Please do not think that I am dismissing experience, knowledge, subject matter expertise, or training. I am not. But I have learned those things are secondary. For any teacher, the two most powerful factors in teaching effectiveness are a teacher's visible passion for teaching, and having genuine high expectations and belief in the children. Children can tell when it's real – and they respond! And as I watched teachers (and sat through hundreds of parent-teacher nights and conferences), another factor became clear – far and away the most important characteristic in the child that made a difference is when those children had parents who shared the exact same passion and expectations for their sons and daughters.

One of the best things in my life has been sharing time with, and watching, great teachers unlock the promise in our children despite all the mandates that directly tie the hands of teachers and prevent teaching. I always enjoyed sitting in the back of an English class where I could watch two exceptional young women get through to urban high school students, breathing life into *To Kill a Mockingbird*, or *Of Mice and Men*. Every year I would eavesdrop on physics classes tracking bubblehead dolls on bungee-cord drops down a stairwell, or battling with homemade catapults. I smiled every time students would share with me about teachers they really liked. Parents would be genuinely surprised at how often the talk in the teacher lunchroom is about our pride in children who are doing better and better each week, despite the system.

But over the years, as I looked at the best teachers, something finally dawned on me. The very best ones were not the ones the system expected to excel. They were exceptional because of something far different, something that an "outsider" like James Ryan in his passage below, seems to have figured out faster than I did. They encouraged as much as taught.

> *(James Ryan is a motivational educator, homeschool parent, nationally recognized developer of improved systems for major organizations, and a best-selling author with Steve Forbes. He lives in Virginia.)*

(James Ryan) Motivation, passion, and coaching our children

A home school teacher dismays the parents of a child when she advises that the child should go into 3rd grade rather than the goal of 4th when transitioning from home school to private school. The teacher believed that working memory and attention may be limiting factors.

How could a child, who had always before been identified as gifted, slow down so much in one year? The parents take action. First, they find a test of working memory – read a long number and recite it backwards from memory. The parents test this using a credit card number. The daughter gets a quick glance and the card is turned over. How many can she recite backwards from memory? The results is all – a very rare result for any child.

So, it's not a working memory issue as thought by the home school teacher. Next, one parent becomes a coach for his daughter with a goal of helping her pass the 3rd grade standardized test in 4 weeks, even though the child had recently passed the 2nd grade test with only average results.

Did the child achieve the goal? Yes, with flying colors. How could a parent allow his child to achieve more in 30 days than was achieved in the prior 7 months? The parent used leadership and coaching techniques proven in industry to motivate, remove self-limiting blocks, and empower the student to teach themselves. Want more motivated students? Allow teachers to become better leaders – it's a science anyone can learn. Teachers lead students and some lead better than others.

Want high performing students? Teach less, coach more.

What James Ryan identified is an aspect of homeschooling that I always underestimated. We always talk about the benefits of small class sizes, and the need to encourage and motivate our students. Homeschooling takes those two concepts to their pinnacle.

(Chapter 11)
Failure – Cheating and rampant cronyism in schools

Few parents realize the scope of corruption and cronyism in our schools. Because it is so hard for teachers to take the career-threatening risk of reporting such incidents, most instances are never seen or reach the news. You do not want to be a whistleblower in a school – unless you really don't need a job!

Despite the lack of all the additional reports teachers could have reported, , the Washington Post[20] confirmed cheating scandals in thirty-seven states, and was convinced that there were far more actual incidents than were ever discovered.

Here are just a few examples – the tip of the iceberg in a problem that infests almost every urban high school. Later (chapter 20) we detail rampant corruption and cronyism in appointments and assignments that has undermined teacher faith in their own administration.

New Jersey DOE Deposition: *"…corruption, cronyism, favoritism, racism, and discrimination that has plagued the District for decades…"*[21]

UK Daily Standard: *"Culture of cronyism is at the very heart of education."*[22]

The Village Voice: *Even by New York standards it was an astonishing display of venality…all caught on video. That tape, accompanying a report released April 29 by board of education investigators, epitomized corruption in School District 12. The footage was…one snapshot from years of systemic graft that has undermined the health, education, and welfare of tens of thousands of New York children…the scorching report that details widespread corruption, nepotism, and cronyism in the Bronx school district.*[23]

Ann Arbor News: *"…district is the former home of first-year Ypsilanti Superintendent Dedrick Martin, which raised questions of nepotism prior to the meeting. The vote came after board members voiced*

---

[20] *Atlanta Test cheating: Tip of the iceberg?*, Washington Post April 2013
[21] New Jersey DOE hearing, Sep 2011
[22] UK Daily Standard, Jun 2007
[23] Village Voice, May 1993

concerns over Moore's qualifications, the hiring process, his salary and why current principal Jon Brown couldn't be retained."[24]

San Bernardino Sentinel: "...the San Bernardino City Unified School District's former assistant superintendent of human resources and its current associate superintendent and chief administrative officer, has engaged in numerous examples of nepotism, cronyism and race-driven favoritism, according to an independent hearing officer who looked into the district's personnel practices."[25]

AJC: "A DeKalb grand jury reindicted (sic) former school Superintendent Crawford Lewis last week. There are new developments in the criminal case against former DeKalb school chief Crawford Lewis and construction manager Pat Reid, developments that only underscore the imperative to take an unflinching and unapologetic look at who holds which positions in the district and how they got them."[26]

Dallas, Tx: "Favoritism, cronyism and friendships will no longer be the criteria for selecting new principals," said Bea Martinez, a former president of the North Texas LULAC chapter. "It's not about adults, it's about children."[27]

Fairfield, CA: School administrators are investigating a grade-changing scandal involving at least seven students at Armijo High School-- and they say there's no indication the students had anything to do with it.[28]

Philadelphia, PA: A city principal and four teachers helped young children cheat on standardized tests by changing their answers and reviewing questions beforehand, prosecutors charged as they announced a widespread, ongoing grand jury investigation. Attorney General Kathleen Kane accused the defendants Thursday of "perpetuating a culture of cheating" on the Pennsylvania System of School Assessment tests over a five-year period. The grand jury found that after the cheating at their inner-city school stopped in 2012, the percentage of students who scored well on the tests dropped dramatically. Fifth-grade reading proficiency fell from 50 percent to 16 percent at Cayuga Elementary School, and math proficiency from 62 percent to 22 percent, authorities said.[29]

---

[24] Ann Arbor MI News, April 2010
[25] San Bernardino Sentinel, April 2012
[26] AJC, May 2012
[27] Dallas News, May 2013
[28] News10 ABC, Sacramento, CA, 22 Nov 14
[29] Associated Press, 7 Aug 14

Washington, DC: *District of Columbia schools officials say they've found cheating at 11 schools during the last school year. It says "critical violations" of testing integrity were found at seven public schools and four charter schools. Test results from those schools will be thrown out. The audit was released on the same day it was revealed that city school officials knew in early 2009 about possible widespread cheating. An internal memo shows that an analyst found 191 teachers at 70 schools may have erased their students' wrong answers and filled in the right ones.*[30]

El Paso, TX: *A federal judge sentenced the former superintendent of El Paso Independent School District to more than three years in prison Friday for his participation in a conspiracy to improve the district's high-stakes tests scores by removing low-performing students from classrooms. Lorenzo Garcia's scheme to prevent hundreds of sophomores from taking the accountability tests fooled authorities into believing that academic standards had improved in his West Texas district – resulting in a boost in federal funds and personal bonuses totaling at least $56,000. Garcia pleaded guilty to two fraud counts in June; one in the testing scandal and another in which he misled the school board so that his lover would receive a $450,000 no-bid contract to produce school materials.*[31]

Detroit, MI: *I found Detroit Public Schools to be a magnificent vessel of wholesale theft and graft. Not one area of management escaped the thieves and defrauders: One high school food service worker stuffed as much as $200 daily from lunchroom sales into her apron and bra. A teacher and her mother, a contract accountant, placed $500,000 worth of orders for supplies from a sham company they had created. Ten people collectively stole more than 1,500 laptops. Even sworn police officers assigned to my security detail committed fraud, submitting phony overtime reports. I chose a former FBI executive as my inspector general to root out waste, fraud and abuse. The laptop thieves were charged with operating a criminal enterprise under the Racketeer Influenced and Corrupt Organizations Act. Many culprits pleaded guilty or were convicted by a jury. Washington was sentenced to seven years in prison.*[32]

---

[30] Huffington Post, 6 Dec 13
[31] Associated Press, 12 May 12
[32] *Corruption is destroying America's schools*, Richmond Times-Dispatch, 22 Jul 14

(Chapter 12)
Failure – Resistance to Common Core and Standardized Testing

Nine states[33] have already rejected common core, with more rejections anticipated. There are three major reasons for the evolving failure of common core – the first two are (potentially) solvable, but the last one is deadly.

- (Potentially solvable) The widespread negative unintended consequences of standardized testing that lead to dumbed-down education and "teaching-to-the-test."
- (Potentially solvable) Controversies over some of the content in common core
- (Deadly) Technical, design, and rollout issues

Even if we somehow resolved every subjective common core content question to everyone's satisfaction, and magically cured the dumbing-down of education that occurs when we focus on standardized test results, Common Core would still fail because of severe DoE failures in design, management, and rollout.

Teaching to the test

In chapter 18 we cover the first point in detail. Teachers forced to teach-to-the-test is directly responsible for dumbing down education. Here is just one actual example:

> *Anonymous is a retired high school English teacher from California. She describes a very common impact of standardized testing on teachers and students. Like most teachers, she prefers to not reveal her name in order to avoid retribution from school administrators for speaking out.*
>
> **(Anonymous) California STAR Testing – Yet another example of pressure on teachers to teach-to-the-test and to change failing grades**
>
> With state testing becoming a pressure cooker, my high school principal had teachers take time out of our regular curriculum to prep with specific test questions. She also held a student only rally in which students were promised a class

---

[33] As of Nov 2014

grade bump if their scores were higher than last year's. We discussed grade bumping at our department meetings, and my English department refused to give a higher grade to a student for what they did on one test, concluding that what they did in class was the only fair way to assign their grades.

Sure enough, students demanded grade changes after the test. One student with 50% demanded a passing grade. When I refused, her parents threatened to go to the school board, sue, etc.

My principal tried to throw me under the bus by repeatedly making me meet with the irate mother and crying student. After two heated meetings, I called the union. The union president sat in on the next meeting telling both the principal and mother that only a teacher can change a grade.

My principal then came up with a rally flyer. It said that students whose scores improved could receive a 6% bump in their class grade. She said I <u>had</u> to change the grade since students received this written notice. Another meeting was called. Armed with a copy of the flyer, I told both mother and student I would honor it and give her the 6%. Her grade, however, would not change because 56% is not a passing grade.

Content issues – a major topic not for this book

The second reason, content issues in some subjects (History, English and Biology seem to be the most visible), are very controversial. There are deep, genuine concerns by many parents and teachers about some topics and how they are covered. While I might have a personal opinion on a few of those issues, luckily none of them impact the one topic I am qualified to discuss, math – all voices seem to still agree that 2 + 2 = 4. Those content issues are for a different discussion than this book.

Can standardized testing measure intangibles?

A submission by noted educator Dr. Lois Jarmin, below, exposed a critical subtlety that I had completely missed about standard testing when researching this topic for the 1st edition of *Lifting the Curtain* – one that is only visible when a teacher's view from within the classroom is presented. Dr. Jarmin raises the much bigger question of:

how can we present such subjective and intangible topics as music and the arts under the structure of codified education and standardized "…choose 'A,' 'B,' 'C,' or 'D' answers?

> *Dr. Lois A. Jarman is high school modern languages teacher in Maryland. She has been a foreign language educator for more than 15 years, and has taught French, Spanish, and Latin. She has served on curriculum committees and presented at conferences on teaching in the target language.*

(Dr. Jarmin) The future of Music and Arts under "education reform"

Albert Einstein said "the true sign of intelligence is not knowledge but imagination." On a trip to the art gallery, my students and I had a guided tour of French masterpieces led by two docents. I had prepared my students in advance with a mini-art unit conducted completely in French-our tour, however, was in English.

In front of various paintings, the docents would ask questions about what the students saw and their thoughts about the artwork. The discourse was intriguing and imaginative. My students were sharing ideas that put together what they had learned in many classes – psychology, history, math…. It was amazing to observe my students experience art in this way.

On the ride home, I pondered the experience and the likelihood future trips like this might not be able to continue under education reforms. There was no "bubble-in" answer sheet to accompany our activity. There was no way to accurately measure the learning that occurred during the museum visit. How could that possibly be quantified? Without quantifying the experience, how could I be evaluated as a teacher?

The more I thought about it, the greater my fear became that this type of activity won't have much of a future in reform education. With a focus on test results, there will be no time for these experiences, no room for events that expand imagination. I see tremendous value in learning through experience. I've watched my students grow this way.

I've yet to see growth through testing.

The same issue – the difficulty of standardized assessments for the music and arts -- was raised by Nathaniel C. Ashbaugh. He is a highly qualified performing artist and music educator, teaching middle school music in New Mexico.

This quote from an administrator is embedded in my nightmares—"You are correct, but that's not the way we do things here." This was uttered in response to factual, research-based, data-driven statements made in support of students who wish to be involved in music class but are denied because of their test scores. The blame lies not on site administrators, but on the new "common-core standards."

Whether the available time for the music course is usurped for test preparation classes, or the student is denied access to the music course due to low test scores, the child loses.

Common core is not the solution to the education deficiencies as perceived by its designers. Music, in its simplest, purest form, is the solution. It is a *fact* that learning music makes neurological pathways stronger, and develops these pathways where they previously did not exist. It is a *fact* that music supports all other subjects that are valued so highly.

Yet, statements such as the one above are still made, in ignorance of that fact. "Common-Core Standards" mean music teachers are forced to make cumbersome attempts at making a "square peg fit in a round hole" by being forced to include math lessons and different focus points from testing deficiencies in their music lesson plans, visible to anyone every day, instead of teaching a subject that is already, and has been for centuries, common-core.

The problem with education is that these facts are ignored, and administrators need to refrain from taking students out of music. After all, the *fact* is that music increases test scores *and* self-esteem all at the same time. Common Core – please let us do it right and make music available to every child.

Common core – "…It couldda bin a contendah!"

When it comes to common core, I will sound as though I am talking out of both sides of my mouth. I like the new *math* framework, even though I dread seeing it enter my high school classes. For math, at least, it has the *potential* to be a truly exceptional upgrade to teaching – it goes back 30 years to the idea of having students *understand* math, rather than *remember* steps. In truth, the most successful math teachers already use such an approach, despite all the system does to try to dumb down instruction so that "everybody passes."

Yet many of our most successful teachers, even us curmudgeonly math types, are strongly against the new core for technical reasons. We are highly concerned that what could (and should!) have been a big step forward in math education has been so mishandled by inept career DoE bureaucrats that it will be just another major failure of a poorly implemented bureaucratic mandate.

Even if everything else was magically fixed, common core is untenable, even the good parts, because those who are responsible for its implementation are neither qualified nor experienced to roll out and manage a project anywhere close to this level of technical complexity. Common core is a huge project, easily comparable to the technical scope of the Obamacare website rollout. No matter what you think of the healthcare policy itself, love it or hate it, the technical part of the rollout was yet another exercise in complete bureaucratic incompetence.

Common core is directly comparable to "...a healthcare website" rolled out by bureaucrats who have never worked in IT, or "...a teacher evaluation system" implemented by bureaucrats who have no knowledge or experience in HR best practices, or any of the dozens of recent bureaucratic failures that have dominated the news.

Implementation timeline mismanagement:

> One technical cause for the rejection of common core by so many states is the typical ineptitude by the career bureaucrats in DoE cubicles that once again produced a poorly thought-out implementation and rollout of a new mandate. This year, standardized math test for sophomores in high school will have significant content based upon the new approach to math — *even though those students have just started to see the very different learning approach in their classes.* A sensible and professional implementation and rollout would have been phased over 4-5 years — starting the content in elementary school, expand it in middle school, and be ready for high

school testing when those students had experienced the needed lead-in to the new approach.

Many teachers and administrators fear a major drop off in standardized test scores this year (with the resulting deadly school sanctions and staff firings) because students will not be ready for the new style of questions after just a few months of working with them. Personally, I expect a bloodbath in math scores, unless state DoEs do what Massachusetts has routinely done in the past – hide the failure by quietly lowering the passing requirement for the year's test when they don't want parents and legislators to see that too many children are failing under their watch.

High costs, and weak or non-existent support materials:

The second problem is both the major cost and lack of materials and textbooks for an "immediate" rollout before such materials can be professionally prepared. Schools are being forced to purchase new books consistent with the new common core, yet many of the "new and improved" common core text books are little more than quick-and-dirty reworks of existing texts by publishers rushing to capitalize on new sales possibilities. Even a wannabe author like me knows that it takes time and a lot of effort to design a new textbook based upon a significant change in approach – plus all the related lessons, homework, projects, etc. *Most* of these new books are so weak that they will have to be scrapped and replaced (at even more cost) down the line.

Meanwhile, school budgets have to prepare for the significant indirect expense for the rollout of a new common core – new testing materials, preparation of curricula, and replacement text books all place a very large financial burden on high schools.

Curricula – missing in action:

Third, as usual, the bureaucratic approach to rolling out a new program the scope of common core relied on classroom teachers to pick up the pieces and make it work. I spent many days, pulled from my classroom, as my math department struggled to prepare for common core. Every school has had to divert weeks of teacher time to try to create new curricula for all the courses – because the career bureaucrats in state and federal DoEs did not bother to include such materials in their rollout plans.

A laundry list of core standards, no matter how good, is not a curriculum.

And none of the subjective issues are the real reason why Common Core "...couldda been a contendah," but never had the chance. Even a "perfect" Common Core (in terms of content) still needs professional management and planning to succeed.

An Original Survey of Teachers and Students

(Chapter 13)
Setting the table – Teacher and Student Views

Before you can solve a problem, it is critical to understand its scope and magnitude. A significant difficulty in trying to analyze what is happening today in education is that the statistics we really need to see – information about student attitudes, parent expectations, and current classroom methods – *simply did not exist until I decided to design and conduct an extensive survey of students and teachers*. We have all the data we can handle on teacher salaries, class size, test scores, graduation rates, and racial/social classifications. But the real indicators of the crisis in education remain largely hidden.

Ironically, despite all the surveys that have been accomplished regarding schools, there is almost no current public information about student and teacher opinions, and about what students and teachers think is happening in education.

We seem to have asked everyone <u>outside</u> of the school building what is wrong with education, but ignored the views of everyone <u>inside</u> the building!

A second problem is that we all have a tendency to mistake the symptoms for the causes. The question should not be "…how do we punish schools that cheat on standard tests?" but rather should be "…why have so many schools had cheating scandals?" The factors listed in the first chapters of this book are symptoms. In subsequent chapters we identify why they occur.

This book is based upon three years of active research, surveying, interviewing, and speaking to hundreds of students and teachers in urban high schools throughout the northeast. In addition, it reflects the past decade as a classroom math teacher in an urban high school.

I must again emphasize that the estimates are biased towards conditions in urban high schools – and certainly overstate some of the problems for some schools. Because such statistics will vary greatly in different school districts (*especially elementary school versus high school comparisons*) please look at the magnitudes and scope of the issues rather than at the specific numbers! What matters is that a "lot" of students cheat and a "lot" of parents don't care. Whether the actual percentage for factor "X" in another school system is "20%" rather than "50%" is of far lesser importance than the fact that <u>either percentage is far too problematic for the system to succeed</u>.

Published studies on student and teacher attitudes are very rare. In 2008 Perri Applegate at the University of Oklahoma[34] conducted an excellent analysis of what led to success in rural school educations. The crux of the findings was apparently lost on many educators – success did <u>not</u> come from the normal education metrics, or from suitcases full of money for education, but rather from effective co-responsibility between parent, teacher, and student to foster an attitude of success. Midgley, Feldlaufer and Eccles in 1989[35] did a study that is still relevant today about the strong effect a teacher's attitude towards students has on how the student performs. Barkley[36] presents a compelling argument that children can only learn from a teacher if they like that teacher. There are a handful of treatises on classroom attitudes written in the 1980s that are still relevant today.

However, there are no known recent public studies about how <u>students</u> and <u>teachers</u> actually feel about education, and about the core issues facing education today.

Thus, over three years in 2012 and 2014, I conducted an intensive survey of students and teachers to address the real issues confronting today's educational system – cheating, student effort, parental involvement, and expectations of all stakeholders in a child's education. Most of the survey results were from students and teachers in metropolitan cities surrounding Boston, Massachusetts – towns such as Lowell, Revere, Chelsea, Saugus, Lawrence, and Woburn. For those readers unfamiliar with the Boston area, none of these towns would be considered "affluent suburbs," all have a very high percentage of students who qualify for free or reduced lunch, and all have a history of "low performance" as defined by the state DoE.

The results were sobering. We can argue over whether the children had an accurate perception of conditions (I believe that they did!) or challenge a particular finding as being unrealistically high or low for other geographies, but the magnitude of the issues still remains. These students succinctly identified the <u>symptoms</u> that have been caused by systemic failures in education.

Both surveys were anonymous. Many students also chose to volunteer important insights via the four optional questions at the end of the survey. The instructions emphasized that the questions were not about the student who was filling out the survey, but rather what he/she feels is accurate for the <u>other</u> students in the school. To put the answers in perspective, these students

---

[34] Science Daily, June 2013
[35] *Student/Teacher Relations and Attitudes towards Mathematics Before and After the Transition to Junior High School.* Carol Midgley, Harriett Feldhaufer and Jacqueline Eccles, 1989
[36] Wow! Adding Pizzazz to Teaching and Learning, Stephen G. Barkley

typically took five or six classes per week, and the class size for almost all of these students was twenty-five to thirty.

The survey of teachers turned out to be far more difficult to accomplish than I ever envisioned when I started this project. With 20-20 hindsight, I should have anticipated the resistance by teachers to complete such a questionnaire. *I had to be very careful when I approached teachers in my own school, because teachers had a strong fear of retaliation by administration if their participation was discovered.* Fortunately, I was able to use my contacts in other schools, from years of coaching, to obtain most of my survey teacher responses.

There were two major reasons for so many teachers fearing to be part of the survey:

> The overwhelming majority of the concerns were fear that the results would not be anonymous, and that their schools would be able to identify their participation in the survey if the results appeared critical of the school. This was seen by the teachers as something that would end up being reflected in their evaluations, get them on the administration "poop list," and would eliminate any chance they would receive any of the extra pay assignments that are so important to most teachers. (Chapter 5 concentrates on the issue of school administrators bullying of teachers using the threat of censure or lack of assignments as a weapon.) I often heard the comment "…if anyone asks, I did not fill this out for you…" when teachers took the survey.

> Second, many teachers were sincerely worried that anyone would risk drawing even more criticism down on them by publicizing critical views about teaching and education. As will be discussed at length later, teachers are more and more defensive about their occupations because of the widespread attacks and criticisms teachers receive.

The teacher survey paralleled the student questionnaire topics, and also added questions about administration, regulations, and parents. On the questions that overlapped, it is fascinating to compare the student and teacher perceptions of the same issue. Most of the time, the two perceptions were very close together.

It is easy to write off student opinions on education – but based upon comparing them to the teacher results and my own anecdotal experience – these students were spot on!

(Chapter 14)
The Student and Teacher Survey Results[37]

How much homework do you think <u>other</u> students average for all classes combined <u>at home</u> (not including class work, on the bus, or in the morning in cafeteria) for the <u>whole week</u>?

The results of this question would be no surprise to any veteran teacher. The typical urban high school student today in this survey did far less homework in a *week* than most of their parents used to do in a *single night*. Total at-home homework for the week averaged just 1.5 hours.

Even more telling was the distribution. Only 3% of all students did more than an hour each night of homework. 46% did less than 15 minutes homework per night, including the 16% who did not do any homework at all.

Student Results:

Average hours/week:	*1.5 hours*
None	16%
0-1 hours/week	30%
1-2 hours/week	31%
3-5 hours/week	20%
More than 5 hours/week	3%

Teacher results:

Average hours/week:	*1.2 hours*

Homework in today's urban high schools is becoming a dying concept, and has lost much of its powerful effectiveness in helping children master concepts. Without the practice and reinforcement offered by well-planned homework, it is simply not possible for a student to master and retain high school material. There is a direct and obvious correlation between the reduction in homework and the reduction in educational performance.

---

[37] Survey detail and methodology is summarized at LiftingTheCurtain.com

The raw numbers in this response underestimate the scope of the problem. In addition to the children who do little or no homework, many more willingly accept zeroes, and many simply copy another student's homework on the bus or in the cafeteria each morning. When I put all these factors together, combined with years of classroom experience, I believe that no more than 25% of today's urban high school students gain any meaningful educational benefit from today's homework assignments.

Please remember – this is just a *symptom, and is not a cause*. It is one of the core factors responsible for undermining today's education. In subsequent chapters we look at the vital question of "…why is this happening to homework?"

I'll be late for dinner, hon. Still four more homes to go where parents expect me to make sure their kids do their homework.

However, homework is an excellent indicator of a symptom that can point to an actual reason for such a systemic failure, if we just lift the curtain a bit. If a handful of students did no homework, we could dismiss it as an anomaly. But when 46% of urban high school students do less than one hour of home work in an entire week, then the problem goes well beyond an anomaly. *A significant and rapidly growing minority of urban high school parents believe that it is the teacher's job to ensure a child does required homework.*

This result is closely related to several additional survey questions (copying homework, parents who do not care what grades a student gets, and students who do not care what grades they get). For a growing minority of students in today's urban high schools, a good teacher can do little to ensure a child even attempts homework at home each night.

Teachers clearly own part of the responsibility for homework (making fair, manageable, relevant assignments and properly grading them), but homework can only succeed if the parent and child assume co-responsibility. Many of the students (and their parents) in this survey took no responsibility for accomplishing homework.

How many of the other students do you think study, at home, to prepare for tests?

Only 14% of all urban high school students actually prepare at home the night before a test. As bad as the finding on this question is, it is even worse if you look underneath the aggregate. There is a strong cross-correlation between test preparation and class level (standard/CP/honors), and between test preparation and testing format (open-ended versus multiple choice). If you remove honors students from the totals, the figure drops to 8%. If the student also expects the test to be open response, then the figure rises to 23%.

Very telling, if you look at the distribution, was that the *highest* estimate by any student was that only one-third of students study before a test.

Student results:

Study before a test:	*14%*
Study before a test (excluding honors):	*8%*
Study before a test (if tests are open response, not multiple choice):	*23%*

Teacher results:

Study before a test:	*12%*

This result is a one of the best examples from the survey of a symptom that must be looked at systemically. Failure to study before a test is one symptom that results from a tightly interrelated group of factors – including overuse of multiple choice tests, intentionally dumbed-down tests, opportunities for do-overs and extra credit to pull up bad grades, low parental involvement, student attitudes, and lowered expectations.

These answers aren't simple. To paraphrase a famous Washington saxophone player – it's the system, stupid.

How many <u>other</u> students in a typical class do you think copy homework from another student?

This is one of the results that actually is much lower than I expected. According to the students, "only" 29% of students copy homework on the bus or in the cafeteria in the morning. Even with 20-20 hindsight, I expected a much higher number.

Student results:

Percent of students who copy homework: *29%*

Teacher results:

Percent of students who copy homework: *37%*

This result, even if accurate, is misleading. It does not include those students who willingly take a zero on homework assignments. In my years of teaching I found that roughly 6-8 children in a class of 30 will have no qualms about taking a zero for homework, and do not seem to care about the grade. These are often the same students who fail tests, yet never come in for extra help.

**Hurry up and finish your homework, Kevin!
I need to copy it before the bell or I'll miss breakfast!**

If I factor in students willingly taking zeroes, it results in the following:

(Survey) Percent of students who copy *homework:*	29%
(Opinion) Percent who take *zeroes* rather than do the *homework:*	20 – 27%
(Total) Did not attempt their own *homework:*	49 – 56%

While the numbers are high, they are remarkably consistent with the finding of the earlier questions.

How many of the tests given in your school are multiple choice versus open response?

This result will certainly seem innocuous to most people, yet it should bother every parent a great deal. As will be discussed at length later, the overuse of multiple choice tests is a destructive factor in today's education. And, despite the many pressures on teachers that force them to use multiple choice, this is an area where teachers must try to improve the system, *despite* the system.

First, a quick definition of how I am using these terms. By "open response" I mean that the answers are written details – perhaps a paragraph for a history or English question, or showing the detailed steps for a math problem. By "multiple choice" I include both the traditional "A-B-C-D-E" choice format, and also fill-in-the-blanks formats (such as "Lincoln was president during the _____ war.").

Student results:

Percent of tests that are multiple choice: 56%

Teacher results:

Percent of tests that are multiple choice: 67%

Teachers have little choice but to use multiple choice tests rather than open-ended tests. Many school administrations consciously embraced and urged use of multiple choice in the hopelessly false premise of "...preparing our students to take standardized tests." Often the class size makes open-ended questions nearly impossible to grade and process.

To understand the pressure to use multiple choice tests (other than when administrations require it in the misguided view that it helps students get ready for standardized testing), consider a typical English teacher who teaches a standard-level class of 30 students. He/she assigns an open response essay (two pages) on *To Kill a Mockingbird*. To properly read, edit, analyze, annotate corrections and suggestions, and grade such an essay would take a professional editor 15-20 minutes, *each*. (If this was simple copyediting, an editing pro could finish two typed pages in 4-8 minutes. However, this is a "developmental editing" project – errors need to be annotated and explained, and reading is compounded by bad handwriting. This results in a much longer editing requirement.) Multiply that by 30 students in the class and you have a total of 8-10 *hours* to correct just one test for one class. If that English teacher teaches four classes, then those forty hours of essay correction are added at night, in addition to the 30 hours of weekly base duties of teaching those four classes and administrative duties and the 10-15 hours of homework correction and class planning. An 80-hour workweek for a high school English teacher is far different from the "part time teaching position" many people envision.

So, given the realities of this timeframe to completely correct an open-ended test, there are just two options. Both options occur. Option one is that the essay is fully reviewed, but some of the factors the teacher finds that influence the grade are never annotated onto the paper. This does allow an accurate and responsible grade, but means the student gets a paper back with no clear relationship between the grade and what was handed in. It also can make it appear that "bad" work is acceptable. The second option is to use multiple choice tests, or have part of the test be multiple choice, so that grading for all those students can be done in a timely manner.

As much as I understand the pressure to use multiple choice tests (been there, done that, have the t-shirt), they always have a strong negative impact on the quality of education for our children. It's a deadly trap, and it is up to us, as teachers, to absolutely minimize their use despite what the system and class sizes forces us to do. Multiple choice focuses the child's education more on remembering facts than on understanding ideas – a recipe for educational failure. Multiple choice tests mean that the student can do 99% of the problem right and get it "wrong" because of a small mistake. Worse, the students never know why something was wrong, so that they can learn from their mistake. I have had untold numbers of new students over the years who think they are "dumb" and cannot do math, when it turned out (looking at their detailed work, not just the answer) that they were simply having brainfarts on small parts of the problem.

Here is a simple math example to make the point:

(Student answers with "8.7" (instead of the correct "10") and gets a zero for the answer – even though the student completely understood the material).

The problem uses Pythagoras (remember – the old $C^2 = A^2 + B^2$?)

$C^2 = A^2 + B^2$ ← Student nailed it – used correct formula
$C^2 = 6^2 + 8^2$ ← excellent, correctly substituted
$C^2 = 12 + 64$ ← **oops, brainfart!** $6^2 = 36$, not 12
$C^2 = 76$ ← correct, except used the incorrect 12
$C = \sqrt{76}$ ← correct, saw the need to use a square root
$C = 8.7$ ← final answer as entered on multiple choice

Since this is a multiple choice answer, the teacher never sees the work and just marks it wrong. The student gets a zero for this problem, thinks he/she is dumb, says "…I can't do Pythagoras," and has no idea where they went wrong. Actually, this is the work of an "A" student who just had a brainfart on squaring the number six.

As if the bad education impact of multiple choice tests is not enough, they also contribute strongly to cheating. It is very easy, with just a sideways glance that will never be caught, even by a vigilant teacher, to copy a multiple choice checkmark. Classrooms are so overcrowded and desks are so close together that it is hard for a student to *not* see adjacent tests. In addition, many multiple choice tests are created from test generator software, and are repeated class-to-class, and year-to-year. The kids pass them down to the next class. Children actively steal copies of the teacher version of textbooks, and steal copies of the test generator software, to get the tests in advance. Saving multiple choice tests for your friends has become a cottage industry in many urban high schools.

Yes, there is pressure because of large class sizes (almost all of my classes the past few years have 30 students per class crammed into a classroom designed for 20) to use multiple choice. And yes, there are misguided administrations that still want us to use multiple choice because standardized tests are largely multiple choice questions. Yet we, as teachers, must find ways to make absolutely the minimum possible use of multiple choice where at all possible.

Multiple choice tests are a deadly weakness in today's education. We need to absolutely minimize their use!

How many classes in your school do you think regularly allow do-overs or extra credit assignments to pull up a failing grade?

I wrote this section about do-overs last, when covering the student survey results, because I kept getting deeply disturbed every time I looked at the data. Do-overs are a symptom whose cause will get a *lot* of ink later in this book. Phony do-overs, the "curve," and "...extra credit packets to pull up your grade" do nothing except let children pass without earning it, while teaching them that they can "succeed" even with no effort. This is a disaster for any chance at good education.

Student result:

Percent of your teachers that allow do-overs, etc.: 51%

Teacher result:

Percent of teachers in the school that allow do-overs, etc.: 55%

There is unbelievable pressure on teachers to pass every student regardless of the child's effort. (The reasons for that pressure are covered in great detail later – we are still looking at the problems, not their causes.) The result is that even many of the best teachers have caved under the intense DoE and administration pressure, and find ways to pass everyone.

I must emphasize something again – this excessive use of make-up assignments is a symptom, not the problem itself. The issue is not "…how do we stop allowing do-overs?" but rather is "…why do good teachers cave in and do them at all?"

How many <u>other</u> students in a typical class do you think cheat on weekly tests?

Many things contribute to cheating – and all are major topics later in this book. For now, the issue is to quantify how prevalent cheating is in schools today.

Student result:

Percent of children who cheat on tests: 20%

Teacher result:

Percent of children who cheat on tests: 15%

According to the students, five or six children in every class are cheating. Yet this statistic understates the problem of cheating in school because of an oversight in my survey design. I believe that the result, based upon the way the question was worded, is accurate. However, in the choice of wording I forgot to include cheating <u>outside</u> of tests – plagiarized reports, copied assignments, etc.

*No Mr. West, I would never cheat!
I was just rubbing my forehead.*

That one in five children cheat on tests is no surprise to teachers. Even with close vigilance while proctoring a test, cheating is easy. Multiple choice test answers on another student's desk can easily be seen with a brief glance with eyes covered by a strategically located hand. Cell phones are prohibited in schools not just because they are a distraction or discipline issue, but even more so because they have become a remarkably effective way to cheat. Many schools use "common tests" so that all classes take the same test, which means that answer sheets can be passed class-to-class. Many schools also use common exams for midterms and finals, and do not change them year-to-year. By period "two," the results from period "one" testing are in the hands of a dozen students. In period "one," chances are good that a couple students had last year's exam.

One of the optional comments by a student in the 2013 survey showed an extreme perspective on the problem:

"I don't think I've ever tooken (sic) a test without people cheating"[38]

Once again – been there, done that. Two years ago I had a struggling math student get the correct answer to a very difficult test problem, even though his work was not even close to anything that could have achieved that answer. Since all my tests are open response, it was very

---

[38] Anon, Student Survey 2013

easy to detect that cheating had occurred. (It's like having the students work show "2+2 = 4", but he gives the correct answer of "946.221." Clearly something "odd" happened for him to get the right answer from totally the wrong work!) But I was baffled, because I am very careful when proctoring tests, and based upon his seating I saw that both students he might have copied had a different answer.

It turns out that the blunder was mine – one I soon corrected. He had "forgotten" his calculator, so I let him use his cell phone as a calculator. He simply took a photo of the question, sent it to a friend, and soon got a return message with the answer. Needless to say, cell phones were never allowed to be used as calculators from that day forward. Fool me once, shame on you, fool me twice…

Plagiarism on projects and reports is rampant, and a serious problem for all teachers. Whole reports are cut-and-pasted from web sources. Projects are often no more than squares of papers downloaded from the web and pasted onto a poster board. And the most critical factor here is <u>not</u> that children plagiarize, it is that they genuinely do not understand why it is wrong. This is the same moral gray area that makes it perfectly fine to download pirated songs, software, or games. I remember jumping in when I heard a group of boys bragging about the games they had downloaded from pirate sites. When I tried to get them to see this was stealing, what stunned me most was <u>not</u> the reply "…why should I pay for this when I can download it for free?" What really hurt was recognizing that look of bewilderment on the child's face, with no comprehension of how I could possibly see anything wrong with "…downloading free stuff."

The corollary in education is "…why should I take the time to write this report when I can download it for free?"

How many of the <u>other</u> students, in all the classes you have taken this year, do not seem to really care what they get for grades?

This is an important question, and a remarkable indicator of the problems facing schools today.

Student result:

Percent of students who do <u>not</u> care what grades they get: 23%

Teacher result:

Percent of students who do <u>not</u> care what grades they get: 24%

It would be easy to downplay this result. Many people might feel that this is children *pretending* to not care. But the reality is that a sizable part of today's students (almost one in four, per the students themselves) genuinely do not care. All that matters is that they get through the day, end up graduating, and don't do so badly that they draw the attention of their parents.

The lack of caring is reflected in many areas – homework, class work, test preparation, and attendance at extra help sessions. All teachers have at least one night a week where they stay late to help children. It is common for the extra help sessions to be attended by the best students who probably do not really need it, and be ignored by almost all of the failing students who should be there.

This problem is worsening, tangibly, every year.

As little as four years ago (back in 2008, as I write this paragraph in 2013) I would have put the percentage of students who did not really care at less than 5%, not the 23% the kids think (and I agree) is the case today. But the real problem is how rapidly this is growing. This year's freshman class (the class of 2016) has taken lack of caring to a new and very disturbing level. I would estimate that a full third of the freshmen I have taught this year, because of a rare assignment (for me) to 9th grade classes, simply do not care. When they flunk a test, it is a source of pride. They laugh and giggle as they proudly announce to the class that "…I got a 42!" I had two instances of freshmen this year choosing to not make up a quiz they missed, and take a zero "…nah, I'm still passing even with the zero."

Yesterday, as I write this, I was in the back of a freshman English class when they were taking their final for another teacher. They had to write two pages on a book (*To Kill a Mockingbird*) they had read the prior two terms. Part way through, several children started complaining that the test was "…too hard." Then one complained "…and you won't even show us the parts in the book that have the answers." (They had the books on their desks and were allowed to refer to them for the final.) The English teacher handled it with remarkable patience and effectiveness. But I was once again struck by how much this new freshman class *expected and demanded* that someone do the work for them. They had no comprehension why it was reasonable to ask them to open the book, and look for themselves.

And not a single parent of a failing 9th grader came to either parent-teacher night this year. Not one. (Please remember, the sample size for this observation is just two classes of 2016 freshman at this point – not nearly enough to draw a statistically meaningful conclusion.)

I am hoping this year's freshman class is an anomaly, and not a valid indicator of a trend. My concerned view seems to be shared by all the other teachers I have spoken to about the class. Stay tuned on this one!

Overall, how many teachers in your school do you think really do care about how well students do in classes?

This result is very discouraging, and the result has to be primarily laid at the feet of teachers despite all the external causes (to be covered later) that influence poor teacher attitudes. Even when I factor in an adjustment for a probable survey methodology error, the percentage is still unacceptable.

Student result:

Percent of teachers who really do care about their students: 27%

Teacher result:

This question was not asked of teachers

The raw figure suggests that students believe over 70% of teachers do not care. Even if we cut the estimate in half, the order of magnitude is still an educational disaster. For today's children, unlike most of us in school decades earlier, there is a very tight correlation between educational results and whether or not the child thinks the teacher likes him/her. An absolute fact for the majority of students today is that most can only learn from a teacher if they like that teacher.[39] Now, that is not true for all teacher-student relationships, but it certainly is accurate for *most* students in the schools I have researched.

Of course this 27% student figure understates the percentage of teachers who do care, because the survey does not do a good job of factoring in the teenager frame of reference. Far more teachers than this really do care about their students. The survey should have had additional questions that would have allowed me to separate out those

---

[39] *Wow! Adding Pizzazz to Teaching and Learning*, Barkley

students whose dislike for discipline or authority at all, or dislike of school, led them to dislike any adult who imposed a structure on them. Such a student would, due to poor survey design, easily chalk this up to "...the teacher doesn't care."

However, the percentage of teachers who do project an attitude of disinterest or dislike for children still is far too large. (The issue of teacher burnout is covered in chapter 24.) Many of these seem to be just going through the motions. Two students picked up on this and said it very succinctly in the survey comments:

"Fire the teachers that don't want to be here."[40]

"Teachers don't like to teach and tend to block a lot of things out."[41]

Over the years I have seen a handful of teachers who simply should not be teaching because of the way they treated children. Fortunately, as in *any* business that has employees, there are just a few of these in each school. Perhaps 5% of teachers fall into this category. A common denominator seems to be that they do not know how to discipline, are very uncomfortable when there is a difficult situation, and therefore resort to yelling, threatening, and insulting for any level of offense. We call these teachers the "screamers," whose only approach to discipline is yelling at the students. They are totally dismissive of the children, and then wonder why the children are disrespectful in return.

Just a handful of such teachers can taint the atmosphere of an entire school.

If the only problem was this angry 5%, we could deal with that in schools. But there is a much larger group of teachers that is of much greater concern. These are the ones I discuss at length in "Systemic Failure #6" (Chapter 24) where I look at the bunker mentality of many teachers that has resulted from having to work within the current system. The handful of angry, hateful teachers needs to be fired – they are unworthy of the title of teacher. The more significant problem is the much larger group of teachers that has caved in, and has become highly defensive because of what the system forces them to do every day. This issue can be reversed, but only by fixing the systemic problems that caused their deteriorating attitudes.

---

[40] Adriel, Student Survey 2013
[41] Mark, Student Survey 2013

Overall, how many parents of students you know do you think really <u>do</u> care about how well their children do in classes?

Anyone reading this result should be very concerned. I am sure there are schools that would receive a much more favorable result if surveyed, but this symptom is one of the most telling indicators of all that ails public education.

Student result:

Percent of parents who really <u>do</u> care about grades: *37%*

Teacher result:

Percent of parents who really <u>do</u> care about grades: *31%*

The red flag here is the implied corollary to this statistic. It suggests that over 60% of parents do <u>not</u> really care about student performance.

Normally I would be tempted to temper this figure by the same approach I cited with the "teachers who care" question. After all, a rite of passage for teenagers is to mistake imposing structure for lack of caring. However, while I know the …60% don't care…" figure is too high, I am deeply troubled by the knowledge that the actual figure is still a very high number, and certainly is <u>more than a third</u> of parents I have witnessed.

I interviewed many teachers about this result. Their overall assessment was chilling – a strong belief that perhaps *only one in four parents* is really invested in how their child does at school. I searched for any source of hard data (other than my teacher and student survey) that might support or challenge this notion, but found only one published source – a very suspect US Census finding for 2008 that is covered below.

One of the strongest statistical examples of this lack of parent interest is by tabulating the results of parent-teacher nights the past few years. In the teacher survey (a question following this one) just 4% of the parents of struggling students requested to attend parent-teacher nights and conferences actually showed up. My results parallel this survey result. Over the past decade, I have attended twenty parent-teacher nights, two per year. On average, I had a total of about 175 students in my chasses each year.

(Students) Typical number of students in all my classes: 175
(Problem students) Number of parents requested to attend   12
    to discuss concerns with their child's performance:
(Parents of problem students) Number of invited parents
    who attended: 1 (8%)
(Parents of good students) Number of parents of students who were
    doing well who attended: 18
Total attendance: 19 (11%)
(No-show parents) who did not choose to attend   156 (89%)
    Parent-Teacher conferences:

The import of the above summary is that over a ten year period an average of just 11% of all parents attended Parent-Teacher night. If we look only at those parents requested to attend so that we could discuss issues with their child's education, *a staggering 92% of requested parents did not bother to show up.* I can recall literally dozens of instance where an ally in guidance tried many times to set up a time for a private meeting, yet the parent never attended.

The above student data, and my own anecdotal data, is almost the opposite of an "official" government estimate on parent involvement. According to the U.S. Census Bureau,[42] 83% of High School parents are active parents who have attended PTA and parent-teacher activities, and 61% of parents attend "regularly" scheduled conferences.

(The survey question is flawed to the point of being statistically unreliable by professional econometric standards – after all, how many parents, when asked, will admit they do not attend? It is like asking a survey question "Do you beat your kids?" and then reporting the "fact" that 99.8% of parents "never" beat their children.)

In addition, the question's wording would allow a parent who attended just one meeting early in elementary school check the "yes" box. The detail in the census report also suggests that most of the interactions occurred in elementary school, with a big drop off in high school participation.

The US Census data (flawed as it is) is chilling – even at face value it means nearly 40% of parents are willing to admit they do not attend regular parent-teacher conferences. The supporting data indicates this 40% figure rises

---

[42] *Parent Involvement*, US Government Census Bureau 2007

dramatically if we look only at high school involvement, and do not include attendance back in elementary school.

The one group that is very active in attending meetings or conferences are the parents of SPED children – and sadly many of those meeting are for parent demands that end up hurting their children far more than helping. (SPED is a separate issue covered on "Systemic failure #4" in chapter 22.

(Teachers only) On a scale of 1 (very little support) to 5 (strong support) – how do you feel administration supports teachers when there is a conflict with a parent?

The result: 3.0 (mixed support)

The distribution of the raw data is very telling for this issue. Only 7% of teachers felt they got strong support, and 29% of the teachers reported little or very little support.

1	(very little)	12%	⎤
			⎦ 29%
2		17%	
3		41%	
4		23%	⎤
			⎦ 30%
5	(strong)	7%	

An urban high school teacher who does not get support from administration when there is a difference with a parent is in a deadly no-win situation. Either you must cave in to the demand (at the expense of the child's education by giving the child credit for something they did not learn or earn) or you sign up for days of nasty confrontation, strong pressure, and the risk the strong displeasure of administration. The parent can easily go around the teacher, directly to guidance, SPED, and even the principal, in order to try to get a grade changed, challenge a disciplinary action, or get an overdue assignment waved.

The best guidance professionals, by nature, want to resolve confrontations by negotiation and compromise – i.e. give the student another chance or a do-over. Weak principals just want the problem to go away before it reaches the school committee or causes a decline in passing/graduation rates for students – i.e. give the student another chance or do-over. The student just wants to get out of trouble – i.e. get a second chance or a do-over. No one in this equation, other than the teacher, wants to see the student actually learn the material in question. And it simply doesn't matter that the same pattern of performance surfaces in several of the student's other courses.

Regardless of facts, it is up to the teacher to "…fix this problem." And far too often the parent succeeds in getting a weak principal to force the teacher to change the grade.

In the best schools I visited and surveyed, administrations were credited with strongly supporting good teachers. The principal, before answering the parent, would look at the student records, look at the teacher history, and decide if the specific issue for the student was part of a pattern, or was just an anomaly that really did need fixing. If the principal determined that it might be a teacher issue, the principal would quietly meet with the teacher and look for the best way to correct the situation.

Yes, sometimes the teacher is wrong!

If the principal saw a pattern suggesting that the child was equally failing elsewhere, the principal would have a joint meeting with the parents to firmly suggest a course of action for future efforts (not changing the past results!) that would help the child improve.

Yes, sometimes the teacher is *not* wrong.

The fact that 70% of the teachers in this survey had a neutral or negative view of administration support, and only 30% had a positive view, is a strong indicator of the defensive posture most teachers have now assumed.

(Teachers only) How many interactions a month do you feel an average teacher at your school must deal with a difficult, confrontational, parent?

The result: 3.1 difficult confrontations per month

These confrontational interactions occurred in four different ways – telephone calls, emails, visits to the school (rare), and indirect through other departments (guidance, the principal, and SPED). The figure was quite a bit higher than I expected, although when I formed the questionnaire I was not thinking of the indirect confrontations when the parent first calls guidance or the principal to complain. For many of these 3.1 incidents the teacher never hears directly from the parent, and ultimately "…gets the message" via principal, SPED, or guidance feedback on a call received by one (or more!) of them.

(Teachers only) How many written (email or letter) positive comments do you receive from parents in a typical year?

    The result: 1.7 per year

This is a sad statistic. Perhaps it says more about evolving societal trends on saying "thank you" than it does about education.

The question was included because I was looking to gain hard data about a very intangible concept that might only make sense to a Vietnam Veteran from back in the 60s and 70s. The question I hoped to pin down for teachers was: "How much negative feedback and criticism do you receive that you believe is completely unfair? These are criticisms for actions you took that either you think were good and honorable, or were actions out of your control that are blamed on you?"

(A fellow Vietnam Vet would instantly get this. Few Vietnam vets were the "baby killers" all were painted as being. None that I know of were responsible for starting the war. A teenage soldier has little impact on the generals and Secretaries of State who were responsible for sending our troops over there. Yet the blame laid at the feet of 20-year-old kids returning from Vietnam colored their entire lives – just as such criticism would impact teachers.)

Teachers certainly have faults and problems, but it has not yet been proven that teachers are responsible for global warming or the death of baby seals. Yet many of the loudest critics of teachers can never see behind the curtain to the things where teachers really _do_ deserve strong criticism, and instead blame them for anything else that is visibly wrong with education. The incentive for this book was listening to talk radio in Boston during my morning commutes to school. This highly respected Boston talk show host[43] blamed everything short of a lunar eclipse on teacher faults. (I actually liked most of her views, and enjoyed hearing her perspectives on areas of difference.) She blamed teachers for bullying incidents regardless of

---

[43] Margery Eagan, WTKK talk radio (now discontinued)

the way the child had been brought up at home. She blamed teachers for declining graduation even when children never came to school.

Then, one day the light bulb went off. I realized that even people who really care about education could not possibly know what really happened inside our classrooms. How could they? This is one "elephant in the room" that no one outside the school would ever know was trampling everything in its path. *The system is amazingly effective in hiding its problems.*

It is all very easy to know the answers when you have never been inside a school to see the rest of the story. It is akin to one of the greatest book titles I have ever seen (someday I have <u>got</u> to read it!) "*I was a really good mom before I had kids.*" [44] Any parent listening to the "parenting advice" of someone who has no children will instantly smile at reading that title. Perhaps the title of this book should have been "*I was a really good teacher before I stepped into a classroom.*"

The bottom line – in addition to their faults, teachers operate under the cloud of constant criticism for things out of their control, and for things where the critic simply has no clue. (This is the topic for "Systemic Failure #6" in chapter 24.)

(Teachers only) **If your school has parent-teacher nights, what percent of the parents of <u>struggling students</u> actually do attend?**

> The result: 4%
>
> This is a terrible statistic that was even lower than I expected. If 96% of the parents of struggling students cannot be bothered to attend a conference aimed at helping their children, then the system has no chance of helping this child succeed in his/her education.

(Teachers only) **If your school has parent-teacher nights, what percent of the parents who attend are parents of students who are already doing well in your classes?**

> The result: 87%
>
> No surprise here. The parents we beg to attend are no-shows. The parents of the successful students are active and involved.

---

[44] *I was a Really Good Mom Before I Had Kids*, Trisha Ashworth

Methinks there is cause-and-effect here for those with eyes to see past the symptoms to the actual causes of some of the problems with education.

(Teachers only) When you request a formal parent conference (any of in-guidance, in-classroom, at parent-teacher night, in-SPED, etc.) for a struggling or problem student, what percent of the time does the parent not respond?

The result: 71%

According to teachers, even if we look beyond parent-teacher night to also include direct requests for a meeting to discuss a struggling child's education, the parents still do not attend. The most common response is "…thank you for the information, I will deal with Billy on this…" so that, in their view, they avoid any meeting – whether or not they actually intend to talk to "Billy."

The old partnership of co-responsibility between parent, teacher, and student is broken.

(Teachers only) In your typical teaching year, what percentage of your time do you estimate is spent on tasks that you believe do not contribute to a student's education in any meaningful way?

The result: 32%

Every year state DOEs (Departments of Education) come up with more and more ill-conceived requirements to place on classroom teaching. The bureaucratic mandates that flood schools today are at the point where a significant part of teacher effort does nothing to help educate our children. In school year 2012-2013 alone, I was out of my classroom for eighteen days (at least half of which had absolutely no discernible educational value to our students). This total does not include the even larger impact of all the DoE mandates I had to incorporate into my classroom that had absolutely no educational value.

- 2 full days for "Professional Development"
- 8 days where we let children out so that the last hour and a half I could be part of a teacher team to write public relations plans for the school. This was all a part of writing a large document used as part of the periodic accreditation process

for the school. It had 10-12 teachers, unqualified in the area of public relations, writing a PR plan to be read by bureaucrats who had no experience in PR, and had no way of evaluating whether or not the plan was real or would be activated.
- 7 half days lost to proctor mandated state testing
- 1 half day to attend a state-mandated annual review of restraint training for handling student fights
- 1 half day to attend a state-mandated annual review of standard test administration procedures
- 1 half day to attend a state-mandated annual review of bullying
- 3 days to help write new curricula for classes that would be in accordance with developing new core standards

The above days are just the ones that were taken out of classroom time. They do not include two monthly meetings after school for teachers, or time spent in a course, after school, covering the new 2014 core standards. They also do not include weekly hall and cafeteria monitoring assignments.

Classroom procedure changes included activities as silly and useless as daily posting of a sign referencing the specific core standard (a reference akin to the Dewey Decimal System that refers to a paragraph in the state common core standards, such as P2.31.5.3) being taught that day. I can think of nothing accomplished to educate a child by that requirement, other than to meet some inexperienced bureaucrat's "check-the-box" idea of how to teach.

Taking one-third of our teacher's time for meaningless DoE mandates is a disaster

(Teachers only) On a scale of 1 (very easy) to 5 (very difficult) – how easy is it for the school to correct or replace tenured teachers?

The result: 4.6 (Difficult)

1	(very easy)	0%
2		0%
3		4%

4		27%
5	(very difficult)	68%

(Note: This question solely refers to dismissals for poor classroom teaching, *and does not include firing for misconduct*.)

That not a single teacher responded with either a "1" or a "2" is very telling here. If there had been an option "6 – no way in hell" I suspect it would have received votes.

The hard truth is well known to most people. This is one where the talk show hosts have it right – it is nearly impossible to get rid of a bad teacher. Unless that teacher is caught with the proverbial smoking gun for non-teaching issues (stealing, sexual contact, drinking, drugs, bullying, etc.) then the teacher will teach forever. In the past ten years I have seen four teachers dismissed for "poor teaching" during their first (untenured) years. I have seen three other teachers dismissed for alleged misconduct. I have never heard of a tenured teacher being dismissed for poor teaching effectiveness, even when all of us knew of teachers who should not be in a classroom.

New rules and procedures that are finally being rolled out for teacher evaluations might help this, somewhat. However, most teachers believe that even after the new procedures, it will remain nearly impossible to replace a bad teacher.

(Teachers only) On a scale of 1 (decisions are based upon cronyism) to 5 (decisions are fair and impartial) – how much faith do you have in your schools process for assigning additional paid duties such as coaching positions, department heads, and club leaders? Please consider whether you believe the process is fair, impartial and selects the best person possible.

The result: 2.5 (decisions largely cronyism)

1	(cronyism)	28%	⎫
2		32%	⎬ 60%
			⎭
3		17%	
4		9%	⎫
			⎬ 23%

5   (impartial)   14%

This is a major topic in a chapter (Systemic failure #2) later in this book. Again, it is a question never asked or researched by those who "...were really good teachers without ever stepping into a classroom." The fact that *60% of these teachers felt that cronyism was the full or main reason for appointments* to paid duties (coaching, club advisors, department heads, etc.) is one of the most powerful negative impacts on teacher attitudes, teacher effort, and merit pay perceptions.

(Teachers only) On a scale of 1 (very little impact) to 5 (very strong impact) – how much do you think the need to pass standard state testing impacts both course content and teaching methods?

The result: 4.1 (strong impact)

1   (very little)   0%
2   4%
3   23%
4   34%
5   (very strong)   39%

It is interesting that no one chose "very little," and only 4% chose "1." Even though many of these teachers were in courses that do not have standardized state testing, they all saw the impact on curricula.

The pressure from state Departments of Education, teachers, and parents to find a way to pass children regardless of performance is enormous. Schools have dropped electives to add special preparatory courses for the standardized tests, and center their curricula on those questions they expect the tests to ask. Many classes have the "MCAS question of the week" (substitute your state exam for the Massachusetts MCAS test cited here). Administrations dedicate significant time to compiling and studying estimators of expected student performance. Parents are notified if a child is on the "risk of failing" list. Extra after school programs are run for struggling students.

State testing impacts all schools every day. If that school has dropped to their state's equivalent of the Massachusetts level 3 or 4, then the focus becomes an obsession.

(Teachers only) On a scale of 1 (not qualified) to 5 (highly qualified), how qualified do you feel your school administration is qualified to lead

your school and handle issues such as legislation, relations with town government, budgets, personnel matters, building maintenance, security, and curricula?

    The result: 2.8 (somewhat qualified)

1	(not qualified)	22%	⎤
2		24%	⎬ 46%
3		20%	⎦
4		17%	⎤ 34%
5	(highly qualified)	17%	⎦

Overall, teachers felt that <u>almost half</u> of all administrations are either little qualified or not qualified to run the school. By contrast, just one-third felt administrations were qualified or highly qualified.

This finding speaks directly to "Systemic Issue #2 – chapter 20," and is <u>not</u> about the character of these principals, but rather about their degree of preparation and training to lead an organization this complex.

(Optional <u>Student-only</u> question) What is the <u>best</u> thing about your education at this school?

    (Quote without comment – Interesting comments offered by students in the open-response section of the survey. Grammar and spelling as written.)

- *"The teachers"*
- *"Most of the time learning can be fun"*
- *"I feel we have really good teachers."*
- *"Friendly teachers"*
- *"The way teachers interact with their students"*
- *"It's fairly well taught. I learn a good amount."*
- *"Teachers are hands on with students"*
- *"The teachers are mostly nice and it helps me not be afraid to ask a question."*
- *"Having good teachers that explain and not just rush through"*
- *"Most teachers make the material easier to understand"*
- *"One of my teachers actually expect (sic) something out of his students and the way he teaches made (it) my best subject when last year it was my worst."*

(Optional Student-only question) What is the worst thing about your education at this school?

> (Quote almost without comment – Interesting comments offered by students in the open-response section of the survey. Grammar and spelling as written.)

- *"Class sizes"*
- *"The lack of work that is given. Personally I rather be challenged than be given a free pass."*
- *"Some teachers just seem to give work and have you do all the work without much explaining much of the lesson."*
- *"The limited availability of classes."*
- *"Some teachers don't really prepare us for tests"*
- *"Too much homework"*
- *"Sometimes teachers will just show you how to do something rather than teach."*
  (Editor's note: Amazing how accurate and insightful that comment is by a teenager who understands the difference between presenting and teaching!)
- *It takes a long time and I have to wait for other people to catch up."*
- *"Some teachers force you to learn at their pace, and not your own."*
- *"Mr. Russell."*
  (Editor's note: Actually, there were a dozen instances of this comment from students in my classes who took the survey ☺)
- *"Having to take pool. What's the purpose they don't even teach you how to swim the teachers are always on their iPads and iPhones"*
- *"We don't really get to make up are old class work or homework up.*
- *"Most teachers don't seem to care about what students get for grades or give them opportunities to bring there grades up"*
- *"Move through topics to quickly"*
- *"Most of the teachers just don't seem to care and understand, I only know of 2 who do."*
- *"It's to hard"*
- *"Pool!"*
- *"Teachers don't really 'teach' enough they just give us work and expect us to know what to do."*
- *"Pool"*
- *"Some teachers confuse us by the way they teach."*
- *"We don't get a lot of time to learn a topic"*
- *"Some teachers just give us notes and then don't explain the rest."*

- *"How early we have to wake up"*
- *"Having you that kids cheat and get away with it."*
- *"Some teachers don't care about the students"*
- *"Constantly throwing homework at us"*
- *"Some teachers don't really explain the work."*
- *"Some of the teachers that don't teach much."*
- *"There are a lot of teachers that don't do anything but sit at their desk. Some of them can't control a class."*
- *"Most teachers don't really explain the work they are giving us, they don't understand that people have different ways of learning, some are slower than others."*
- Most of the teachers honestly don't care about the students. Teachers don't like to teach and tend to block a lot of things out."
- *"The classes are crowded and I can't concentrate on my work."*
- *"The work they give us is stupid is like they don't want to challenge is to do something bigger."*

(Optional <u>Student-only</u> question) What is the most important thing the school should change that would help you get a better education?

(Quote without comment – Interesting comments offered by students in the open-response section of the survey. Grammar and spelling as written.)

- *"up to date computers"*
- *"Teachers that actually care and know how to teach."*
- *"Teachers care more about our test grades."*
- *"More fun activities and projects to do."*
- *"Better technology"*
- *"Better clubs, more activities"*
- *"Get better teachers."*
- *"Add another period to just work on homework"*
- *"Have more understanding teachers who really care."*
- *"Get rid of MCAS"*
- *"They should give us more extra credit package"*
- *"I think they should let us do some things that will help us learn like listening to music"*
- *"After school program"*
- *"Nothing, really I like how this school works"*
- *A point in time where you get a free period to do homework'*
- *"More hands-on activities and field trips"*

- *"Smaller classes so a teacher can see if a kid is cheating"*
- *"Teachers should teach without making the lesson complicated"*
- *"Get the teachers to interact and try for the kids to learn something."*
- *"They should care for what happens to us and they just don't."*
- *"The teachers shouldn't be on their period every day."*
- *"Fire the teachers that don't want to be here."*
- *"Get teachers that actually care."*

(Optional <u>Student-only</u> question) Any other comments?

(Quote without comment – Interesting comments offered by students in the open-response section of the survey. Grammar and spelling as written.)

- *"Teachers should learn how to keep their students interested. You can't learn if you are bored out of your mind."*
- *"I used to think that all teachers were the same just passing kids along."*
- *""Other schools have classes/clubs that have students who is more interested than others."*
- *"Some teachers really suck at teaching kids."*
- *"Students complain all the time about one certain teacher and nobody does anything about it because they don't care."*
- *"I don't think I've tooken (sic) a test without people cheating."*

Three Myths We Must Debunk

(Chapter 15)
Myth #1 – Children don't want to learn anymore

It is somehow human nature that we are far more aware of the negatives in our lives, and miss a lot of the positives. In an odd way, that is probably a good thing – one essential to early human survival, and one that any soldier, police officer, or a person walking down a dark street would certainly appreciate. But, like all powerful things in our lives, there often are two sides to the issue. And this natural focus on the negatives is rarely shown more clearly than in some widespread negative views of education.

The negative here is on one of the most subtle and deadly perceptions that has hurt our children more than anything else in education – the widespread view that children don't want to work and learn in school anymore.

It is easy to fall into the trap of believing children no longer care, or just do the minimum in school to get by. After all, there is a large minority (a numerical minority, not a demographic one) of children in every urban high school that clearly demonstrates those exact *symptoms*. Note that I carefully use the word "symptom" rather than "cause" – because there is a huge difference between the two that is the crux of this attitude.

> *Anonymous is a college professor in Pennsylvania. She provides an exceptional view of what happens to students when the education system fails them. We "graduate" students who come from a dumbed-down system that emphasized remembering over understanding? Like most teachers, anonymous prefers to not reveal a name in order to avoid retribution from school administrators for speaking out.*

> **(Anonymous) Students who only learn facts, but with no frame of reference to make those facts have meaning**

> I empower students, believing that student empowerment enables freedom for academic growth and discovery. But what happens when students think that they are entitled to take advantage of that freedom as they see fit? Answering as a community college instructor who saw this first-hand working with recent high school graduates: classroom anarchy.

> My class of paramedic students did not feel the communications skills I was teaching were relevant to their profession, so not only did they

> brashly verbalize their opinions as such, they wielded the freedom I gave them as weapons of destruction, ruining lectures I had spent hours preparing, mocking subject matter that was, indeed, relevant to them, and degrading and disregarding the authority of the classroom. They showed utter disrespect for instruction that didn't seem to explicitly support or entertain what they deemed as "important."
>
> But the underlying issue is that these students didn't know *how* to assess what was truly important in a well-rounded education nor *how* to learn. They entered college without any understanding of what is *really* important to them. It is scary to realize that people who don't know how to, essentially, *think* are on the front lines as some of my community's first responders.

So first – the bad news. This minority is real. Based upon the three years of research, 700-plus surveys of students and teachers, and hundreds of interviews that went into writing this book, and based upon ten years in an urban high school teaching math to inclusion classes, standard level classes, and classes that averaged well over half on SPED IEPs, the facts are compelling.

Just consider these findings:

- The average amount of homework for urban high school students in a week is less than their parents did in a night – 1.5 hours, total. Only 14% study for a test the next day.
- 27% of students (the large numerical minority I keep referencing) do not care what grade they get as long as they pass and graduate
- Urban high school students believe that 37% of their parents do not care what grades they get as long as they pass and graduate

The real question is "why?" – is the attitude because children no longer have the drive and interest in learning? Or is it due to something else hidden behind the curtain of the school entryway? Well, surprise! *It's not the children!*

The overwhelming finding was that almost all children, even including the most stereotypical disadvantaged students, still want to learn, and jump on the opportunity to feel genuine pride in mastering a topic.

I know – been there, done that, and have the t-shirt (one that teases me as a "Grandma Magnet" given to me by my students!). I have had the joy of watching classes full of kids who started out that way, yet ended up excited about as dry a topic as high school math. I've been in the back of the room watching an English class come alive when discussing *The Things They Carried*, or *To Kill a Mockingbird*. I've smiled seeing a physics class competition pit homemade catapults against each other. And I've watched child after child become reengaged in learning, turn "just passing" into B's and A's, leave that "minority," and change their whole attitude about school.

Why? To paraphrase a famous Washington saxophone player – *it's the pride stupid!*

You see, the children change when they have the chance to feel pride in what they do! To them, it is not about learning. A rare few have a planning horizon much farther than the upcoming weekend – the long-term value of solving an equation or dissecting a frog is not even on their radar. They know they have to learn it (or so they have been told) but they, as yet, have little clue as to why other than the bromide "…you need it to get into college." There is no teacher on the planet that has never heard the student question "when will I ever use this?" a thousand times. But there is something that nearly every child understands – the great feeling of pride when you earn a difficult accomplishment.

At the end of the student survey in chapter 14, there were open-ended questions about what is best, worst, and needs changing in school. The results amazed me because of all the comments asking for more challenge. Here are just a few examples of my favorites:

> *"The work they give us is stupid is (sic) like they don't want to challenge us to do something bigger." (Cat)*
>
> [Worst thing about school] *"The lack of work that is given. Personally I rather (sic) be challenged than given a free pass." (Fatima)*
>
> *"I used to think all teachers were the same just passing kids along." (Nick)*
>
> *"One of my teachers actually expect (sic) something out of his students and the way he teaches made math my best subject when last year it was my worst." (Mark#1)*
>
> *"We don't learn. We just sit there playing with our thumbs waiting for teachers to give a crap. Some people actually want an education." (Kayla)*

Our education system has been so dumbed-down, and so focused on pushing any student through high school, that the children have learned they do not have to work to pass – the school will make sure they will regardless of effort.

While there are, of course, many students who work to excel despite the system, it is up to all of us who teach to somehow excite and motivate children that our education system is actively demotivating. It is the single most difficult challenge for all the great teachers who have to counter the systemic failures in urban high school education every day, and every class.

But what happens when that great English teacher, or that curmudgeonly Physics teacher really invests the time to reverse the attitude and generate pride? Amazing success. Last year I had the joy of teaching a very special CP math class for seniors that is a perfect example of what our children really want. As juniors, every one of the students had been in standard level math classes for three years. 90% were on SPED IEPs. Most had never done well in math. In any high school, if you have been in the standard track for three years, there is zero chance you can move to a CP class for your senior year. You simply are too far behind the curriculum for the CP track.

Well, this class was different! By midyear they had blown through the standard curriculum. It was yet another case of great children somehow deciding they wanted more. Courtney, the feisty "trouble maker" started enjoying the challenges and helping others learn the material. Dago, the paper airplane master ("incoming!"), and Ray, the class comic, would tease each other continuously, yet compete with each other to solve problems. Candice, the hall walker, would put down her cell phone and wrestle with tough problems. Nick, "I don't need math, I play basketball", became engaged and challenged because of the support of his coach and the help of a superb co-teacher in the class. The whole class decided they wanted CP work for the rest of the year – so with the co-teacher playing a very important positive role, we dove into Algebra I CP material, and went back over most of the Geometry CP material they had never seen. It was amazing and joyful to watch. They loved it.

You see, they had discovered pride in themselves – earned pride for mastering something they knew was a real challenge. Most of these students had started out in that "large minority" who appeared to only want to do the minimum to pass and graduate. But when they had the chance to feel pride in an earned accomplishment (there was nothing given to any of them on a silver platter – no do-overs, no extra credit assignments, no easy multiple choice exams...) they left the "minority" in a heartbeat!

So, in their senior year those 20 students accomplished something new to my school, and we believe new to the entire state of Massachusetts. For the first time we can find in any state, a special senior CP "Transition to Algebra II" course was set up for students who had been locked into standard level classes for the prior three years. Far more students than we could fit asked to be enrolled in that senior class. It turned out to be one of the most joyful classes I have ever had the honor to watch.

Author and retired teacher James Howson clearly sees the need focus upon our children's underlying need to feel accomplishments:

> James Howson is the author of "American Education: A Nat. Blueprint for the Future," and is a retired middle school En~~~~ ~~ Connecticut. Here is his analysis:

(James Howson) Teamwork to restore student pride

For Education to really work in the 21st century, schools must have a clear mission. I believe our mission should be what I call the 3 C's: Commitment, Community, and Cooperation! During the 2014 election season our politicians continued to play the "Blame" game. Instead of facing problems head on, our nation has become a "reactionary society." We put in a much-needed stop sign only after someone is killed. Our communities have enough policemen and firefighters only after mobs and fires increase, and it makes national news. What's going to be the "Education Reaction" when our country realizes too late that our Education system needs to be fixed right now?

Schools, teachers, parents, and communities need to get tough, to stand committed and cooperate together as one voice! Schools do not like to get tough – if we make parents mad, they won't pass the budget. Teachers do not like to tell students that they are not doing well (Who does?), so social promotions have become a fact of life – we do not want to ruin a child's "self-esteem." Yet, students appreciate honesty and in the long run they will thank you – you can count on it. Parents do not want to admit that their children are not perfect. Believe me when I say that "realistic" love is much more long-lasting to them than "...my child can do nothing wrong" love.

Finally, communities need to work closely with and support schools. This is not about just parents, or just teachers, or just students – it is about all of us. As a caring society, we must all be in this together!

One final example of an individual student shows how powerful newfound pride can be in a child's life.

> *"I did good (sic) in math this year because you pushed me and told me I could do it. I went from a 57 to a 96 in a matter of three months. Thank you for everything and showing me I am smart and can do math and do it correctly."*
> (Kayla)

This is a Special Ed student who had always failed math and was absolutely convinced she was "stupid." It turned out she just had some gaps from 7th grade math that surfaced in all her high school work and generated wrong answers. We fixed that, and she earned B's and A's for the second half of junior year, and all her senior year. I still remember the day she got her first A on a test. She started crying right in front of the entire class, and asked me if she could call her mom (cell phones were not permitted to be used in school). I let her call, and watched the joy on her face as she smiled through all the tears to say "…Mom, I just got an 'A' in math." That was a Friday afternoon. I went home and was on cloud nine for the whole weekend. One Kayla in a teacher's life cancels out a whole lot of tough times. I framed that letter on my wall at home – it encourages me every time I glance at it. It was the day Kayla learned something every child should know, "…*showing me I am smart.*"

So yes, there is a minority of students who start out "…just wanting to pass and graduate" and appear not to care. But any battle-scarred teacher can tell you that they only *start* this way. We can change them. And, they want to change, but just don't know it yet. When a teacher sees that light of pride finally go on, it is absolutely the best feeling you will ever know. The only "dumb" children are the ones we dumb-down by a bad system, because even a great teacher cannot always overcome all the obstacles to teaching because of inept bureaucracies, conflicting mandates, and the unintended consequence of well-meaning legislation.

(Chapter 16)
Myth #2 – The main problem with education is too many bad teachers

It has become the norm to place all blame for the failure on teachers. Now of course there are a few bad teachers in every school, just as there are a handful of bad employees in any organization. In high schools, those few bad teachers tend to be very visible. And since school administrators and career DoE bureaucrats carefully hide the most severe problems they caused in high school education from everyone outside the school, then those "bad" teachers become the lightning rod for the host of conditions that remain unseen.

However, three or four bad teachers out of more than a hundred good ones in a school, or a handful of creeps nationwide each year out of 7,2000,000 teachers in 99,000 schools,[45] are just a small part of the #6 (Chapter 24) problem on a list of serious issues that have destroyed our schools. The first five reasons are far more deadly, and are the reason even the best teachers are now giving up.

That is the tragedy when trying to fix this disgrace – parents, the people we most need to help us change these failures, have no clue how serious the problems are that pervade the educational system – they have been carefully hidden from them by school administrators and career DoE bureaucrats. Perhaps that is changing because of all the highly visible national instances of corruption and ineptitude in government bureaucracies that have dominated the news for the past year. VA bonuses, IRS targeting, healthcare rollout ineptitude, GSA lavish parties, State Department cover-ups, and administrative "misleading statements" are just a few of the examples of what is wrong with bureaucracies –the impact of no accountability and few qualifications for those making major systemic decisions.

At that is the nub of it – an urban high school is a bureaucracy. Its policies are set by career bureaucrats with no accountability and with little or no educational experience outside their cubicles. Even the senior DoE bureaucrats who once were teachers have not been in a classroom for years – and have no direct experience with the huge destructive changes in education that have been concentrated in the past five years. The school administration is headed by principals (and/or superintendents) who might have been good teachers, but have no management/leadership experience and are not held accountable for their actions. The results are inevitable.

---

[45] Profile America Facts, US Census, 27 Jun 11

I know – been there, done that, and have the t-shirt to prove it. Like many other teachers over the past couple years, I finally lost faith in the system, despite my love for children and teaching, when I realized that good teachers were no longer enough to counter all the failures of the educational system. Even Parnelli Jones in his prime could not win a race if his car had three flat tires and a blown manifold.

Teaching can only be fixed from outside the classroom, and those who should be leading the charge to fix it – legislators, parents, Departments of Education, and school administrators (and some teachers) – are the very ones causing the problems.

A personal note might help put this book into perspective for the reader. Teaching is a job I felt I was born for, and by any standard I was a good teacher. I love what I do, and nothing on this planet gives me more joy then helping children be proud of what they earned and accomplished in school. For the last ten years in urban high schools, my students always were tops in the school in standardized tests, and outperformed most of the best high schools in the entire state.

Now, the purpose of this crass braggadocio is not to be vainglorious. It is to emphasize that even successful teachers – those with a passion for teaching and who love helping children succeed – can no longer overcome all the obstacles that education places in the way of motivating, engaging, and teaching our children.

Those high standardized test results were from teaching in a <u>vocational</u> school serving ten inner city communities. These "voke" students were in academics just half the time compared to traditional high schools (the other half was spent in shop). Sixty percent of the students were ESL, SPED, and/or free lunch. Yet my students *did* succeed, *loved* what they were achieving, and could match their abilities against the wealthiest fulltime suburban high schools in the state. They looked forward to coming to math class. Three of my last five years the entire junior class signed a petition started by the students to try to get administration to assign me to teach seniors. (I normally had sophomores and juniors, only.) Guidance was routinely flooded with dozens of parent requests each year to have children transferred to my class.

The point of such crass "patting-myself-on-the-back?" Despite being a good teacher with a passion for children, I watched the system morph into one that actively worked to *prevent* me from helping these children succeed. I watched more and more inane micromanagement, forced on teachers by DoE requirements, that did nothing to aid the teaching process. I watched teachers, with far better credentials and results than mine, walk out the door to "normal" jobs.

Worse, I saw many more teachers give up, and just go with the flow by dumbing down their own teaching to meet the demands of the system. I saw some very good teachers become very mediocre teachers.

Why? Today's educational system guarantees failure. It ensures that many, except the most self-motivated students, will soon learn they can coast through school. It eliminates pride and accountability in both children and their parents. It lowers expectations to the point where we expect little, and barely get that. After years of being beaten down by all the failures of the system, the best teachers become ashamed at being forced to instruct children the way today's teachers must run their classrooms. *And then they either leave, or dumb themselves down to the teaching level forced by our legislators, bureaucrats, and a growing numerical minority of parents.* The system punishes those who most love and cherish teaching our children. It punishes the children most of all.

We are failing. Our children will pay the price for decades to come. And yet, there is hope. This can be completely turned around by addressing all of the top issues.

Yes, that includes priority #6 on the list – eliminating a handful of bad teachers.

(Chapter 17)
Myth #3 – All we need to fix education is more funding

For years we all have heard the incessant pleas for "…more funding" as the solution to all of education's problems. It seemed that nothing more simplistic than throwing millions of new tax dollars at our school budgets was the only answer that DoEs, teacher unions, and legislators saw as ways to turn around the deplorable trends in our schools.

"Fix the buildings…" and "…reduce class size" and "put more money into technology" are about as far as our career DoE bureaucrats and legislators seem able to see. And, of course, "…just fire all the teachers" who were blamed for doing a poor job of teaching our children under a set of bureaucratic mandates that directly *prevent* even the best teachers from teaching.

Just look at three facts to see how ineffective just throwing money at problems that need systemic policy changes has been. These are the signs of an abject policy failure:[46]

- Total spending on K-12 education in the period 2005 to 2011 rose more than 250 billion dollars.
- The 2014 estimated state, federal and local total spending on education is expected to be up more than 40% from just eight years ago.
- On average, 25% of state budgets go to education
- Yet, in 2014 ACT and SAT both reported that less than one-half of all students who were tested had a high school education sufficient to let them be ready for college.

Throwing money at the problem – no matter how much legislators love to encourage contributions from supporters of "more spending", and no matter how much career bureaucrats in DoEs like the guaranteed lifetime positions with no accountability – *simply has not worked.* The situation has deeply worsened in the last five years. Why? Because it is far easier for legislators and bureaucrats to spend money than it is to actually deal with the real issues teachers face every day in their classrooms.

As one indication of that, I mailed out nearly 50 letters and copies of the 1st edition of *Lifting the Curtain* to state legislators in Massachusetts. Each mailing

---

[46] US Census and NCES

had specific suggestions of things legislation could do to help, many with immediate impact, for the most serious issues. *Of the eleven recommendations presented in chapter 27, nine actually reduce funding needs!* Yet, not a single Massachusetts legislator or member of the Massachusetts leadership even bothered to reply or acknowledge receipt of the package. My own local legislator, one whom you would think might answer just to curry a vote, could not be bothered with something as unimportant to him as our children's education. But, of course, none of these legislators had any problem running to events that offered donations from groups requesting more funding for schools.

Changes that help and cost less? Is that possible? Absolutely. Here's a small sample:

- At least half of PDP courses are a costly farce – adding nothing to a teacher's ability to teach, and yet required to meet annual PDP mandates.
- We treat teachers as though they were pedophiles if they try to break up a fight *before* a child is seriously injured and actually bleeding – preferring to avoid the cost of lawsuits for "incidental touching" while stopping a fight, rather than to protect the children from harm.
- We set such low requirements for a person to "qualify" to be a principal – trivial night courses from degree mills for someone we expect to run a 15 million dollar corporation with 400 employees, unions, complex DoE mandates, local politics, bullying and lockdown responsibilities, budgets, the safety of 1,500 students – that few principals have anything even close to the experience or training to manage an organization of such demands and complexity.
- We let failing students "make up" an entire failed year of a course with a simplistic two-week, half-time summer school.
- We let those same students miss 12-18 days of "excused" absences, and ignore the learning they never got.

But maybe, just maybe, the bow of the ship inching towards a new direction, away from the iceberg that is in education's path?

I am encouraged by a handful of *very* small signs. We've saw 26,000 visitors and followers to our blog (LiftingTheCurtainOnEducation.Wordpress.com) in just the first 12 weeks after it was launched, almost all by teachers gaining the courage to be heard on the *real* issues, and despite the environment of intimidation and cronyism in our schools against teachers who speak out. In Massachusetts, a state teacher's union that always seemed to be focused only on PAC activities has made an apparent shift in the past three months, under new leadership, to actually discuss educational issues and try to understand what teachers really need to succeed. (Prior to the leadership change, 81% of emails over a 10 month period were to support, donate, or write legislators as part of PAC activities – and the other 19% about very simplistic teacher issues.) Websites and blogs that avoided the topic of the systemic failures in education as "too controversial" are now actively covering it and even posting reviews. Every time I see another "share" or "follow" or "like" or review I take heart – because each one is a courageous teacher voice speaking out to help our children. Only the legislators and career DoE bureaucrats continue to ignore the real issues.

More money is not the solution. It's a greedy, shameful copout. Indeed, many of the actions that would have the most immediate positive impact would actually cost less. But sadly, each money sink is defended vigorously by those who benefit from a hand in the cookie jar, while teacher voices are rarely heard.

The Eight Systemic Causes of Education Failure

(Chapter 18)
The symptoms of failure are not the causes of failure

In the prior sections we listed a lot of issues. Without exception, all of them were symptoms of a much greater problem. Unfortunately, most news and commentary about schools focus just on these symptoms, and ignore the real causes.. It is akin to the silliness if we were to tell a driver found at the bottom of a cliff to stop bleeding, because bleeding is dangerous and messy, when the real issue is how to stop him from getting drunk and driving off the cliff in the first place.

The primary *symptoms* cover a litany of popular views of education:

- Poor grades
- Poor graduation rates
- Truancy
- Loss of Music and the Arts
- Little time spent by students on homework
- Little time spent by students preparing for tests
- Rise in homeschooling
- Cheating by copying assignments from other students
- Cheating by plagiarism
- Cheating by teachers and administrators on standardized tests
- Overuse of multiple-choice testing
- Focus on preparation for standardized test taking
- Phony projects to allow failing students to pass without doing passing work
- Students who do not care about their educational performance
- Teachers who do not care about the students
- Parents who do not care about the educational performance of their child
- Teachers who are not good at teaching
- Cronyism and corruption in appointments within the school
- Principals not qualified to lead a complex organization

The intent of this book, so far, has been to show how much is hidden behind the curtain that parents never get a chance to see. But what has been shown so far are symptoms – the causes of those symptoms are far more controversial, because many of them are in failures of programs that have high goals we all support. The real problems are systemic – pervading and influencing everything that happens in a school.

- Systemic failure #1: Unintended consequences of well-meaning laws
- Systemic failure #2: Unqualified administrators and rampant cronyism
- Systemic failure #3: Inclusion classes where everyone loses
- Systemic failure #4: Special Education – Hijacked by parents
- Systemic failure #5: "Educator" – our newest four-letter word
- Systemic failure #6: Burned out teachers
- Systemic failure #7: The untouchables – parents and teacher unions
- Systemic failure #8: Rewards unrelated to performance

The solutions exist. The solutions are painful. But even the most painful solution is far better than we are doing to today's children.

(Chapter 19)
Systemic Failure #1: Unintended Consequences – good intentions gone horribly wrong

Overview: Education has fallen victim to quick fixes, and well-meaning programs that never envisioned the disastrous long-term consequences of their actions. Despite very good intentions, these programs have proven to seriously hurt education by lowering expectations, fostering cheating, destroying child incentive and effort, removing student accountability, and dumbing down education to the point of ineffectiveness.

In less than 20 years, we have gone from holding teachers, parents, and students co-responsible for a student's performance, to often holding the teacher solely responsible. There is little question that the authors of programs such as No Child Left Behind were individuals who genuinely loved children and wanted education to improve for all schools. Yet these programs ended up having exactly the opposite impact.

They have been a disaster.

Nothing has hurt education more over the past two decades than the unintended consequences of well-meaning ideas. Of all the problems facing schools today, this is far and away the most deadly issue. I suspect that had I the opportunity to personally know the individuals who authored many of the federal and state education programs of the past 20 years, I would truly admire and respect those who came up with such a wonderful concept as "No Child Left Behind." That phrase, in four short words, encapsulates everything I believe about teaching. I enthusiastically supported NCLB when it was launched. Even with 20/20 hindsight, based upon *what I envisioned then* I would still be an enthusiastic supporter of the NCLB concept.

But it turns out that I was wrong. Horribly wrong. The real impact of these programs has been to undermine a student's personal effort and accountability, degrade educational success, and hold teachers responsible for many factors largely out of their control.

Despite twenty years of well-meaning programs, and trillions of dollars spent, education in 2013 is worse than at any time in our history. In 2013, both ACT and SAT testing services reported that most high school graduates were not prepared for college – and that does not even include all those students who never applied to college.

> *"Just over 1 in 4 (26%) ACT-tested high school graduates met all four ACT College Readiness Benchmarks in 2013.*[47]

Only 43 percent of test-takers in 2013 met the SAT's definition of being prepared for college, a statistic that has remained stagnant since 2009. [48]

Instead of the lofty goals of those who crafted NCLB and related programs, the direct impact that started to appear in the years after enactment were horribly destructive:

- First of all, we have taken away from children the possibility of failure – mandating their "success" to the point where a rapidly increasing majority of students know they *do not have to try* in order to graduate from high school. The "system" now <u>forces</u> teachers to find a way to pass them regardless of effort – phony do-overs and extra credit, dumbed-down teaching, "adjusted" grades, and even outright cheating – or else the teacher is held accountable for the failure.

- Second, the ages-old education partnership of teacher, student, and parents has been eroded to the point where teachers are often held <u>solely</u> responsible for the performance of a student, while the student and a growing numerical minority of parents often take no co-responsibility. Teachers are expected to motivate and raise today's children, despite the growing minority of parents who demonstrate no effective interest in their child's education.

Any reader would certainly have to question the above claim that programs like "No Child Left Behind" and "Race to the Top" are directly responsible for this. It would be natural to think that a good teacher can motivate such students and make a difference. But the real answer is that teachers can do little today to counter everything the system has created.

And that leads to a central premise of this book:

> *The problems in schools are systemic. A small part of the problem is a few bad teachers. The much larger problem is a system that turns many good teachers into mediocre ones, and that takes all responsibility for student performance away from the student and parents.*

A parallel to Dickens' Oliver Twist might be helpful. Yes, there were bad children back in Dickens' London. Yes, there were those who stole food or were pickpockets. Yes, stealing is bad. But before we throw all the street children into jail, we might want to look at the 1800's systemic problems in Dickens' London – starvation, famine, poorhouse slavery, and

---

[47] ACT, *The Condition of Career and College Readiness,* September 2013
[48] Huffington Post, 16 Sep 13

disease. That starving children turn to theft of a cabbage should not be a shock. One way to "solve" the stealing and pickpocket problem would have been to imprison all the street children. But the better way might be to look at how to end the disease and famine, and a system that let people like Fagin and the Artful Dodger flourish.

The parallel today? We want to just fire all the teachers, even though what the good teachers <u>really</u> need is someone to help end the disease and famine in the educational system. Dickens had it right.

Teachers certainly are <u>co</u>-responsible, along with parents and the student, for student performance. Yet the present system holds them <u>solely</u> responsibility, with no enforceable responsibility held by students and parents. Thankfully, there are still parents and students who choose to take up the co-responsibility that the system enables them to shun.

The original intent – great goals we can all embrace

> Just look for a moment at this list of goals that I hope any parent, legislator, or teacher would immediately embrace. *I heartily endorse every one of these goals*. These were certainly the goals behind NCLB, Race to the Top, and a host of other educational initiatives enacted since NCLB.
>
> - Teachers and administrators should be held accountable for inadequate teaching.
> - No child should ever have to fail school because of an inadequate education.
> - Standardized testing will ensure that all schools are providing the fundamentals of a good education, and will identify underperforming schools.
> - A school must serve all students, and not provide a lesser educational opportunity to students of a particular subset of the population – such as a racial or income group.
> - Schools must recognize and accommodate student disabilities that make traditional teaching methods less effective.
> - The state must set basic core standards for every topic to ensure that all students cover essential material.

Now, compare the above wonderful goals to what they have actually become in practice. They have been twisted and deformed into mandates that have undermined teaching at every level.

Great Goals – undermined by inept DoE implementation and mandates

Teacher accountability

The goal: Teachers and administrators should be held accountable for inadequate teaching:

The unintended consequences of this excellent goal have had a deadly impact on education. Teachers and high school administrators now are routinely held *solely* accountable for the results of conditions over which they have little or no control. This has lead to demoralized teachers, intentionally dumbed-down education, misuse of Special Education (SPED) programs, widespread cheating, and a teaching methodology that emphasizes remembering enough to pass a weekly test rather than learning to understand the material.

Teachers certainly are co-responsible for student performance, *along with the students themselves, and the parents.* I personally believe that teachers have the most responsibility among the three parties – and that great teachers can <u>sometimes</u> overcome even the three obstacles of students with poor effort, no-show parents who do not bother to support their children's education process, and inane bureaucratic mandates.

But over the past 20 years, teachers somehow have become <u>solely</u> responsible for student performance. Urban high schools can be taken over by the state, and both teachers and administrators fired, if children have low grades, low standardized test scores, or low graduation rates – regardless of what caused those failures. One possible reason for such failures is a bad teacher – but there are many more causes that can overcome even the work of a great teacher.

Just consider an example that sounds improbable to someone outside the classroom, but occurs <u>many times each week</u> in <u>every</u> urban high school in the country. A student (John Doe) is failing, and the student…

- …missed many school days (some "excused" and most simple truancy),
- …does no homework,

- ...has parents who ignore any requests for conferences or meetings,
- ...has parents who take no responsibility for getting the child to attend school
- ...does no classwork,
- ...fails most/all tests,
- ...has serious and repetitive disciplinary and attitude issues,
- ...has been disciplined (sent to in-house, emails to parents, etc.) for recurring lack of effort and attitude issues, but resulting in no positive impact on the child or parents
- ...openly does not care what grades he/she gets.

This all-too-common example is considered a failure by the school and teacher in today's system! Just 25 or so students like this out of 1200 are enough to drive a school's graduation and test scores to the danger zone. My current school has at least 200 like this. And the education of the other 1000 great students gets held hostage to systems focused solely on getting the 200 to pass.

That prior line is so critical to understanding what is destroying education that I repeat it here: **The education of 1000 great students gets held hostage to systems focused solely on getting the 200 to pass.**

The above "John Doe" example is far from rare. Consider what happens when a school that has many students that match that pattern. In a report by the Boston Public Schools (BPS) in 2007, BPS estimated 4500 current Boston school children were likely to drop out because of factors that include a history of missing *more* than one day each week of school.[49] Such students would certainly result in lower graduation rates and low standardized test scores. These, in turn, would cause the school to be judged deficient. Either result puts the school teachers and administration at risk of immediate dismissal.

The impact of either result means that teachers and administrators will be fired because 4,500 sets of parents did not care enough to get their

---

[49] Boston Public Schools, 26 September 2007

children to board the school bus and attend school — and the teachers were "deficient" because they were unable to teach geometry to an empty chair.

The above begs the question that is at the very heart of "unintended consequences of well-meaning goals." What possible action, even by a superb teacher, can cause an empty chair to pass a test and graduate? What possible action, even by a great teacher, could get the above example (one of 4,500 in just one US school district!) to get on the school bus?

Great job, class! Billy's been absent for a couple days again, but his chair gets another "A" for the week. His parents think he might be at a Red Sox game this time.

The pressure to pass children comes from many places, but none worse than state Departments of Education. Passing rates and graduation rates are a key factor in deciding the status of a school and whether or not the state will take over an "underperforming" school. So administrations are under strong pressure to pass students, and they in turn shift that pressure onto the teachers. Parents lobby with irate visits and phone calls (especially if the child is a SPED student) to get the grade changed. Guidance shows up outside the classroom to ask "…it's up to you, of course, but is there anything Johnny can do to raise his grade to a 65?"

Teachers soon learn they must pass "Johnny" or face strong consequences. They can either cave in to the pressure and find an excuse to raise a grade, or they can just dumb down the tests so anyone can pass. Everyone loses either way. And when the choice is the dumbed-down classroom, then the best students suffer most. Very few children do not fall into the trap of the "free ride" that so many teachers feel forced to give.

> *The impact of forcing teachers to pass children who should be allowed to fail pervades urban high schools. Unfortunately, as this vignette indicates, the practice is just as common in the rural schools I did not directly survey. Joanne P. is a retired high school English teacher from Wisconsin who taught for ten years at a small rural school. Her love and frustration with teaching mirrors that of hundreds of teachers I interviewed. As she told me, "...I came into teaching for the sheer love of teaching my passion. For every moment of frustration, there were a dozen of joy, and though, in the end, the house still won, I don't regret a minute."*

> Mandates, we have a lot of them. Administrative strangling, we have that, too. And don't forget parents. The best of them bona fide blessings and the worst...well, they can frustrate a teacher more than anyone else. Almost.

> But, as long as we can make a difference, it's all worth it. That's why my biggest teaching frustrations come on this front. When someone robs my students of the one single thing they need most, I get angry.

> They need the truth.

> Take "Donnie." A nice kid – personable, eager, sincere – *and promoted beyond his ability*. When I get him, he's a senior, planning to go to college. And I want him to go, but he won't make it, not with his English skills, which are on about a sixth grade level. So I help him as much as I can, and he tries hard, but doesn't make enough progress. He doesn't pass. That's OK, I think, I'll coach him over the summer. Summer school can help. Let him graduate later. He can still make it.

But, no. The principal changes his F to a D in the name of accommodation, lets him graduate, and he flunks out of the local junior college the first semester. A child of color, an immigrant with a rough upbringing, and we lied to him. We failed him, the very one we want to help most.

Shame on us.

Yet despite the "easy path" open to so many of our children, most of the children in my survey really wanted to learn. When I did this survey, my favorite comments were from students, like the following examples, who still wanted to excel at what they did:

> Worst thing about school: "The lack of work that is given. Personally I rather (sic) be challenged than given a free pass." [50]
>
> Any comments?: "I used to think all teachers were the same just passing kids along. But Mr. X changed that." (Editor's note: Name replaced with "X" for this book.) [51]
>
> Best thing about school: "One of my teachers actually expect (sic) something out of his students and the way he teaches made math my best subject when last year it was my worst."[52]
>
> Most important to change: "The work they give us is stupid is (sic) like they don't want to challenge us to do something bigger."[53]
>
> Worst thing about school: "We don't learn. We just sit there playing with our thumbs waiting for teachers to give a crap. Some people actually want an education."[54]

---

[50] Fatima, Student Survey 2013
[51] Nick, Student Survey 2013
[52] Mark, Student Survey 2013
[53] Catalina, Student Survey 2013
[54] Kayla, Student Survey 2013

> Worst thing about school: My teachers think I'm incapable of doing work because I'm in standard. I want a challenge.[55]

Now, truth in advertising, I have to attest that I am not objective on the topic of how great children can be, and how they are the most important thing on this planet. *Children are the passion in my life.* I am not objective when I am driven to try to help them succeed, and to know that awesome feeling inside when they earned something.

Why? My stepfather was a pedophile of the most vile sort. What he did to me and to my older sister Karen is still, decades later, beyond comprehension to me. We both ended up leaving home as soon as we reached 17 or 18, and neither of us ever returned. From the research I have seen, there is a disturbing chance Karen and I could have turned out to be the same as my stepfather, but by good fortune we both turned out just the opposite.

For Karen, it was to become a medical professional who devoted her life to helping people. When she died early, at age 40 from cancer, *hundreds* of "strangers" who had been touched by her life attended the funeral. I lost my best friend that day. So many times over the years, when times were rough for either of us, we would invent a reason to give our spouses so that we could meet at a small restaurant called Finnerty's in Wayland, Massachusetts, and just talk. I was "playing chess" in Boston, and Karen was "out shopping." Because of our past, talking to others about problems was always hard for both of us. Karen had an amazing ability to listen and understand. I never realized back then that what I learned about listening from Karen would be one of the most important gifts I was ever given in my life. Every day in school I am surrounded by children who desperately need an adult just to listen, even if we disagree. Listening is one of the greatest acts of love an adult can give a child. Karen showed me that. She is the finest person I have ever known, and ever will be the goal for what I hope to be.

---

[55] Julia, Student Survey 2013

For me, it was children. I still remember the scene. I was probably 19 or so, and was standing down by home plate looking at a child rounding third, arms up in celebration, grinning ear to ear. I don't remember the specifics, but the picture is burned into my memory. I was coaching a little league team, and the boy must have been scoring a winning run, or something. But I still remember to this day the thought that came to me as I looked at the boy. "Every child should be able to feel that way. I want to help other children feel that way, the way I never did."

So – I am not objective, and wear on my sleeve at all times, my love for children and passion for helping them earn such a feeling. There is no job on earth more suited to make that happen than being a teacher.

Every child should know the joy of earned pride.

And the truth is that every child <u>can</u> be able to feel that way. The self-fulfilling prophecy of today's education (children are dumb, so we will dumb down the teaching, so we end up making them dumb) has to be broken. Every time we give a child a free ride via a phony do-over or extra credit packet, we hurt the child. We dumb them down. And then we seem surprised to see children act exactly the way we taught them to be.

A free ride through high school is <u>not</u> an act of love or kindness!

Over the years I have received letters from many parents and students who also loved the chance to <u>earn</u> their success, and <u>earn</u> their pride in what they did. Just consider the following examples – given not from some vainglorious attempt to brag, but as a reflection of kids that the system wrote off, yet who ended up receiving the most precious gift they would ever get – genuine pride in the accomplishments they earned.

"I did good (sic) in math this year because you pushed me and told me I could do it. I went from a 57 to a 96 in a matter of three months. Thank you for everything and showing me I am smart and can do math and do it correctly."[56]

> Note: This is a Special Ed student who had always failed math and was absolutely convinced she was "stupid." It turned out she just had some gaps from 7th grade math that surfaced in all her high school work and generated wrong answers. We fixed that, and she <u>earned</u> Bs and As for the second half of junior year, and all her senior year. I still remember the day she got her first A on a test. She started crying right in front of the entire class, and asked me if she could call her mom (cell phones were not permitted to be used in school). I let her call, and watched the joy on her face as she smiled through all the tears to say "…Mom, I just got an 'A' in math." That was a Friday afternoon. I went home and was on cloud nine for the whole weekend. One Kayla in a teacher's life cancels out a whole lot of tough times. I framed that letter on my wall at home – it encourages me every time I glance at it.

"Hey Russel (sic) I wanted to thank you for helping me in math, and believing me when no one else did dispite (sic) my parents efforts."[57]

> Note: This student was a well-known discipline problem who had a history of substance-abuse issues along with her poor grades. She ended up discovering she was "smart," and by term three of her sophomore year I had her tutoring weak students in class that I would team up with her. I had the joy of watching as her growing confidence in math started changing her attitude in all areas. She ended up making some of the hardest life choices a child can be

---

[56] Kayla, 2011 letter
[57] Amandee, 2011 email

asked to make, changing so many of the choices that were hurting her. What a wonderful young lady she is becoming.

I wish I had access to examples from other teachers so that the message was not lost in what looks like bragging. All teachers have letters they save and cherish like these. But the message is clear – children *want* to learn, children *are* smart, children blossom with *earned* pride.

The only dumb ones are the ones we teach to be dumb.

Of course, none of us in administration would ever ask you to change a student's grade. However, would any teacher who plans to flunk a student this year please take the steps to your left.

The pressure to pass children who did not learn enough to warrant passing, most often because the child did not make any significant attempt to pass, is strong. In Massachusetts, if a school drops below "Level Two"[58] then everything that school administration does becomes focused upon being able to report higher graduation rates and higher MCAS scores. (MCAS – the Massachusetts version of standardized tests.) I have been in meetings held because the school dropped to "level three" where administrators announced to the assembled teachers that *"…if we do not raise our MCAS grades*

---

[58] *Massachusetts Framework for District Accountability and Assistance*, August 2012

this year, then half of you will no longer be here next year." The impact of such a mandate is that all the classes start to teach to the test rather than educate the students, electives are replaced by supplemental test-taking classes, and there is tremendous incentive for cheating by students, teachers, and administrators.

The graduation rate pressure becomes very visible, especially for seniors each year. Seniors who missed weeks of school are suddenly showing up to school a half hour early to get "catch-up credit" for missed days – by wandering the halls and chatting with their friends. Teachers must find any way possible for "Joan" to make up tests missed many weeks ago, and for "Mikey" to write a paper that was due last fall. And please be clear, the "grades" on those make-up assignments will all be passing grades, even if they are never read. A low graduation rate is one of the factors that can drive a school into the dreaded "Level Four" or "Level Five."

We think we are helping children, this way. Yet we end up hurting the rest of their lives every time we give them an unearned "free pass."

The pressure from guidance is frequent, but far more subtle. I have always sympathized with guidance, because they receive most of the direct pressure from the parents, and I suspect that the average guidance person receives several very nasty calls each week from irate parents. Guidance professionals know that they cannot officially ask for a grade change in the case of a failing student, and that a teacher's grade cannot be overridden by guidance or administration. The best guidance pros also know both the teachers and students involved, and know when looking at a make-up effort might be warranted. The weaker guidance members want to avoid return calls from parents at all costs. The result is a few times each month where guidance approaches a teacher to ask "…is there any way Sigmund can raise his grade to pass?"

School principals are far less subtle. There is no question that a teacher's application to coach the baseball team or lead the LGBT club hangs in the balance. When a principal tells a teacher "…I'd like to see what we can do to let Susie pass…" the pressure quickly rises to bullying levels. In the context of pressure from DOE mandates and school classifications, parents, and administration about grades, very few teachers have the courage to say "no."

Parents, via meetings, phone calls, and emails, exert great pressure on guidance and teachers. Sadly, the overwhelming bulk of these irate demands to raise a grade come from the parents of children who try the least, and with parents who take almost no apparent interest in their child's education unless the child is actually failing. As a rule, 90% of the involved, "good" parents who are invested in their child's education never request a grade change – but instead ask what their child needs to do *going forward* to improve grades. Conversely, two-thirds of the parents of failing kids do not seem to even notice or respond in any way, while many of the remaining third make angry efforts to get the grade changed *without* the child doing anything meaningful to earn a grade change.

Summer school is another example of a terrible symptom of a major systemic failure in education. If a child is one of the rare ones that actually *is* allowed to fail for poor performance and effort, they can "pass" the year via a summer school that is even more of an openly dumbed-down travesty than the Massachusetts MCAS test. The child spends two weeks, half days – *the equivalent of one week of normal school* – and if the child can get a D-minus on a quick summary of a handful of topics, they "pass" the year. Often the only requirement to qualify for summer school (instead of having to repeat the year) is that the student "achieves" a grade higher than "X" (typically 50% or 55%) for the actual school year. In today's schools, it is nearly impossible to get a grade below a 50!

This concept of teacher responsibility is endemic to more and more of today's parents. Just three weeks ago (as I write this section in April of 2013) I was at a parent-teacher night when I heard yelling from down the hall. An irate mother was screaming at an English teacher about her son's failing grades. The child had a long history in that class, and in his other classes, of doing no class work and blowing off most assignments. When the teacher pointed to all the zeroes for homework and class work grades, she screamed *"It's your job to motivate your students."* I was amazed at how calm the English teacher remained. Finally, he simply asked *"What part do you and your son play in the grades he gets?"* The answer? She jumped up with *"You're not doing your job!"* and then stormed out of the room to seek the principal.

As bad as this event sounds, it gets even worse in most urban high schools when it goes to a principal with little or no leadership experience and ability. Too often, the principal will avoid conflict and possible issues with school failure rates by siding with the parents – undermining the teacher and cementing a pattern of failure for that student for the rest of the student's school years.

Even a great teacher cannot teach an empty chair, nor motivate a child who has no incentive from home to succeed.

Poor student performance certainly can, and does occur due to poor teaching. The system must develop far more effective ways of correcting, or eliminating poor teachers. However, this is, and must be, a separate topic from teacher accountability. Even the best teachers are now being held solely responsible for performance, effort, and attitude issues that used to be the joint responsibility of the student, parent and teacher.

The loser in this process is the student who learns he/she can "pass" regardless of effort. It results in a sentence that will recur many times in this document: *Children can only achieve the best if they know they can fail.*

The most alarming unintended consequence of holding teachers solely responsible for grades is that we now have a new generation of children entering high schools with a set of expectations and entitlement that guarantees increasing failures in education. The freshmen class of 2016 (the current freshmen class in May of 2013 as I write this) is one of the first to enter high school after spending their entire elementary and middle school education under the influence of a system that has taken all responsibility for their performance away from them.

Now, of course there are exceptions, and there are many great students and parents who accept their co-responsibility and work hard to earn their performance. But, for a disturbing percentage of these students a teacher can only feel helpless (and hopeless) when looking at their attitude. Failing tests is "no biggie" to this growing minority of students – it is actually a point of pride shared with other students amid giggles. Homework is ignored, because a zero grade simply doesn't matter. Rampant cheating and plagiarism is expected.

The bottom line: One of the most important fix we can do that will greatly benefit our children is to reinstate the co-responsible trinity of parent, teacher, and student. Yet this will be by far the most difficult fix to achieve. A growing minority of no-show parents is helping to destroy education because a dysfunctional system encourages lack of co-responsibility with the teacher by students and parents. There is almost nothing a teacher can do to overcome a student who does not care because his/her parents do not care.

No failures:

The goal: No child should ever have to fail school because of an inadequate education.

Again, this is a lofty and excellent goal that had destructive unintended consequences. The disaster here was when "…not allowing failure" due to bad teaching morphed into "…not allowing failure" for anyone, any time, for any reason. We started "passing" children who should never have been allowed to pass.

> *One of the most important messages in this book, painfully learned from years of teaching and helping weak students excel, surfaces here – we can never expect children to start succeeding until we start allowing them to fail.* **We must start letting them fail!**

As also discussed in the above section about teacher accountability, there is strong pressure for teachers to pass all children in every class, regardless of effort or performance. Failures, graduation rates, and standardized test results are the three triggers – *regardless of the reason for the occurrences* – that can lead to immediate dismissal of administrators and teachers, and state takeover of a school.

Jacqueline Goodwin, a retired high school LOTE teacher from New York, shares her experiences with forced promotion:

(Jacqueline Goodwin) Children being cheated out of their education when teachers are forced to

pass students who should be allowed to fail, restart, and then succeed

Settling for the map instead of the territory – this is the principle passed on to our students when educators are pressured to allow extra credit assignments and retakes of assessments. In certain cases this is a necessary and compassionate action, but for the most part the practice defeats the purpose and integrity of our education system. For it implies that only the grade matters.

And this philosophy affects all students–both the overachievers, where grades impact college selection and potential scholarships, as well as the underachievers who simply need the grade so they can graduate. Extra-credit and test retakes send a message that it doesn't matter what you learn and understand as long as you attain a certain grade.

The long-term picture must be considered if the current system is to produce contributing and productive members of society. When a student is promoted without an understanding of the materials–due to an inflated grade achieved by supplemental assignments–he or she is unprepared for success at the new level. This perpetuates the "need" for the crutch of extra credit assignments as well as the expectation that they will be permitted.

The act of pressuring teachers to continually allow additional credit is based on distrust of the system and students – distrust that neither the system nor students can achieve what they have set out to do – to educate and to be educated.

Education is much more than a number, just as the territory is much more than the map.

Now here is the crux of the issue – one that cannot be supported with hard, factual data yet one that is the hardest "fact" for those outside of the walls of a school to accept – today, until we make changes to fix the problems, *20% of current students in urban high schools have earned their failure, and must* *be allowed to fail, due to almost no effort, little interest in trying, and parents who are no-shows. <u>Failing them is an act of caring that will help them quickly turn this around</u>. Only by failing <u>for just one or two terms</u> will they be able to reset their effort and begin to easily and quickly earn the passing grades that always had been an untapped possibility for them.*

To put this 20% figure into perspective, a decline in standardized test scores of just 5% could trigger closure of a school. In a school of 1000 students, if just 50 were the kind I described above (and not the 200+ I actually claim) that is far more than enough needed to drop a Massachusetts school down to the danger levels of performance.

So we focus everything in the high school on getting the 50 to pass. Education for all students is held hostage by the performance of a numerical minority who do not try.

All we need to do to reverse this is to allow the child to fail <u>just one term</u>! 90% of them will immediately get the message, and in the resiliency of children they will immediately adapt to the new "rules." The rest of the year they will work and earn far better grades, and it will change their life for the better!

There is absolutely nothing a teacher can do to influence most of these to try to pass under the current system. A great teacher can overcome so great an obstacle for a handful of such students, but has no chance of turning around <u>all</u> of them. It has become common for people with little understanding about the reality of today's schools to say "*...it is the teacher's job to motivate the student.*" Few statements more frustrate a good teacher. The truth is <u>no</u> – it is absolutely <u>not</u> the teacher's responsibility! *It is the responsibility of the teacher to reinforce and strengthen the motivation provided by the parents.* We have the child for just five hours out of the 168 hours in a week. The degree of success in motivating is impacted by the kind of home life the student has, his/her friends, and a host of other factors well beyond the influence of the teacher.

To paraphrase a well-known Washington DC housewife, "*...it takes a village*" to motivate a child.

It is easy to underestimate how difficult it is to overcome this culture of entitlement and lack of effort. I have such a passion for teaching and challenging students that I have had good luck over the years turning around many such students. Yet there are always a handful where I am unable to overcome all that works against their success. I believe in our children today – they are far smarter, and far more eager to learn and earn reasons for pride than anyone outside the system seems to understand. I am not even in the top half of teachers in my math department in terms of experience and teaching skills, yet this "...winning by letting them fail" approach works for me, and for the handful of teachers I know with the courage to risk the ire of parents and school administrators by failing a child for just one term. One term is almost always all it takes – and the child benefits for the rest of their school years, and for the rest of their lives. My students know how much I care, and that I believe in them. They know I have high expectations for them. They know I do everything in my power to explain the material to them.

And they know I will fail them.

The same scenario has played out in my classes for year after year. Such students fail term one, and then are shocked when I point to the statement I had them sign at the start of the year that says "...absolutely no extra-credit packets or do-overs." They immediately head to guidance to ask to be moved to an easier class. Thankfully, the best guidance people know me and my approach, and send them back to class with the correct admonition – "...try harder and get some extra help until you get caught up." The rest of the pattern is staggering in the consistency of the result: halfway through term two they start working. By term three they are earning Bs. Earning! Nothing given! By term four they are getting As, are so proud they could burst, and are down in guidance asking to be in my class again next year.

95% average in math for the entire year!

These are the same classes, including students who started out by not trying, that lead the entire school and match the very top schools in the state in standardized test scores. These are the students who cherish wearing the geeky T-shirt I give to the top 10 students each year in my "Slow Group" – to qualify you must have a grade for the entire year of at least 95%. These are the classes that flock to the board every two weeks when the latest "Slow Group" listing is posted to see if they are listed in the top ten.

Pride is contagious!

(Intentionally blurred)
Can't wait to see if in top ten!

Please note – these results are due to two factors – and <u>neither</u> factor has anything to do with being a "good teacher." A "garden-variety" teacher could achieve the exact same results. Factor #1 is my high expectations for e very student. I start with the knowledge that all students are smart, want to learn, and are nothing like the stereotype calling for dumbed-down instruction that is forced by the system today. I believe in them. Kids are much smarter than adults in quickly figuring out whether or not a teacher really cares. So I don't dumb down the class, I make it harder!

Education has been dumbed down to make the <u>system</u> look good, not because of the needs of the students!

The second factor is that I am willing to fail them. I have the willpower (some think a better label is "feistiness!") to put up with the irate parents, the initial outraged student entitlement speeches, and the pressure from administration and SPED to find a way to pass them.

For the record, I have students (and their parents) sign a set of "expectations" I have for them at the start of each year. It is very specific about "…you get what you get the first time through."

Here is part of the form I have all students and parents sign:

Grading:

60% - Weekly Quiz
15% - Class attitude and effort
25% - Classwork and Homework

Homework:

Zero credit is given for homework that does not show the work. A page of "answers" is not homework.

Do-overs, extra credit packets, etc:

This one is simple: <u>never</u>. With the rare exception of an IEP-specific reason, I never allow do-overs for bad grades, or provide extra credit packets to pull a grade up. Your grade is what you earn the <u>first</u> time through.

Make-up of missed quizzes:

You have <u>one week</u>, <u>shop week</u>, to make up a quiz you miss. At the end of the shop week <u>following</u> a missed quiz, if you did not come in to make up the quiz or see me to schedule a make-up, then you will get a zero for that quiz with no opportunity for a retest. If you need extra help before the retest, it is up to you to see me and schedule extra help.

Scheduling make-ups and extra help:

Once again, simple answer: it is completely up to you. I will not chase you. I am available Thursday after school, early mornings before school (usually here by 7:15 or so unless traffic problems) and even third period if your shop will let you out. Come see me and schedule help or a retest. If you get a zero and don't come in – and later come to me with "…I was busy…" or "…I forgot…" or "…I had to work …" "…an elephant fell on my brother…" then my reply will be "I feel your pain, but you still get a zero."

Most teachers, like most people everywhere, are very uncomfortable if there is great conflict. And believe me, when a child is flunking these days there will be great conflict. Parents are on the phone to the teacher, sending emails, calling guidance, playing the SPED card, and calling the principal – all to get the grade changed without the child actually doing something to earn a change. Very few people anywhere can withstand that kind of pressure, including teachers. Compare it to the "assistant manager" at a Burger King with an out-of-control customer screaming about a poorly cooked hamburger. The customer can get as nasty as he/she wants, even with no valid reason – and the manager usually gives up rather than battle against it.

A classic case for me was "Gertrude."

> Gertrude was a bright young girl who entered term four with a cumulative average for the prior three terms and midterm of just 48. A grade of 65 was needed to pass for the year. If you "do the math," she needed to average about 130 on all her remaining tests, homework and final exam in order to pass. Obviously, grades of 130 could not happen without a break in the math space-time continuum.
>
> But I had faith in this girl for some reason, despite every apparent reason to the contrary. I could tell that she was very bright, and despite her bad disciplinary record I felt that she was really a "good kid" at heart. But she never tried (doodled and daydreamed all class), did little or no homework, rarely passed a test, never came in for extra help, and missed a lot of classes. Her missed classes were due to truancy, cutting class for "hall walking," and some were for "excused" reasons. She had a pretty long history of disciplinary issues and in-house detentions. She refused any effort to get her to come for extra help, attend peer tutoring, etc.
>
> As I always did with such cases, I let her fail when everything else I tried did not work.
>
> At the start of term four her parents came in to guidance for a joint meeting to "demand" a grade change. Their entire view was "...*what are you* [the teacher] *going to do to*

pull up her grade in math?" Despite the parents, I decided to give Gertrude a chance, so I offered to put her on what I call a "program." If she would…

- …come in <u>every</u> Thursday night for the remaining six weeks of school for extra help
- …pass all of her term four tests with at least a "C"
- …come in a dozen additional hours either before school (I agreed to come in an hour early each day), my lunch time, or my free time each day
- …go over earlier work and let her <u>earn</u> a make-up grade for it

…then I would revisit her Term 1-2 grades to allow her to pass. I emphasized again and again that any grade change was dependent upon significant extra effort, and there was so little time left in the school year that missing even a single time would be a problem that could void the "contract." Everyone – Gertrude, parents, and guidance agreed on the plan.

So, the first week, Gertrude does not show for anything. The next week she also is nowhere to be found. I emailed the mother and got back the reply: *"With our schedule, no one can bring her in before school. She missed last Thursday night because she was in detention. She missed this Thursday because she had to work. She should be there next week."* But even in week three, there was no Gertrude to be seen. *"I forgot."*

I emailed the parents that I was sorry she did not keep her part of the deal, but we were out of time for her to make up the material and that she would flunk for the year. The poop then hit the fan, resulting in my suddenly being called out of a class I was teaching to come down to the principal's office. When I arrived, not knowing the meeting topic, I was surprised to find the parents sitting there. A weak principal had called me out of a classroom with no notice, and never mentioned the parents were waiting in his office.

The parent's tone was nasty from minute one – *"…you are a liar, you promised to change her grade."* They had endless excuses for why Gertrude should not have been expected to do her part of the "contract," but I must still live up to mine. The principal kept silent during the meeting, offering no help and no support. After ten minutes of their nastiness, the principal, the latest member of the clique to get the position, and not qualified for handling that level of conflict, actually left the room and said "...*I'll cover your class for you since you'll need more time to work this out.*" Rather than help exert leadership and defuse the situation, the principal was so over his head and cowed by the conflict that he cut and ran. Sadly, he had a reputation for doing anything possible to avoid conflicts like this when a teacher needed help. (This principal was an excellent example of good teachers who do not make good principals – see the next chapter in this book.)

The moral of the story? This case is not an exception in today's education – it is the rule. These two parents had such a sense of entitlement that they could not even comprehend how their daughter needed to earn a passing grade. I now understood how Gertrude, who I still believe was a good kid, could develop such an approach to education with two dysfunctional parents like hers. In the guise of "helping" their daughter, these two parents were destroying her chance at an education.

Teachers deal with this level of parent every week.

With all the pressure to pass children who do not try, and with little help from parents for this sizable minority of students, schools have to resort to one of three approaches to ensure that "no child is left behind."

- One is phony methods to allow students to "pull up" their grades – do-overs, extra credit packages, and make-up assignments. Most of these are never even read or graded – just used as the excuse to "pass" the child.

- Second is dumbed-down instruction so that even no-try students might pass. Of course, the real losers in this approach are the two-thirds of students who are great kids who want to learn.

- The third is outright cheating – the extreme case. A grade will simply be "changed," or a standardized test scandal will occur.

Surprise – the kids quickly figured out that the system would find a way to pass them, and they now milk the system! Do you blame the students?

By the mid 2000s, both children and parents had learned that students will not be allowed to fail, even if the cause is little or no effort by the child, and no educational support from the parent. Failing students routinely are given test do-overs, extra credit packages to pull up their grades, and outright grade changes to ensure they do not fail, <u>regardless</u> of effort or performance. We now have a culture where children expect to pass regardless of their effort.

The bottom line: <u>The only way a child can succeed is to know they can fail.</u> This is true in life, and is true in education. The students in the one-third that get passed without learning anything are being cheated out of the rest of their lives by a system that dooms them to failure. The two-thirds that really want to learn have to live with dumbed-down teaching, and will pay a price for their entire careers.

Standardized testing:

The goal: Standardized testing will ensure that all schools are providing all the fundamentals of a good education, and identify underperforming schools.

[Author's note: The specifics and examples in this section are largely centered on the math portions of standardized tests. As a math teacher, I can speak to this area, but am not qualified to speak with the same level of confidence to English, Biology, or other topic areas. However, based upon interviews and discussions with many other teachers, the experiences and conclusions I draw for math are largely transferrable to these other topics.]

Standardized testing is an absolute joke. Every year I see questions on the Massachusetts math MCAS test for high school sophomores ("number one" in the nation since you only need 29% to "pass") that are barely worthy of being given to middle school children. The test has been dumbed down to the point of being useless as an indicator of high school ability. When the students do badly in a year, the state DoE simply drops the minimum passing score to make sure the real failure rate remains hidden.

MCAS has become little more than a farce designed to make the state and career DoE bureaucrats look good, while covering up the abject failure of their policies in educating our children.

The problem of terrible education hidden by over-inflated standardized test results is not limited to Massachusetts. According to an ACT placement test summary for 2013, only one quarter of 2013 U.S. high school graduates are ready for college work in all four core subjects.

[Editor's note: Underlines added to original]

> *"The ACT reported that 31 percent of all high school graduates were not ready for any college coursework requiring English, science, math, or reading skills. The other 69 percent of test takers met at least one of the four subject area standards. Just a quarter of this year's high school graduates cleared the bar in all four subjects."*[59]

This ACT report is a horrible indictment on the state of high school education. According to the Massachusetts Department of Education, more than 90% of all students "passed" standardized testing to determine whether they were "proficient" in these four topics. Yet ACT finds that only 31% actually received a high school education sufficient to meet college requirements.

The difference between the inflated Massachusetts DOE claim of 90%, and the ACT findings of 31%, is a DoE system designed to carefully hide our failures behind a curtain of dumbed-down standardized tests and inflated results.

A sampling of recent MCAS questions makes this point all too clearly, showing how much the high school tests have been dumbed down by being salted with many middle school

---

[59] *ACT: Third of High School grads not college ready*, ABC News, 21 August 2013

questions – and then the bar adjusted down to allow passing with just 29% of such easy questions:[60]

- Simplify the following (2 pts):   5(y + 3)

- What is the average value of: 10, 5, 6, 8, 0, 10, 10, 7

- What is the value of (2 pts):   -8 + (6 – 2)^3

- What is the circumference* of a circle with a diameter of 8 inches?

- What is the value of: 5(9 - 3)^2 ÷ 3

- Simplify the following: 12(y + 89)

- What is closest to √50?   6.4, 6.8, 7.1, 7.5

- Manuel typed 2974 words in 51 minutes. Which is closest to his average words per minute?   20, 40, 60, 100

- Simplify: 6x – 3 – 4x + 8

- What is the volume* of a right circular cylinder with a diameter of 6 and a height of 10?   188, 283, 471, 1131

   * MCAS provides the needed formula on
     a separate sheet)

Worse, please consider high school topics that are rarely or never on MCAS.

- For the past several years, there has not been a single trigonometry (sine, cosine…) problem.

- There have been no quadratic formula questions.

- Until two years ago there had been no chord/tangent of circles questions.

---

[60] http://www.doe.mass.edu/mcas/testitems.html

- There have never been questions about the volume or surface area of irregular shapes.

- Systems problems are always the easiest form – either simple substitution problems, or elimination problems where one variable already cancels out.

- Etc., etc., etc.!

Each year MCAS has a retest in the November timeframe for students that failed the MCAS the prior spring. This version is intentionally and openly dumbed-down <u>even further</u> so that students face a far easier test than the one they failed. The questions chosen are always from the types of questions that most students passed the prior year, and intentionally omit those questions that gave students the most trouble.

This is the "test" that students must pass with just 29% correct. (A few years earlier, in order for the bureaucrats to hide how poorly the entire state did on one MCAS math test, they temporarily lowered the year's passing requirement for that year to just 25%.) At 29% a student passes, but "needs improvement." To be in the <u>highest</u> MCAS proficiency level, you need to get less than half of these largely middle school questions correct. And yet, many high school students fail MCAS, or just barely pass. So this leads to the main problem with standardized tests – they are over-simplified tests centered on middle school math and the most basic portions of high school math.

The tests have been so simplified that the results are little more than a way to ensure that schools and the state look good and <u>appear</u> to be educating the children. They fail completely as an indicator of actual high school knowledge.

Every year when I start my new high school math classes, I always give the children a "pop quiz" that is not graded, but gives me a chance to see where the children stand on math. The "test" has always included eight <u>very</u> simple problems that cover basic middle school math. I give this to all new sophomores and juniors (and freshmen classes on the rare times I have been assigned ninth graders.) An example of the questions is the following:

$$4*3 \div 3*4$$

This is a very basic elementary school PEMDAS problem. It is a topic that should have been learned by fifth or sixth grade, and completely mastered by the end of middle school. (My granddaughter, 4th grade, actually solved it the first time.) Yet for my new sophomores, more than two-thirds get this problem wrong! The correct answer is 16, though the most common incorrect answer is 1. Without diving into a level of detail that only another math teacher would find interesting, the bottom line is that *two-thirds of these students have learned PEMDAS incorrectly,* and PEMDAS is as fundamental as knowing your multiplication tables to getting the right answer to any math problem

Here is the result from this test of four sophomore classes in 2011 and 2012:

$4*3 \div 3*4$	65% wrong
$3x - 2(4x - 10) + 5$ (Simplify)	88% wrong
35% of 660 (with a calculator!)	71% wrong
6, 1, 2, 0, 3, 0, 7, 9 (mean, mode, median, range)	82% wrong
Given circle with C=145, what is the area?	86% wrong
$3x + 2(x - 10) = 2x + 100$	76% wrong
Area of irregular shape (rectangle plus triangle)	91% wrong
$32 - 6(42 - 6)^2/2*10$	63% wrong

For freshmen, the result is even worse, with the percentage wrong on the first 3*4/4*3 question an alarming 93%.

This is a deadly result, and it is not an indictment of students – it is a red flag about the failure of the educational system. A child can have an IQ of two hundred and totally understand every new high school problem, but if they cannot do PEMDAS, they will get most *of their high school questions wrong. And the hidden indictment underlying these results is that the gap in middle school knowledge was not discovered and corrected in high school – the sophomores still could not do PEMDAS. 65% of these sophomores are fated to get most high school math problems wrong because they could not do the underlying arithmetic.*

High school math builds upon the fundamentals learned in elementary and middle school. It simply adds a top layer of new material. At the top might be a geometry volume question, but as soon as you substitute something into a formula for volume, the next step is middle school math, and the actual computations are elementary school math. A child could perfectly understand the high school material, yet fail badly because of the underlying middle school gaps.

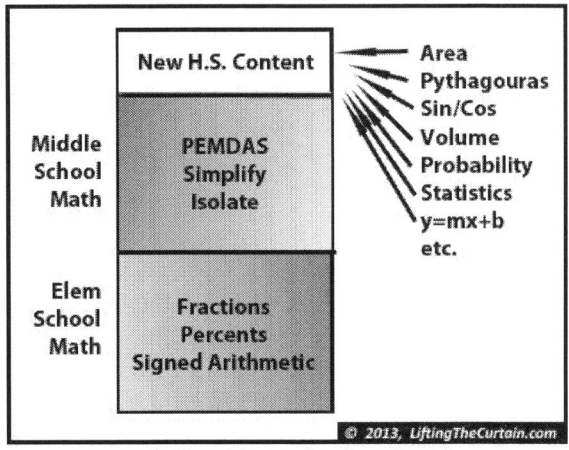

90% of EVERY high school math problem is exactly the same – just the top line changes

The system only adds to the problem. Overuse of multiple choice questions means that the teacher never sees the underlying problem, and just sees and grades a "wrong" answer. The child thinks he/she cannot do math. The mandate to use every available minute of the class to meet educational core standards, (and to somehow also meet added mandates for inclusion classes, SPED, Administration, etc.) means that the high school classes can never go back and "fix" the middle school problem they inherited. We have to get the student "ready" to pass the next standardized test – there is no time to go "backwards" to cover middle school gaps, even if that is exactly what we need to do to give the child a chance to pass the new material.

Class work, and even the text books themselves, become centered on passing the state test, rather than teaching the material. Children spend hours of "learning time" sitting in front of computers taking and retaking practice tests – *even though students learn absolutely nothing by taking practice tests on material they do not know!* To see the silliness in this concept, picture "practicing" to pass a Latin test by reading passages in Latin, if you didn't understand the language to start with!

The curricula of math classes (remember, as a math teacher I am using math examples, but the same applies for all standardized tests) gets centered on those topics expected on the standardized test. This focus on standardized tests ends up hurting the very education process it hoped to help.

- First, it is a further incentive to dumb down education, above and beyond the pressure to pass all children. Since the test emphasizes dumbed-down middle school math, and very simple versions of high school math, then we start teaching to that expected dumbed-down level. Given the history of MCAS, a math teacher is tempted to shortchange teaching trig (a high school topic never on MCAS) and substitute more time on computing averages (a middle school topic that is always a major topic on MCAS). Circular logic reaches out and bites us again – we dumb down the test to make students pass, we dumb down the teaching to make students be prepared for the test, the students get a dumbed-down education, the students become "dumb," we need to further dumb down the test to let students pass…. Brilliant!

- We start devoting a significant amount of teaching effort to "test taking strategies," rather than just teaching the base material. I am embarrassed to watch good teachers forced by school administrators to show students how to plug in each of the four multiple choice answers to see which one gives the correct answer for a "volume" problem, rather than just teaching the same children to understand "volume."

These tests are so critical to school and student evaluation, and have such a dramatic impact on teacher careers, that there are increasing incidences of mass cheating by both students and teachers. Those outside of the system will have a hard time believing or comprehending the intensity of the pressure on teachers to make sure their students pass standardized testing, *or else*. The Washington Post reported confirmed cheating scandals in <u>thirty-seven states</u>, and was convinced that there were far more actual incidents than were ever discovered. On this one, the Washington Post is absolutely correct. They summed up the reasons for the cheating as follows:

> *"Anyone following school reform over the past decade knows exactly what happened. Under No Child Left Behind, President George W. Bush's chief education initiative, and then Race to the Top, President Obama's central education program, placed increasingly high stakes on standardized test scores. They had to go up, or else there would be negative consequences not just for students but schools and teachers and principals."* [61]

Another comment from FairTest seems to go too far in trying to rationalize reprehensible behavior by administrators and teachers who cheated, but it does accurately describe the pressure to cheat in the widely publicized Atlanta school district scandal:

> *Over time, the unreasonable pressure to meet annual APS [Atlanta Public Schools] targets led some employees to cheat on the CRCT [Criterion Referenced Competency Tests]. The refusal of Beverly Hall and her top administrators to accept anything other than satisfying targets created an environment where achieving the desired end result was more important than the students' education.* [62]

The tragedy with standardized testing is the vicious self-fulfilling prophecy of failure when teaching to the test: the more you focus on the expected questions on the standardized test, the less you have time to teach the full curricula, and the less the children learn and understand the material they need – resulting in more failed tests and even more pressure on teachers to "…teach to the test." The medicine makes the situation worse. You end up with an

---

[61] *Atlanta Test cheating: Tip of the iceberg?*, Washington Post April 2013
[62] National Center for Fair and Open Testing, April 2013

"education" based upon remembering facts and test-taking strategies, and *not* on ever understanding the material.

Our children's education is only effective when good teachers help them <u>understand</u> the material, and is useless if we just drill them to <u>remember</u> steps and facts.

Most outside the classroom do see that what is labeled a "…school failure" means they did not show gains on <u>all</u> 36 <u>factors</u> required by the well-meaning, but disastrous legislation of No Child Left Behind and Race to the Top. Miss just one of the 36, even if by just a few tenths of a percent, and the school can be relegated, or in extreme cases taken over. The penalties to the school are so great that the entire curricula gets pushed aside in a school-wide focus on test preparation.

I sat in one assembly of teachers where the principal made the stakes very clear – "If we do not pull up results in all categories this year, half of you will not be returning next year." Failing the state test creates a destructive cycle of dumbed-down courses that mean our children never receive the education teachers dearly want to give them, but are prevented from giving by the unintended consequences of the well-meaning NCLB mandates.

For non-teachers reading this, the key is AYP – annual yearly progress. Nine groups of students across four categories are evaluated. Here is the actual description (the reference to MCAS is the Massachusetts state test) from the Massachusetts DoE:[63]

> AYP is important because it measures progress of **all** groups of students. In the past, schools could appear to be providing a good education if the average scores were high. In reality, these averages often hid the fact that specific groups of students were not making academic progress. **Today, if just one student group at a school does not meet an AYP goal, then the school does not make AYP for that year.** In this way, schools are held accountable for making sure all groups of student

---

[63] NCLB Standards, Massachusetts DoE

make progress, even those who have been left behind in the past. Student groups include:

- All students in the school
- White
- African American
- Hispanic
- Native American
- Asian
- Economically disadvantaged
- English language learners
- Students with disabilities

AYP determinations are based on four factors:

- Participation – At least 95% of students must participate in MCAS tests
- Performance or Improvement – Based on students' scores on MCAS tests
- Attendance (for elementary & middle schools) – at least 92% annual attendance rates or 1% improvement in attendance
- Graduation rate for high schools – A graduation rate of at least 65% or show improvement

The following passage is a heartbreaking look at how children pay the price for a focus on standardized testing at the expense of teaching. Monica S is a high school SPED teacher in New York. Her passage reflects a view I saw in almost all of the urban high schools I researched, interviewed and surveyed. What sets Monica S's submission apart was how well it shows how teaching-to-the-test dominates the entire school – it disrupts teaching, takes teachers out of the classroom, creates endless meetings, ties up and wastes budgets and resources, and ends up making the situation far worse for our children. She even mentions one of my favorite examples of inept mandates by unqualified career bureaucrats at DoE – the useless "Core Standard Whiteboard Posting" (see chapter 23) that sucks yet another 2-3 minutes away from teaching, in every class.

Monica S has been teaching for 25 years. The majority of her experience is in middle school resource room/remedial reading and writing. She also taught at the high school level for three years. Monica is National Board Certified in Exceptionality.

Failing State Tests, Failing Our Students

Our school did not make the mandated annual yearly progress. Of the 36 different categories of mandated "improvement" required, a school can "fail" if it misses any by as little as tenths of a percent. The result for us is that everything we do in our school this year is now focused upon getting children to pass this year's test.

Our community is struggling economically. Drugs and dysfunction, even homelessness, are commonplace. We have high teacher turnover and low school funding. State testing doesn't address any of these issues that also directly impact school performance.

So our school has come up with the finances for professional development from "experts" on the common core standards. We are paying for coaches for our principals, and mentors for newly hired teachers. We pay for substitute teachers (taking us out of the classroom) so we can be trained on how to implement the new teacher evaluation system. Yet our students are using twenty year old text books and outdated technology.

We have added grade level meetings, subject area meetings, CARE team meetings, leadership team meetings, and more parent meetings to our weekly staff and IEP meetings.

I arrive at work at 6:30 a.m. to enter grades from papers I corrected the night before. I am praying the one copier in the building will work this morning. I am writing down the common core standards for today's lesson on the old shower wall "white board" when Joey stops by. He asks if he can come in after school for extra help on a reading assignment. It was the third time in two weeks I had to say, "I'm sorry, but not today. I have a meeting."

A few tenths we missed by in our scores mean we cannot teach this year, we just do test preparation. Failing the state test forces us to fail our students.

The bottom line: Today's standardized tests badly hurt the education of our children. A challenging standardized test, one that conforms to a legitimate high school curricula, would still be a positive thing for education. But the tests we have, and the way they are administered and used to evaluate schools, has backfired from the original intent.

Inclusion classes and Special Education (Chapters 21 and 22)

The inclusion goal: A school must serve all students, and not provide a lesser educational opportunity to students of a particular subset of the population – such as a racial or income group.

The Special Education goal: Schools must recognize and accommodate student disabilities that make traditional learning methods less effective.

[Editor's note: Both special education and inclusion classes are prime examples of destructive unintended consequences of well-meaning mandates. However, the failure in these two areas are so widespread, so destructive, and so significant that they warrant separate chapters in this book. *Please see "Systemic Failure #4 (Chapter 21) – Inclusion classes where everyone loses" and "Systemic Failure #5 (Chapter 22) Special Education – hijacked by a minority of parents" later in this book.*]

Conclusion: Unintended consequences have created a generation of failure

None of us saw the long-term negative impact of programs centered on the great-sounding, but completely destructive concept that a child can not be allowed to fail. We have ended up creating a culture of failure, where failure is expected, and failure is accepted. We fell into the circular logic trap of thinking today's children were too dumb to learn as we did, so we dumb down their education, so the children become dumb.

For many of today's students, there is no longer any perceived short-term consequence for poor performance. Failing is "…no big thing." A growing numerical minority of the parents we deal with every day seem to share that same view. Teachers know that there are long-term impacts from a weak education that will negatively shape the child's entire life, but can do less and less to change that perspective.

Still, today, the most common question a teacher hears is "…when will I ever need this in real life." I always answer the same way. "Maybe never, but that will be because you had many great options to choose from when you start to work, and you were able to choose one that didn't need this topic." But I also tell them that the key here is to give them lots of options. I don't want any child I have taught to start their careers having to settle for one of the few possibilities open to them. I tell them: "If you come back to me in five years and tell me you never used any of this, I will only ask you one question – did you end up being able to do something you love to do? If the answer is 'yes, and you really didn't need this math, then I will be in total agreement with you. But if you answer 'no' because you had to settle for a job you didn't like since you didn't know enough math, then I will have failed you as a teacher."

But a fifteen year old is incapable of seeing past next Wednesday. Job prospects when he graduates are, at best, an interesting question. Savings when she retires do not even register on her radar. Thankfully, this is not true for all students, yet. But for perhaps a third of students (and their parents) in urban high schools today, all that matters is that they "pass" and graduate. These are the children whose parents simply don't care "…as long as Jimmy graduates." These are the children that know the schools don't dare fail them so there will be plenty of chances to pull up their grades via phony do-over tests, and make-work extra credit packets that are never even graded. Many of these are the students who have bogus IEPs that get them out of most work.

These are the students who we have doomed to failure because of a bad educational system. And it was all because of the best of intentions.

(Chapter 20)
Systemic Failure #2: Unqualified Administrators and rampant cronyism

[Author's note: This chapter overstates the role of principal for those schools where a superintendent has direct responsibility for many of these issues, instead of the principal.]

Overview: Of course there are exceptions, but <u>most</u> new principals are not qualified to run an organization the size and complexity of a typical school. A significant minority of new principals got their position via cronyism. All too often the new principal is just the next good old boy (or girl) nearing retirement who wants the large pension boost that occurs in retirement plans based upon the last years of income.

With a weak certification "earned" from an online degree mill offering puff courses, and with no leadership or management experience before assuming the position, they have no clue how to make the tough choices principals face every day. All they can do is "check the boxes" and take care of their friends. A sizable minority raises cronyism to the level of corruption. Most, with no prior experience as a leader, rely upon bullying and cronyism to enforce their policies

Sadly, a great teacher rarely will become a competent principal.

Twenty or so years ago, the personal qualifications of a principal were perhaps the single most important factor in determining the success and environment of a school. At the risk of oversimplification, a great principal back then could make a great school, and a weak principal could still run a pretty good school. Parents were invested in their child's education, and students knew that excellence was expected and possible. But since that time, the unintended consequences of draconian rules and regulations that did not exist in the 1980s have dominated what the principal can control in a school.

A great principal still makes a difference, but even the best principal has a far harder job, today, than his/her predecessors from the 1980s ever envisioned. The challenges are a full order of magnitude more difficult. The knowledge and skill set of a principal must encompass far more expertise in matters well beyond the educational challenges faced by the earlier principals.

The following is not a position for an amateur with a couple semesters of "puff" online "leadership" courses from a degree mill:

- Management of 300 employees
- A $15 million budget
- Negotiations with unions
- Negotiations with towns and legislators
- Making difficult budgetary and financial decisions
- Mandated testing requirements
- The safety of 1,500 children
- Laws and mandates on bullying, child restraint
- Social issues including drugs, neighborhood violence
- Social issues including race and gender
- Media scrutiny
- Hundreds of pages of Special Education mandates
- Hundreds of pages of ESL mandates
- Hundreds of pages of inclusion mandates
- Changing core standards
- Changing grants procedures and requirements
- Changes in Perkins, NCLB, Race to the Top
- New mandates on food and cafeteria policies
- Mandates about food, cafeterias, and vending machines
- Mandates about allergies
- School physical security and terrorism
- Crumbling school buildings
- Changing benefit and pension laws
- Providing leadership
- Evaluations and promotions
- Selecting people for assignments
- *And on top of this – all the daily administrative duties of a principal!*

A good-teacher-turned-principal of the 1980s would have no chance when facing the wide scope of today's education leadership challenges.

The problem is simple – the new demands of the position require new skills, but the hiring requirements have not changed from those before bullying laws, mandated testing, town budgetary battles, union fights over benefits, tons of bureaucracy, special education laws, no-show parents, security requirements, and students armed with lawyers and "advocates."

Before the three years research and surveys that led up to publishing this book, there was little data to support the following four statements other than common sense and anecdotal evidence. The survey results were a powerful look at the degree to which unqualified school principals and administrators are hurting our children's education.

Clearly, the following figures might be higher or lower in another set of urban schools, or in suburban or elementary schools. However, it is doubtful that anyone with direct inside knowledge of schools would challenge the order-of-magnitude of the following estimates:

- Just one-third (34%) of all principals/superintendents in place today have the management skills, training, and abilities sufficient to meet the complex demands of today's schools.

- At least two-thirds of all principals/superintendents in place today are functionally unqualified and incompetent (66%) to address today's issues – contributing directly to the deterioration in education.

- The overwhelming majority (60%) of principals/superintendents today base their key extra-pay assignments and promotions on blatant cronyism – undermining all faith and trust in school administrations by teachers and staff.

- A sizable minority of principals/superintendents today, approaching 40% of all in-place principals, have taken open cronyism to a level approaching corruption.

At a time when we desperately need leaders and managers, we have nice people who used to be good teachers, but are now hopelessly over their heads.

With all these additional demands on a principal, ask yourself two questions.

> *First* – what is the typical prior management experience of successful CEOs in $15 million dollar companies with 400+ employees before they were chosen to become CEO?

> *Second* – when a new principal starts his job, with responsibility for 400 employees, a $15 million budget, and 1600 children, what is the largest number of employees he or she had ever supervised? What preparation has he or she had to qualify them to run an organization this large and complex?

Consider the following imaginary scenario in a major corporation – perhaps a company like IBM, or Dell, or Pepsi Cola, or Nabisco.

Mr. Smith has always been one of the best employees ever, and the pride of the accounting department. For the past 20 years he has been an accountant who performed his job with excellence. He reported early each morning to his desk in the middle of accounting department cubicles, and was rarely absent. Anyone familiar with his work typing invoices for the company knew he was reliable and a very hard worker. Everyone loved him.

So in recognition of his superb performance as an accounting clerk, the Board of Directors for IBM decided to make him President.

The board had him take two years of weak online night courses from a degree mill while he continued his fulltime company job as an accountant typing invoices. He was required to pass an easy online program covering very basic business practices that would not even qualify as an introductory course at any major business school. Two years later, he packed up his desk in accounting, and headed to the executive suite. Starting the next Monday he would be suddenly be totally responsible for 400 employees, a $15 million budget, providing leadership, making extremely difficult financial decisions, negotiations with local towns and legislators, union contracts and grievances, constantly changing laws and regulations, media scrutiny about issues ranging from bullying to political correctness, and the behavior and safety of 1500 children.

Seem like a stretch to go from accountant to president? What about from teacher to principal? Yet that is exactly what happens every day in the USA when a (hopefully) good teacher becomes a new principal. If that happened at Pepsi or GE or IBM most stockholders would see what a disaster was likely and would sell their stock the same day before its value plummets. In public schools there is no stock price – the equivalent drop is in student achievement.

(Oh, the answer to the question about the number of employees supervised before becoming principal, above, is probably "none," except he or she might have shared a secretary for a year as Dean of Students on the way to becoming principal.)

Please remember that this discussion is about the system, not about character.

Many of the people who aspire to become principals and superintendents are among the finest people you would ever hope would *teach* your child. But even exceptional teaching skills have almost nothing to do with running a $15 million dollar business with 400 employees and responsibility for the education and safety of 1500 children. The leadership skills and management experience of nearly all first-time principals and superintendents would not even qualify them for middle management in any small corporation. *The typical first-time principal is more like an OJT assistant manager learning the job – except there is no experienced manager to fall back upon.*

For all but the most forward-thinking school committees, extensive teaching experience and the recommendation of the existing superintendent and/or principal is sufficient to insure appointment. Prior experience outside of teaching – such as business management or military leadership – is not considered an important positive qualification. Often the "clique" is openly derisive and hostile to teachers from military or business backgrounds – deriding those from non-traditional backgrounds as "…not real teachers."

To become a principal of almost any high school does not require any prior management experience at all. Instead, a candidate must be able to show a level of "leadership experience" that is about the same as a student must show to get into the National Honor Society.

> *"Throughout your time as a classroom teacher, look for opportunities to sit on and/or chair committees. Visit with your building principal and let them know that you are interested in becoming a principal. Chances are they will give you some increased role to help you prepare you for being in that role or in the very least you can pick their brain concerning principal best practices. Every bit of experience and knowledge will help when you land your first principal's job."*[64]

As an example of how basic the requirements are, consider this actual job posting for a principal. It requires less of the applicant than a posting to be a shift manager at Burger King. These are the total "requirements," not just a summary.

---

[64] *How to become a School Principal*, About.com

> (1) Must possess and maintain proper certification as established by state law and the Department of Public Instruction (DPI).
> (2) Must be aware of current trends and developments in education.
> (3) Must possess related training and/or experience.
> (4) Must possess leadership qualities.
> (5) Must meet any additional qualifications set by the district. [65]

Here is another posting – listing <u>all</u> that is required!

> 1. Ability to meet certification requirements from the State DPI.
> 2. Master's Degree or equivalent.
> 3. Demonstrated ability to exercise the responsibility allocated to the high school.
> 4. A minimum of 3 years previous administrative experience. [66]

Requirements such as these usually refer to two conditions – certification and prior administrative experience – that are used as the catchalls to show capability and experience. Both factors imply far more than they are in reality:

- Prior administrative experience can be service as limited as being a department head, or a position such as dean of students for disciplinary matters. Both are positions that are very limited in scope, normally include supervision of no more than one shared secretary, and are not able to set any policy or make any substantive personnel decisions without review and approval by administration.

- Principal certification programs would not meet the standards of even a middle management position in industry. Most course offerings fall well below that required by any <u>entry-level</u> business courses in a quality MBA program. Full certification can be accomplished via an online course in less than two years, and involves zero actual management responsibility.

   [Editor's note: Underline was added to the original]

   "You'll be exposed to the processes of teaching and learning that drive student-centered decision-making and will learn to adapt your Instructional strategies to meet the needs of all students. Additionally, these programs support your passion to enhance the lives of all individuals through education and community awareness.

   • *Regionally and NCATE* accredited*

---

[65] Somerset School District, Somerset Wisconsin
[66] Waupaca School District, Wisconsin

> - *Choose from four convenient start dates*
> - *45-54 quarter credits – graduate in as few as <u>two years</u>*
> - <u>*Completely online – no campus visits*</u>
> - *Instantly apply what you've learned to your own classroom*
> - *Balanced curriculum through hands-on collaboration and peer Interaction"* [67]

> *These online certification programs, routinely used to "qualify" candidates to be principal based upon just two years of online night courses with a weak curriculum, would not be sufficient to qualify for or a middle manager position in a small commercial business.*

The problem with getting qualified principals is made even worse by the way many principals and superintendents are selected. All too often promotions come from within the same school. While that sounds sensible on the surface, it is actually a very serious problem just waiting to backfire on the school. A promotion from within fails due to a number of factors, even if the person is otherwise an excellent candidate:

- The new principal must now evaluate, lead, promote, appoint extra-pay positions, and discipline those who were his longtime peers just days earlier.

- He/she enters the position with years imbued by the existing culture of the school, and has little or no perspective of how other schools handle similar issues

- There is a natural momentum and resistance to change when coming from within the environment

- The new principal brings baggage – old friends and enemies, favorites, vendettas, and hot buttons.

- His/her experience is heavily shaped by "…the way it has always been done," including by the principal and board that did the hiring.

Ironically, many of the most successful schools are careful to avoid hiring first-time principals, and consciously seek principal candidates who come from outside the school.

The impact of weak, poorly qualified principals impacts all aspects of the school environment:

---

[67] University of Cincinnati course description

Reactive, rather than proactive leadership – checking the boxes

Never before has education had such a strong need for proactive, strong leadership. We face old buildings needing replacement or refurbishment, new technologies, a deluge of new laws and regulations, parents who have opted out of co-responsibility for their students, union issues, rising SPED and ESL constraints, relationships with towns facing tax limits, and dropping educational performance.

Instead of these strong leaders, many of today's principals are just marking time to retirement by checking the boxes. Let's make sure we have computers in every room (whether or not they work) and only serve skim milk at lunch. Let's hold required principal's hearings on disciplinary cases, and attend school board meetings. Let's speak at parent meetings and hold assemblies. Let's sign off on invoices and help interview new hires. Let's organize mandatory state informational meetings.

Outside for the parents to see – new benches and pretty paint
Inside for the students – unusable toilets, and broken water fountains throughout the school – unrepaired for years!

Let's make sure anything the parents might see looks great – the entryway when parents drop off their children looks pretty with new benches and large LCD monitors for announcements, and let's have nice new tile and furniture in the administrative offices and any conference room a parent might see – but ignore the fact that students have gone years without working water fountains and the heating systems in half the classrooms have not worked in years.

Most of all, let's make sure we don't rock the boat, make certain that our sports teams do well, and ensure that our friends get the best extra-pay positions.

Let's keep busy while avoiding the systemic issues. Let's not make the hard decisions – firing the 3-4 bad teachers, encouraging parents to get involved, setting a culture of fairness and trust, raising expectations for our students, making classes more challenging, forbidding easy "make-ups" and "do-overs," cutting expenditures where possible, etc. Don't rock the boat, and absolutely make sure you don't confront and anger any parents that could result in an issue brought before the school board.

Oh, and of course, make sure your friends get the choice assignments.

Classroom heating systems unrepaired and unworking despite five years of requests – but the parent entryway looks beautiful!

After all, if the goal is just to mark time until qualified for the retirement pay boost that accrues with three years as principal, then why not keep our friends happy and just kick the can down the road for the next principal?

Take care of the cronies who got them there

In many inbred schools, leadership is centered on a clique who carefully plans both "whose turn" it is for a promotion, and when that promotion should occur. Often it is the turn of whoever in the clique is closest to retirement, so that person can get the maximum retirement income, and then leave so the next person in the clique can go for the job. The retirement system in most geographies contributes to the problem by basing retirement income on the last or highest-paid years (the last three in Massachusetts), so that having three years as principal before retirement is financially *very* attractive – often doubling your retirement income. It incents short-term principals who are far more focused (often very openly so) on getting a maximum retirement income than on contributing anything to the long-term success of the school. When a school suffers from a succession of "…three and out" principals and superintendents focused more on retirement pay than on education, it crushes faith in the system. Been there, done that, have the t-shirt. It had occurred in most of the urban high schools I researched.

*Okay, we're set. Bill makes me principal when he moves to super.
I make Ted the new dean. Mary, you replace me in three years.
We just have to make sure that idiot Jefferson doesn't have a chance.*

Now obviously there are exceptions, and there are very many excellent and qualified principals in the educational system. But the end result of the selection (and retirement) process is that we get many weak principals with a very short-term focus. And with virtually no checks-and-balances for a principal, especially if the principal is there only for a short period heading for retirement, it is nearly impossible to correct the problems.

And for those many principals who got their position via the clique, they are beholden to that clique for the rest of their term. The allegiance shows in many of the decisions they make, and undermines faith in the system by all teachers (the vast majority) who are not in the clique.

High School principals (in some districts it is the superintendent, not the principal) have extraordinary and unquestioned authority to hand out the "cookie jar" positions – extra-pay assignments for coaching, department heads, club leaders, class advisors, head of groups like the National Honor Society or Skills USA, and special positions such as safety coordinator or peer mentoring leader. The principal's authority to make the sole determination of what candidates receive these positions is absolute and not subject to review.

The exercise of this authority is one of the strongest factors undermining trust and faith in administrations. All too often, in *every one of the urban high schools I visited and researched*, the process was seen as predominately centering on the principal's best friends and cronies. This high incidence of clear cronyism largely explains the statistic cited earlier that *sixty percent of the teachers surveyed had little faith in the integrity of administrative assignments.*[68] Very qualified candidates are rejected, and the principal's close friends appointed, far too often in the view of almost all teachers.

The number of such assignments in a typical school is far larger than those outside the school would imagine, and is assigned to a new principal/superintendent with no prior management experience:[69]

- Typically 30-50 extra-pay positions
- Typical annual stipend $2,000 to $25,000 per position
- Coaches, club leaders, department heads, etc.
- Total budget: $250,000 to $400,000 per year.

Few outside the classroom understand the scope of these positions, and the degree to which principals are never held accountable for even the worst examples of cronyism. Here is a <u>partial</u> list from my current school:[70]

- Equipment Manager
- Head Baseball Coach
- Coordinator Intramural Fall (2)
- Assistant Baseball Coach
- Coordinator Intramural Spring (2)
- Head Softball Coach
- Head Football Coach
- Assistant Softball Coach
- Assistant Football Coach (4)
- Head Outdoor Track & Field Coach
- Head Cross Country
- Assistant Outdoor Track & Field Coach
- Head Boys Soccer
- Head Lacrosse Coach
- Assistant Boys Soccer
- Assistant Lacrosse Coach

---

[68] Parent-teacher survey
[69] Public budget data for several Massachusetts school districts
[70] Public postings via email – "The Secretary of State has determined that all e-mails are a public record and may not be kept confidential."

- Head Girls Soccer
- SADD Advisor
- Assistant Girls Soccer
- Freshman Class Advisor
- Head Volleyball Coach
- Sophomore Class Advisor
- Assistant Volleyball Coach
- Junior Class Advisor
- Head Golf Coach
- Senior Class Advisor
- Head Boys Basketball Coach
- Gay Straight Alliance
- Assistant Boys Basketball Coach (2)
- Cheerleader Advisor (Fall & Winter)
- Head Girls Basketball Coach
- Honor Societies Advisor
- Assistant Girls Basketball Coach
- Scholarship Committee Advisor
- Head Hockey Coach
- Student Activity Chairperson
- Assistant Hockey Coach
- Student Council Advisor
- Head Swimming Coach
- Skills USA Advisor
- Assistant Swimming Coach
- Asst. Skills USA Advisor
- Peer Mentoring
- Yearbook Advisor
- Equipment Manager
- Co-op Director
- Safety Coordinator
- STEM Coordinator
- Athletic Director

There are many more not in this incomplete listing, including additional sports positions, department heads, and clubs. Also not listed here are a host of special "opportunities" for paid conferences, summer assignments, and school-paid courses for PDP credit handed out by the same cronyism system.

The principal (or superintendent) has absolute authority to award more than a quarter of a million dollars a year, to anyone he/she chooses, without any requirement to justify or explain the choices to anyone. The authority is absolute. Many schools have policies that the positions must be posted before they can be awarded, but the decision has often been made long before other candidates submit their letter of application.

Absolute power corrupts absolutely[71]

The degree of cronyism in many schools approaches the level of corruption, yet there is no recourse for the victims, and nothing that can be done to stop the practice. Union grievances are easily stonewalled with the simple, and accepted statement "...I made the choice of the candidate I thought most qualified."

Often, for a new principal, it didn't start out that way. In the schools I researched, half of new principals were not just "...the latest crony," and actually appeared to have begun with best intentions and high hopes. They appeared to have been genuinely good people who had been excellent teachers. But within a year or three, those I interviewed saw the same pattern in almost all new principals – once they got comfortable with the system and lack of accountability, they started abusing the power of their new position.

Yet, rather than look to all the individuals who abuse the system, we must focus instead on how the system sets up people to fail.

The results – when a person with no prior management experience suddenly has total and unquestioned authority to hand out more than a quarter million dollars based upon whatever standards he/she chooses – should not be unexpected. Put even the best kid into an unattended candy store, and despite knowing that stealing is bad, a candy bar is likely to eventually disappear from the shelves. If there is no challenge, a second disappears from view. Then a third...

A new manager in a non-education business has had years of experience and *earned* gradually increasing discretion and responsibility as he/she earns promotions. By the time a CEO is handed the cookie jar, he/she has passed years of lesser temptations than a quarter million dollars of discretionary spending, and has passed many examples of that specific kind of leadership test. A new principal is handed the cookie jar for the first time, with no prior training.

Sixty percent of the teachers surveyed felt that cronyism was the full or main reason for appointments. Nationwide, the immense scope of this level of abuse and corruption can be seen when an overwhelming number of teachers, 81%, expect it to occur:

---

[71] John Acton letter dated 1887

NEA report: *"In findings due next week from Education Sector, a Washington think tank, 81% of K-12 teachers surveyed believe that without a union, teachers "would be vulnerable to school politics or administrators who abuse their power."* [72]

[Editor's note: Please see chapter 11 for a list of scandals and corruption in our schools, and see chapter 5 for a look at the pervasive degree of bullying and intimidation of teachers]

Until I started surveying other teachers, I had always hoped that the degree of cronyism and "legal" corruption I had witnessed was an anomaly in schools. But when only 23% of the teachers I surveyed felt such decisions were mostly impartial and fair, and when the NEA states that 81% of teachers nationwide expect abuse of power by principals, this has a devastating impact on education. The abuse of power is so strong and so pervasive that almost no teacher dares take the risk to challenge or report them. *The overwhelming bulk of such abuse and cronyism stays hidden behind the curtain of the school entryway, and never gets seen outside the building.* A complaining teacher (or worse, one who files a grievance that is sure to fail anyway) knows that poor class assignments and lack of any extra-pay assignments will inevitably follow.

When teachers are under fire from many directions, and also cannot trust their own administrations, the result is just what would be expected – anger, defeat, discouragement, and a decline in performance.

Please consider the following real-world examples that might seem extreme cases to someone outside the system, but are actually very common in today's schools.

Please note! The following examples are *not* a criticism of the winning candidates. They are fine people and worthy candidates to apply for the positions. The discussion is about the procedure and the cronyism.

Position: Sports coach (soccer):

Qualification	Candidate "A"	Candidate "B"
League championships	Dozens	few
State finals	5 times	none

---

[72] *NEA membership decline heralds loss of power and influence*, Education News, July 2012

FIFA gold medal for amateur world champions	Yes – starting goalie	None
Teacher at school	Yes - current	Never
Years at school	10+	None
Coaches the daughter of the superintendent on a town soccer team?	No	**Yes**

The choice was candidate "B" despite an announced policy (used by the same superintendent to terminate prior retiring coaches) that all coaching positions would be first given to qualified internal candidates, and would go outside only if there were no internal candidates. Candidate "A" has one of the best coaching records in the state of Massachusetts and had received outstanding teacher evaluations for years – but candidate "B" was awarded the position with no challenge of the decision possible – because he was the coach of the superintendent's daughter.

Position: Secretary to the Superintendent

Qualification	Candidate "A"	Candidate "B"
Years at school	20	1/2
Years experience as secretary to the Principal or Superintendent	13	0
Past evaluations	Outstanding	N/A
Years as school copy center clerk	None	1/2
Superintendent wife's best friend	No	**Yes**

Again, the choice was a good person fully qualified to be considered as a candidate, but one who is put in the position of having a reputation tainted by being known to the rest of the school as getting the position because of cronyism despite an exceptional internal candidate.

For this particular superintendent, the blatant cronyism has gotten to the point where multiple grievances and school committee presentations[73] are in progress or planned to challenge what the local

---

[73] *MTA Grievance versus School Committee*, June 2013

union now feels has risen to the level of near corruption. The school committee and superintendent rejected the initial grievance, as expected. The union knows that there is no chance that such decisions will be reversed in the arbitration hearing that is now pending. The superintendent merely has to state that "I chose the candidate that I feel is best for the position." End of story – such decisions are "legal and proper" for most school committees. The union grievance was not begun with any hope of winning – it was in the outside hope of embarrassing the superintendent to the point where he would scale back his decisions to "normal cronyism" from the extreme levels that had started to show up in his decisions.

When I interviewed at other schools as part of my three years research for this book, I kept finding the same pattern of cronyism and lack of faith in the system. Here is a small sample selected from examples that were common in many of these schools:

- A new Superintendent hires a secretary that is his wife's best friend, despite highly qualified internal candidates

- The new athletic director is the principal's Friday night poker buddy, and immediately gets the AD stipend increased $10,000 at a time important school programs are being cut

- A new SPED paraprofessional is the principal's nanny

- A superintendent requests, and is given, a $20,000 per year raise at a time when the school is facing a budget crisis threatening the termination of many programs and a dozen teachers.

- The head of maintenance is openly permitted to chain smoke in a room on the hallway leading to the cafeteria, despite a school-wide ban on smoking, and many student complaints "…why can teachers smoke if smoking is not allowed in the building?"

- A new coach is chosen who does not work at the school, because he is the coach of the superintendent's daughter in a town league – despite two highly qualified internal candidates.

- A young teacher is hired and then made a coach because he used to be a player on a top administrator's town team.

- Dozens of teachers and paraprofessionals are sons, daughters, or friends of past and present top administrators.

- Closest friends of the principal/superintendent are awarded the key department head or club leader extra-pay positions

- A very weak teacher knowing for filling most of his classes with movies, and with a long history of problems disciplining his class is retained, and given extra-pay assignments because he is the son of a senior administrator.

- The week-long visit by the state recertification board is postponed, completely disrupting school-wide plans and timelines, so that the superintendent can take a vacation in Florida.

- The clique openly discusses and announces" who will be the next dean, principal, superintendent, etc. long before the decision is made – with unfailing accuracy in their "predictions."

- A member of the clique becomes an officer in the teacher union – and actively informs administration of union plans and activities during negotiations.

- Members of the clique actively report potential issues with "problem" teachers to administrators – even searching through that teacher's room and desk during off hours.

- A school is specifically cited for being "filthy" by the state DOE while dozens of teachers report that their requests to fix toilets, failed heating systems, electrical malfunctions, and ventilation systems are routinely ignored – at a time when the school is making a significant investment in all parent-visible areas and administrative offices.

The most disturbing thing about these examples is that they are not rare exceptions. They are common occurrences nationwide, as evidenced by the list of scandals on listed earlier. Based upon personal observation, and visits and interviews with dozens of teachers at many schools, far more than half of all special appointments are made based upon cronyism, not qualifications. And the principals (or superintendents) have full authority to make these appointments without accountability.

"Because they can…"

A few weeks ago I was talking to a teacher who had just been removed from a key special assignment, despite an outstanding track record, and replaced by a member of the clique who had never before had any experience in the position. She was heartbroken. I asked her why they had done it, and she gave a three word answer that summarizes the entire issue of the clique, cronyism, and corruption:

> *"Because they can."*

That this level of blatant cronyism occurs should not be a surprise in a school bureaucracy where the superintendent has basically no checks and balances on his/her decisions. School administrations are a classic bureaucracy. As in any bureaucracy without accountability by the leadership, excesses inevitably occur, and bureaucracies, by definition, have little traditional accountability compared to commercial businesses. Recent highly visible examples of non-accountability excesses at IRS, GSA, ATF, State Department, NSA, and the healthcare rollout have made us far more aware of how pervasive such actions are. (Chapter 11 lists a few examples.)

As just one typical example of how common and inbred bureaucratic cronyism is, in June 2013 the US Inspector General reported on rampant cronyism, despite many "check-the-box" emails and training sessions declaring it "wrong," at the US Department of Energy. The worst part of their finding was that the violators did not even see it as wrong. One example:

> [Editor's note –underlines added to the original]
>
> *"A senior official in the department used his position to secure competitive internships in 2012 for his three college-aged children. In addition, the report found, the senior staffer <u>didn't think he had done anything wrong</u> and defended his actions to investigators, saying doling out favors for family members is a <u>common practice in the department</u>.*
>
> *The report says that while many officials within the department told us they thought jockeying for an internship for family members was a <u>common practice</u>, others told investigators they found the practice 'problematic.'"*[74]

Blatant cronyism, at the level of the soccer coach or secretary examples cited earlier, or like the interns example cited just above, approaches the level of being labeled "corruption" in the eyes of teachers, yet it is perfectly legal and allowed by school bureaucracies. This pattern of behavior by administrators is rampant in urban high schools. "Normal" cronyism that simply involves promoting and selecting the principal's friends within the school occurs at <u>all</u> schools. There are absolutely no checks-and-balances on these decisions, so abuse is natural and growing.

Abuse is easy, *"...because they can."*

Such blatant cronyism is the reason today's teachers have a love-hate relationship with the concept of merit pay. (More on this in Systemic Failure #8 (Chapter 26) – Rewards unrelated to Performance.) Teachers love the concept, but hate the "certainty" that the clique will be awarded the merit pay, regardless of merit.

If all else fails – Good sports teams will cover a lot of sins

There are three cornerstones for a principal trying to get through his/her term without all the failures becoming evident outside the school:

- Misdirection
- Self-promotion
- Bullying and intimidation of potential teacher whistleblowers.

The goal is to make sure everything looks "good" to the overwhelming bulk of parents who never get past the school entryway. Two of the most common approaches to this are promoting "cosmetics" (the appearance of the school administrative offices and entry), and sports.

It would be hard to overstate the degree of emphasis administrations place on sports teams. This is a "comfort zone," and easy area that does not require the hard work and decision-making of budgets, parent involvement, or teacher evaluations. It is often an area where the principal really <u>is</u> somewhat qualified. (After all, in Massachusetts everyone knows they would be a far better manager of the Red Sox or the Bruins than anyone currently holding the position.)

---

[74] *Alleged Nepotism and Wasteful Spending in the Office of Energy Efficiency and Renewable Energy*, US Inspector General, June 2013

But best of all, it is a great distraction from the real problems, and an easy way to trumpet "success" to the parents and school district.

Ms. Jones, make sure we put our technology initiatives on the next school board agenda. We now have a computer in every classroom!

Put nice paint and new benches at the school entryway, and have a couple winning sports teams – maybe nobody will notice the children have no working water fountains, and half the second floor heating systems have been broken for years. Announce that computers are in all of the classrooms, but don't mention that few work. Brag about any student success you can find, but don't mention all the failures. Say budget limits might force cancellation of music and the arts, but carefully hide that the real reason for the cancellations is that all the available class periods for arts are being used for standardized test preparation classes.

The goal is misdirection – if the principal gets them looking one way, the parents will never see the disasters in the other direction.

The bottom line: It is important to restate something from the start of this chapter – this section is not about the person, it is about the systemic failure of the position. When a good man or woman, and likely a good teacher, becomes principal with little or no experience or qualifications to handle today's problems, then the entire school suffers. It is not because the principal starts out being a bad person. It is because the person is qualified to be a great teacher, but is not qualified or trained to be an adequate principal. This is compounded by unlimited authority to make decisions on extra-pay assignments, and few effective checks and balances on decision making.

81% of teachers, nationwide, think principals and administrations abuse their powers. We must fix this.

(Chapter 21)
Systemic Failure #3: Inclusion classes – Everyone loses

Overview: Inclusion classes are directly responsible for more irreparable damage to the education of a generation of our children than any other single systemic failure in this analysis. Despite good intentions, inclusion classes are an abject failure because of simple physics, not because of philosophy. Their failure has nothing to do with what you might think about "equal opportunity" or about the rights of SPED and ESL students. The failure is that they violate the reality that two objects cannot occupy the same place at the same time – pitting several mandated requirements <u>competing</u> against each other for the same block of time, under conditions where <u>no</u> teacher can succeed with all at the same time.

Either the full class period is used to meet <u>mandated</u> core requirements (thus moving too fast for, and not supporting, the inclusion students) or the teacher must skip parts of the mandated core topics to provide time for <u>mandated</u> inclusion accommodations and diversified teaching (thus not providing roughly half of the lesson plan for <u>all</u> the students in the class.)

> [Author's note: This topic is a very difficult topic to criticize without risking strong confrontation. Criticism of inclusion classes often generates anger and personal attacks on the messenger. *It is not uncommon for the critic to be labeled as insensitive, uncaring, racist, not supportive of special needs, or simply as mean-spirited.*
>
> Those angered by the criticism miss a vital point – the criticism is not in any way based upon attitudes about the children in the classes. It is based only on the impossibility of trying to fit 115 minutes of mandated requirements into a 60-70 minute class period – *always hurting the very inclusion children we are all trying to help.* It is often those who are <u>most caring</u> and supportive of inclusion student needs, including teachers like me who <u>ask</u> for these classes, who are most critical of how inclusion classes cheat our inclusion children.]

Inclusion classes have hurt all of our children in schools over the last five years more than any other systemic failure in education. Everyone loses – both the inclusion students, and the non-exclusion students. It is such a lightning rod issue that it is almost impossible to discuss without conflict – yet the damage both to education and to individuals is deadly.

Inclusion classes fail because the <u>mandated</u> requirements to support the inclusion students compete with the <u>mandated</u> requirements of teaching all core standards and sll the <u>mandated</u> administrative requirements.. Simply stated, a teacher needs the full class period to meet the mandated demands of core standard curricula. Yet the <u>additional</u> mandated demands to support inclusion students now use roughly half of every inclusion class – <u>forcing the teacher to skip required material</u>. *It is a lose-lose choice.*

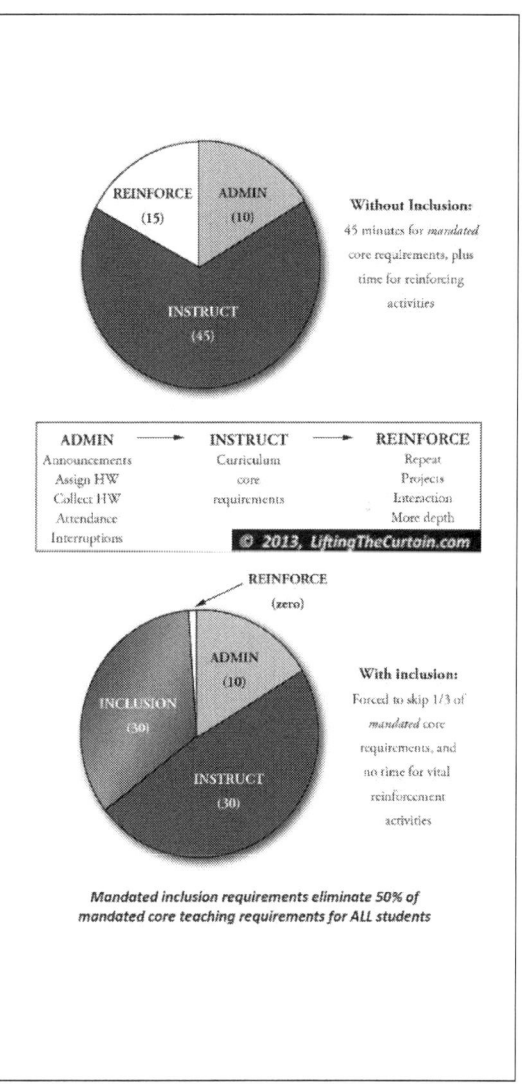

1990: Prior to inclusion, ESL, SPED accommodations and extensive administrative mandates

- No inclusion, ESL, or Sped
- 60-70 minute class
- Mandated curriculum takes 45 minutes to cover
- 15 minutes available for best practices reinforcement: discussion, projects
- 10 minutes for admin and pro-rated assemblies/etc.

2013: After extensive ESL, inclusion, Sped, and administrative mandates

- 30 minutes of mandated accommodations in a typical "standard" urban high school class.
- Available time for curriculum reduced to 30 minutes
- Reinforcement best practices eliminated
- Admin remains at 10 minutes as teachers work around time added for allergies, bullying, LGBT, careers, assemblies, etc.
- **Teacher FORCED to dumb down teaching and eliminate parts of curriculum that will never be taught to the children**

For the bureaucrats and "educators" with little classroom knowledge, inclusion classes sound like a caring idea. But the truth is that inclusion (be it for SPED or ESL reasons) always is a total failure.

- Inclusion waters down the education of <u>all</u> students in the class. Every time the lead teacher (and co-teacher, if applicable) stops the planned instruction to help provide mandated accommodations and diversified individual and group support to the inclusion students, a mandated core requirement must be dropped from the lesson plan.

- A teacher devoting <u>just three minutes</u> per student to each of 10 inclusion students in a class of 25-30 would tie up more than half of the available instruction time that was already needed to cover mandated core material. *(My classes averaged 44% of students requiring mandated accommodations support – often 15 or more, not just the 10 used in this example.)*

- Co-teachers are a Band-Aid that does not work. Many co-teachers are not qualified to teach the subject matter, and so the lead teacher must stop the lesson for the entire class in order to provide most of the inclusion accommodations. Even in those cases where the co-teacher is qualified in the subject, the lead teacher cannot simply continue the mandated lesson plan for the rest of the class while the co-teacher is still helping inclusion students with earlier material. Instead the lead teacher must drop part of the planned lesson to help the co-teacher, by splitting up the support needs.

- If a <u>qualified</u> co-teacher is available for a class, then it will always be better to have that co-teacher be the primary teacher in a separate, smaller class concentrating on just those ten students. The inclusion students would get far better attention, one-on-one time, and teaching via a dedicated, <u>qualified</u> teacher. The non-inclusion students get a dedicated teacher who could cover more of the mandated core requirements.

I love teaching, and always want to be assigned to the classes with struggling students. I always do my best to cover both the mandated core requirements, and the mandated inclusion support requirements. But <u>*every* single day in *every* single inclusion class, I must violate one or more state DoE mandates.</u> In a 70 minute period I am required to fit 115 minutes of mandated requirements.

- 10 minutes – Administration (<u>Mandated</u> attendance, prorated assemblies, lockdown or fire drills, announcements, etc.)
- 45 minutes – Central lesson plan (<u>Mandated</u> core requirements)
- 15 minutes – Reinforcement (Not directly mandated yet, but proven good teaching methodology of repetition, group activities, projects, and interaction to reinforce the lesson plan. These reinforcement activities <u>will be mandated</u> in the new common core rollout next year.)
- 30 minutes – Inclusion support (<u>Mandated</u> accommodations, typically of an average of three minutes each for 10-plus inclusion students in a typical class.)
- 15 minutes – Estimated new Massachusetts SEI support (<u>Mandated</u> accommodations)
- Unpredictable Administrative mandates: Assemblies, fire drills, lockdown drills, evacuation drills, discipline issues, PDP sessions, half days with shortened classes, bullying or allergy discussions, etc.

Obviously these are just average timings. Other teachers certainly will have different views of the amounts and totals. But for <u>every</u> teacher in <u>every</u> school across the USA, the total mandates for *every* inclusion class far exceed the total time to accomplish all those mandates competing for the same limited block of time. There are no exceptions. It is what it is.

> *Jeanie Clemmens does a great job of describing how an inclusion class really operates. Please notice the time she is away from the board helping with the accommodations, using advanced differentiated teaching methods, and obviously deeply caring about the children in the class. Notice also the amount of time the non-inclusion children have to be doing make-work exercises waiting for the teaching to restart. Jeanie Clemmens is a retired high school inclusion teacher for math in Pennsylvania.*

(Jeanie Clemmens) The reality of teaching an inclusion class

Long before I became a certified high school math teacher, I experienced something that has haunted me for years. Our sixth grade class visited the Special Education classroom (in the sixties). The students were relegated to a room in the basement and although it was obvious that the teacher cared a great deal for the non-homogeneous group, it was equally noticeable that they were different. When I started teaching, I was relieved to see that such arcane methods had been abandoned.

Inclusion classrooms of today provide greater social and educational opportunities for special needs students, but they can also benefit the teacher. I think that education would be better if all teaching had aspects of a well-run inclusion class. For one thing, the teacher can establish a pattern that will include all students by gearing the material first to the abilities of the average student. This will ensure maximum learning by the most number of students. If students of lower or greater ability understand on the first go-round, so much the better. If not, a more appropriately targeted approach can be used to draw in the rest of the class. And the second approach helps the average students, because it strengthens what they just learned.

An experienced teacher can address individual learning styles by quietly providing additional support or challenging material and answering questions while visiting each desk. This improves the confidence of each student and removes the social stigma of being singled out as different.

This is the fatal flaw in the wonderful inclusion concept – it has gone horribly wrong due to unintended consequences of plans developed by career DoE bureaucrats who had little understanding of children or education. Even the most caring and dedicated teacher must either cheat all the children (including inclusion students) out of part of the mandated core requirements, or cheat the inclusion students out of their mandated accommodations. **It is not about "racism or insensitivity" – it is about the impossibility of putting 115 minutes of mandated content into a 70 minute period.**

To give the reader insight into the demands of mandated inclusion support into perspective, here is a look at the totals for all of my 2013-2014 classes (excluding my one honors class – which traditionally has few IEP/ESL students):

```
Total students:  123
         IEP:    43  ⎤
         504:     7  ⎬ 54 (44%)
         ESL:     4  ⎦
```

With nearly half of my students needing mandated individual accommodations, there is no choice except to eliminate part of the curriculum each day in order to support these students. Now clearly, the 44% figure is high compared to many non-urban CP classes, and even to the top honors classes in most urban high schools. *But the order-of-magnitude is such that even if a class had just half this amount of inclusion support needs, it still competes with, and forces elimination of, a large portion of every mandated lesson plan.*

In extreme cases, behavioral issues with inclusion classes can completely undermine the effort to teach all members of the class, including the non-inclusion children. As anonymous, an active K-2 teachers from Florida describes, these inclusion issues even occur at the elementary school level. Like most teachers, anonymous prefers to not reveal a name in order to avoid retribution from school administrators for speaking out.

> **(Anonymous) Inclusion – forced whether it helps or it hurts the children's education**
>
> I teach elementary school ESE, and the problems with inclusion have absolutely reached us!
>
> The school tries so hard to keep these kids in "regular" classes, trying intervention after intervention, that the child (and the rest if the class) falls further behind. It's the same in my classes - they place students in a class for students with disabilities, but the focus in this setting is more on academics. It's very appropriate for many, but they will place students who so obviously need more restrictive settings – because the school administrators have to say they tried. This is done even when a student would be better served in a multi- or EBD setting.
>
> Again, even in an ESE classroom, it is disruptive for all the students involved, and precious learning time keeps being wasted for these children so obviously misplaced. My students can make wonderful progress (yes, at a slower pace, but progress nonetheless), but throw a student who tries to punch me all day or stand on tables into the mix, that progress is halted.
>
> It would be refreshing if those making the decisions would spend even a day in an actual classroom teaching, not observing, and then see what kind of decisions they may make.

Consider the following comparison between the class environment that is typical in a standard class in an urban high school, and one that is conducive to the engaging, project-oriented approach teachers enjoy in many suburban school CP/Honors classes. These figures are taken from my research for *Lifting the Curtain*, from looking back at the past 10 years as a classroom math teacher in urban high schools, and from input from hundreds of teachers since the 1st edition was published.

Please remember that an urban high school has a very large percentage of classes that meet this "standard" profile, and very few that match the

"honors" profile. The question is "how are they different?" and "why does an urban standard class environment preclude many teaching initiatives?"

	Standard	CP/Honors
Class Size	28	15
Class time (minutes)	65	65
Inclusion class?	Yes	No
Mandated co-teacher?	Yes	No
Students requiring accommodations	16	1
Minutes per hour allocated to accommodations	**25***	**3**
Minutes per hour allocated to administrative mandates	5**	5**
Minutes per hour left for teaching mandated curriculum (45 required) plus best practices reinforcement/projects (15 required)	**35**	**57**
Percent of parents who "do not care" what grade is received as long as student passes	37%	Unk***
Percent of students who "do not care" what grade is received as long as student passes	27%	Unk***

  * Reduced from 48 down to 25 minutes for accommodations assuming topic-qualified co-teacher and experienced teacher/co-teacher efficiencies
  ** Reduced from 10 assuming experienced teacher efficiencies
  *** Unknown – only urban high schools were surveyed

The same career bureaucrats who developed the fatally-flawed inclusion class idea tried to patch it by requiring that a "co-teacher" be assigned to all inclusion classes. *This has been a bureaucratic failure across the board.* First of all, under the best of circumstances a co-teacher is effective only if the class lesson is stopped so he/she can help struggling students keep up – thus doing nothing to avoid the need to skip mandated core requirements in order to provide time for inclusion support. Co-teachers cannot possibly help those same struggling students if the rest of the class continues to move on with the lesson at a pace aimed to cover all the mandated core standards.

And most of all, many co-teachers or paraprofessionals are of very limited help because most have only very basic knowledge of the subject matter. Many co-teachers have, at best, a competency equivalent to a "C" student in the same class, especially for math and the sciences. *Many paraprofessionals have no subject matter expertise at all, and cannot assist in teaching the base material.* Those co-teachers just become baggage, while the lead teacher is left holding the bag trying to manage an untenable educational challenge.

If you speak to any teacher about co-teachers in inclusion classes, you will hear the same horror stories about paraprofessionals and co-teachers who cannot help teach the subject matter, and often spend more time on the class computer reading emails than "co-teaching." I have been blessed with three great co-teachers over the years, and cursed with many more who contributed little or nothing to the class. Even with the great ones, we ended up having to cheat <u>either</u> the entire class of students by eliminating some mandated topics, or cheated just the inclusion students by trying to cover all the material for such a wide range of abilities.

Ms. Jones, why does your co-teacher always read the newspaper in all our math classes?

Maryann Schneider eloquently describes why inclusion classes fail all out students – inclusion and non-inclusion in the same classroom. The inclusion policies of Career DoE bureaucrats fail simply because DoE is unable to see the wide disconnect between their goals and their policies. The mandates state that inclusion students require different accommodations unneeded by the non-inclusion students in the class, yet ignore this by putting all these different students in a one-size-fits-all learning environment with too many mandates to accomplish in the time available.

Maryann Schneider is a high school Special Education teacher in Pennsylvania.

(Maryann Schneider) Forcing one-size-fits-all mandated teaching onto very different "sizes" of students

Inclusion, like everything else in education, is a trend. When I was in school, kids with severe learning disabilities were not included in the regular education classroom. However, kids with lesser disabilities were, because then they were just labeled "bad," and they were not yet identified with autism, or ODD, or ED, or a million other letters. That came later, after original labels like Educable Mentally Retarded and Trainable Mentally Retarded became passé or politically incorrect. Then came full inclusion, a trend that has been sticking for some time now as our number of students with disabilities continues to grow.

What I know about inclusion is that it is not for everyone.

In 1996 I wrote a Master's Thesis proving how regular education teachers were not equipped to handle special education students included in their classrooms. Then I spent almost 20 years trying to debunk my own research to find ways inclusion *could* work. University requirements for education degrees later changed to automatically include the special education certification. This was important, because parent advocates, paid advocates, expensive lawyers, and stressed out school districts were all jumping on the IDEA (Individuals with Disabilities Education Act) band wagon – rushing to get their children identified as SPED.

The result was children falling through the cracks, and not being placed in the best learning environment to meet their individual needs.

Recently I have become a job coach for special education students who are old enough to hold paying and volunteer jobs in the community. They go through training to learn about holding a job, work ethics and etiquette, and other work-based skills. They observe different fields such as childcare, food service, retail, etc. These students learn meaningful skills, they make valuable contributions to society, and they are self-motivated and eager do a good job. Self-worth and independence are by-products of this program. These same kids could have been the ones lost in a traditional classroom setting.

Most importantly, these children learn to become independent, productive citizens in the community. They learn social skills. I believe more programs such as these are needed to best to serve our special education students. It's time to think outside the box, the four walls of a traditional fully inclusive classroom, that is.

We already know education is not one size fits all, so why pigeon-hole a very unique group of children.

The bottom line: *Inclusion classes have forced teachers to eliminate key parts of the mandated lesson plans in order to meet mandated requirements to support the inclusion students. A teacher has no choice – one or both of the competing mandates must be watered down – it is physically impossible to meet both. Almost always, the teacher is forced to significantly lessen the education of all students in the class. It has nothing to do with "insensitivity," it is just about the number of minutes in an hour.*

(Chapter 22)
Systemic Failure #4: Special Education – Hijacked by parents

> *Up front, a vital caveat: special education is a wonderful concept, a powerful benefit to those who need it, and arguably the most positive achievement of education in the past century. It absolutely is needed and is of great benefit to many students.*
>
> *This chapter is <u>not</u> about the one-third of special education students where the IEP or 504 is a crucial and invaluable asset that can positively changes a child's entire life – <u>it is about the two-thirds of special education students where the IEP is a total farce.</u>*

Few of the problems in education are more frustrating to a teacher than the role of a numerical minority of parents (a mathematical minority, not a demographic one) in today's failing educational system. On average, according to the hundreds of surveys and interviews I conducted during three years of research leading up to publishing *Lifting the Curtain*, teachers have 3.1 hostile interactions with very difficult parents each month. This minority of parents dominates teacher time and effort. And they end up dominating school policy when everything a teacher is mandated to do begins to center on forcing us to find a way to "educate" and pass their children.

Thankfully, <u>most</u> parents, even in the most challenged urban high schools I researched, still are supportive and committed to their children's education.

For teachers, this minority of parents especially hurts us. There is nothing in the nature of a teacher that can accept or understand those parents who don't seem to care about their own children. You don't become a teacher if your heart is anywhere else than all about helping children excel. So when we face the 31% of parents that did not appear to care about their child's education, it's personal and painful to a teacher.

Trying to teach the children of these parents becomes the impossible challenge of trying to motivate a child for 5 hours each *week*, while knowing the child will be in a home and non-school environment for 12-15 hours each *day* that works against everything we try to do. Is it any surprise that these children in urban high schools do an average of just 1.5 total homework hours per week, 29% copy most homework, and 24% routinely take zeroes on homework?[75]

The worst of these parents are the ones who have hijacked the Special Education process, armed with lawyers and paid "advocates," who use IEPs as a way to ensure their child will graduate from high school no matter how little effort the child and parents put into education.

There is no way to verify the actual percentages because the actual SPED data is highly confidential and restricted. However, based upon closely watching thousands of parents and IEPs over the past decade, and listening to hundreds of other teachers –

more than half of all urban high school IEPs are completely unwarranted

– forced by parents who expect their child to fail, and parents who do not choose to spend their time encouraging or helping the child succeed. These parents look at the IEP as a way to ensure passing without interfering with their own lives or schedules. Like the parents at the PTA meeting cited in the "False Introduction," a growing minority of parents, for reasons both understandable and not, does not even make sure their child gets on the school bus in the morning.

Most student IEPs provide crutches and ways to bypass classroom effort that are completely unnecessary for the child. *Less than a third of all IEPs center on real accommodations that are needed by the child.* Many are based upon a highly suspect "diagnosis" of ADHD or some other impediment du jour. Published reports by the CDC show dramatic increases in diagnoses of ADHD:

> *"Parents report that approximately 9.5% of children 4-17 years of age (5.4 million) have been diagnosed with ADHD as of 2007."*
>
> *"The percentage of children with a parent-reported ADHD diagnosis increased by 22% between 2003 and 2007."* [76]

The NY Times reported that 6,400,000 school children have an ADHD diagnosis, up 41% over the past ten years, and up 16% just since 2007. More and more doctors are now starting to openly challenge whether or not the results and diagnoses are real – an opinion that is of no surprise to teachers and SPED professionals. ADHD is the "diagnosis du jour" for parents seeking to use SPED to get their child as much of a "…get out of school free" card as possible. In the NY Times report:

---

[75] Student-teacher survey
[76] CDC, May 2013

[Editor's note: Underline added to original]

"Those are astronomical numbers. I'm floored," said Dr. William Graf, a pediatric neurologist in New Haven and a professor at the Yale School of Medicine. He added, "Mild symptoms are being diagnosed so readily, which goes well beyond the disorder and beyond the zone of ambiguity to <u>pure enhancement</u> of children who are otherwise healthy." [77]

The term "pure enhancement" is doctorspeak for "…a crock of poop."

Almost no IEPs today recognize what most teachers believe should be the underlying principle of <u>every</u> IEP: to help the student get to the point where by the end of his/her senior year, an IEP is not needed. After all, there are no IEPs when the student enters college or begins his/her first job. *They should help a child learn how to learn, given a real disability. They must never be just a way to hand out a "pass" regardless of what is learned.*

In the past several years parents have become very effective, armed with advocates, lawyers, and the clout of threatened discrimination lawsuits, to get two new terrible and educationally-destructive accommodations made part of their child's IEPs.

- <u>Automatic retakes</u>: The student "…can retake any failing test." Almost all IEPs written since 2012 now allow the student to automatically retake a failed test *for any reason* – even if the failure was from absolutely no effort and no preparation.

- <u>50% of the work is an "A"</u>: The student "…gets an 'A' if they only do half of the work expected of all other students, with the grade scaled from there." Amazing – think of the message that sends to the student, and to the rest of the class.

The impact of these two accommodations is deadly.

For the student with the accommodation, it allows failure with no penalty. There would be no problem if the message received by the IEP student was only that hard work earns him/her another chance, because they have a difficulty to surmount.

---

[77] NY Times, March 2013

But that is <u>not</u> the message they get. Twice last week alone, as I write this, I had IEP students who had failed the same test badly (because of zero effort, refusal to accept extra help in class, refusal to come to extra-help sessions, despite full accommodations, and despite the fulltime availability of an outstanding co-teacher in the classroom) and invoked their right to a retest. Both stopped halfway through the retest, and said they would fail again because they had no clue how to do the material. I pointed out how many times they had refused extra help, and that both had done little or no class work. I also reminded them that both had refused to get any extra help on the topics since the original test failure – so how could they expect a different result? Both then asked me to help them do the test problems, and of course I said no. Both asked for a break for an "extra help" session before they finished the test, despite the fact that for more than three weeks they had refused many offers of in-class and after-class extra help. I again said 'no."

Then both asked the killer question that I have grown to hate.

> *"Can we take it down to the resource center and do it there? They will help us do the questions and pass it."*

Our head of the Special Education department would explode if she heard that question, and would severely censure any resource center paraprofessional who dared "cheat" by doing a student's test. Yet there are always people in any SPED department who are exceptions, often because the paraprofessional genuinely believes they are doing something good for the child. Students know that they can always find a "helpful" special education paraprofessional who will ensure that they pass the retest. There was an epilog to this story – the next week I got an email from the SPED paraprofessional for one of the students stating that the student told her "…you wouldn't help them." She offered to do another retest down in the resource center with him.

What should scare any reader outside the classroom is how common this is.

The problem here is not the student – it is the SPED system and the paraprofessional who genuinely thought she was "helping." It is disturbing that these two students expect that I should do the test for them, explain how I am answering each question as I go along, and then hand the test in under their names. But, the real problem here is that the paraprofessional thinks she was doing something good for the child by doing his work for him, and sending the message that it's okay for the student to get another free ride without having to learn anything. Ultimately, it is that student's teachers who have to live with a student who "passed" but never learned the prerequisite material for the next course. We now have a student who now cannot comprehend why subsequent teachers expect him to do his own work.

We have failed that student by setting his expectations of himself so low.

Consider another very real example of teachers being unable to overcome the negative impact of the system – centered on the new and rapidly growing cottage industry of paid student advocates for SPED students. I was in a SPED meeting to review progress for a student who had failed three courses the previous term, including an "F" in History. At the meeting were several of her teachers, SPED representatives, the parent and student. Also attending were a paid student "advocate" and a lawyer, both hired by the parents. The goal of the parents was to get the student's grade for History changed to a passing grade, despite the clear record that the student had failed quizzes, had never submitted assignments, never came in for extra help, and had missed several days of school during the term. The tactic was heavy pressure by the advocate and lawyer to paint the History teacher as "…violating state law by not providing proper accommodations as required by her IEP." The message of the advocate and lawyer was simple: either change the grade, or we will find a way to have you fired, and have the school sued, for violation of state regulations. It didn't matter that there was no indication that the History teacher had actually failed in any requirement of the IEP.

It turned out that the threat was enough when exerted on a young woman just a few years out of college. Even the SPED personnel from the school took the side of the parents to allow some form of second chance. The young teacher folded under the pressure and agreed to allow a retest and late submission of the missing assignments.

But the real result? The teacher "learned her lesson" that you cannot afford to fail a student who deserves to fail. The student learned that she didn't have to work, and would still pass. The parents learned they could get what they wanted – their child to graduate from high school no matter what the child did. The SPED group learned not to challenge this student or parents with their cadre of lawyers and advocates.

But sadly, there was one thing <u>not</u> learned in the process. The student did not have to learn History. She got an all-too-common "get out of jail free" SPED ride.

It would stun most parents how often, when I offer extra help to a struggling student, the IEP student declines with the reply: "Nah, if I fail, I can just retake it down in the resource center, and they'll help me pass it."

For the past few years I have outright disobeyed this retest mandate with a simple con job I foist on special education students with this horrible "automatic retest" accommodation. (BTW – I always let SPED know this in advance, because they need to know it is a bluff should the student come to them. They so love the results that almost always they send the child back to me knowing that, of course, I will allow the required retest if needed.) I just tell the child that "...you have it wrong – the retest is only if the *teacher* determines there was an IEP-specific reason a retest is needed – like not enough time, missed accommodations, or bad test conditions." The result is invariably the same – the student gulps, starts to work harder, and within a few weeks is <u>earning</u> a passing grade on all the tests he/she would have blown off if allowed to get away with playing the IEP card. I still smile with pleasure picturing the dozens of SPED students who fell for that con, soon were earning As and Bs, and who later wrote me letters when they graduated telling me how proud they were to "...finally understand math."

Now a new accommodation is surfacing, the horrible "...gets an 'A' for accomplishing 50% of the work" rule. More and more new IEPs have this accommodation. Parents love it – the ultimate "...get out of school free" card. Their child only has to do half the work for an "A" (even less for a "B"), and gets lots of help on that 50% so he/she actually had to do almost nothing on his/her own to get an "A." It is no-show parent heaven – the child will graduate from high school, nothing else matters.

The problem is that the child gets "As" and graduates, but without learning anything.

The career DoE bureaucrats love special education – it is their cash cow and guarantee of job security. It is an endless opportunity to create mandates, layers of bureaucracy, and guarantee a lifetime job "helping children" no matter how much harm they do.

> [Editor's note: Underline added to original]
>
> *"Why does special ed serve the poor so badly? Part of the answer has to do with its <u>massive, ineffectual, and self-perpetuating bureaucracy</u>. Beneath the federal Office of Special Education Programs, which does research and audits states and school districts, there is a state office, and a localized Special Education Local Plan Area office, and a school district office. This is all on top of whatever counselors, psychologists, therapists, and "educational evaluators" a given school may have working for it. And in some individual states and cities, the situation is even worse. Given this focus on legal liability and procedure, it's little wonder that teaching takes a back seat to paper-pushing."[Special ed teachers] complain they're spending 50 to 60 percent of their time filling out forms," says Kim Reid, a professor at Columbia Teachers' College.* [78]

---

[78] *The Scandal of Special-Ed*, Washington Monthly, August 1999

Meanwhile, teachers and special educators are fighting a losing battle to stem the misuse of special education. They cannot win against an army of lawyers and "advocates." It has only gotten worse since this report back in 2000:

> *"The trouble is that the law pits the single interest of every disabled child against the broader interest of the school and arms his parents with a legal right to a "free and appropriate public education" in "least restrictive environment." Needless to say, the vagueness of these words is a recipe for litigation. A whole cottage industry of lawyers and advocates has grown up to help parents get what they want out of the school system. Furthermore, school districts must pay parents' court fees if they lose. Overburdened, underfunded, and without the expert legal advice parents can draw on, schools tend to give in rather than face a case that could bankrupt them.* [79]

Over the past few years I have been a participant in dozens of IEP meetings and have filled out hundreds of IEP reports. For the overwhelming bulk of those who had "math-related accommodations" I have been overjoyed to be able to write the same thing:

> *"The student is earning Bs and As, and is doing an excellent job with no further need for accommodations other than those routinely given to any student. There are zero apparent IEP-related limitations at all for this student in math. I recommend that the IEP for math be discontinued."*

The above was written for hundreds of my IEP students now earning As and Bs in a CP math course, proud of their work, excited to learn, and starting to show the same performance in all their other courses. These were the same students who had the destructive "...can retake any failing test" accommodations. These are the same students who end up writing me notes, like my most treasured of all notes when Kayla discovered what every child should know: *"...showing me that I am smart..."*

These successes were despite the way special education has been twisted and hijacked, despite the bureaucrats, and despite the parents.

Meanwhile, there is a significant negative personal impact on <u>all</u> students, SPED and non-SPED, something we carefully hide behind the curtain, caused by this dysfunctional spate of conditions:

- The class must be slowed down to try to find a way to pass the two-thirds of IEP students who do not try – thus lessening the education

---

[79] *The Scandal of Special-Ed*, Washington Monthly, August 1999

of <u>all</u> students and leading to lower performance, lower standardized test scores, and less readiness for college and careers.

- Children understand the need to help the students who really need it – the one-third or so with genuine IEPs. But the other IEP students (the two-thirds of the IEP students that the rest of the class <u>knows</u> full well are capable of the workload) will be seen as getting "unfair" help for the material, and no amount of teacher explanation can counter this (accurate) perception.

- The genuine third of IEP students gets tarred with the brush of "retard" because the <u>system</u> puts them in the position where they look bad compared to the rest of the class, and are seen by other students as hurting the rest of the class. The perceptions about the phony two-thirds make it difficult for children to recognize that the remaining one-third has a genuine need for special education.

The bottom line: SPED is an awesome idea, but it fails when children and parents learn they can easily play the "…SPED get-out-of-jail-free" card whenever they want to avoid working. For two-thirds of today's SPED students, the accommodations are completely unneeded and hurt far more than help. For the third or so of SPED students who really do need help, the system is vitally important, but watered down because instead of concentrating time and resources on the third who need it, we let the other two-thirds milk the system. The common accommodation of "…can retake any failed test" is a disaster for children that only hurts them.

(Chapter 23)
Systemic Failure #5: "Bureaucrat" – Our newest four-letter word

Overview: Teachers have learned to deal with no-show parents, students who do not care, lack of textbooks, differentiated learning in classes of 30 students, cronyism, inept principals, and crumbling infrastructures. But there is one stakeholder that still can anger even the most burned-out teacher –bureaucratic "educators" creating mandates that create large burdens, yet do nothing to help education. These are the career bureaucrats that pass down directives on how to teach, with little apparent understanding of teaching.

[Author's note: I apologize up front for the derisive tone of parts of this chapter – it is the one area in education where most teachers have no respect at all for a stakeholder. The negative impact of unqualified career DoE bureaucrats on education is staggering. Perhaps the increased recent national visibility of similar issues of bureaucracy failures at IRS, ATF, VA, HHS, NSA, GSA, and in the healthcare rollout, will give readers some insight into what teachers have had to live with for years. The degree of anger and disdain teachers have for such bureaucrats is widespread.]

Bureaucrats calling themselves "Educators" are killing education.

To most teachers, "educator" has become a four-letter word. It is a word that is very different than the word "teacher." Every month, these "educators" introduce a new teaching "mandate du jour" as the next big thing in classroom instruction. Every few years the core standards are modified. Every year the textbooks re-sequence and add content designed to incent purchase of new books. Every few months the state and federal DOEs pass down inane new regulations.

The central premise of these career DoE bureaucrats calling themselves "educators" seems to be that there is always room for another mandate to be added to the class period – ignoring that an hour's class still only has sixty available minutes, and ignoring that there is not enough time for all the prior mandates. These career bureaucrats don't have to live with their decisions, and have no concept that something which sounds fine in their cubicle back at DOE is completely impossible to achieve in an actual classroom.

Another bad teacher -- he failed to meet all mandated requirements in his 70 minute class

A teacher is "bad" if they do not cover a full sixty minutes of mandated core requirements. A teacher is "bad" if they do not stop the lesson to provide thirty minutes of inclusion accommodations. A teacher is "bad" if they miss that a child is eating something in class that might cause an allergic reaction in another. A teacher is "bad" if they do not monitor every conversation in the class for potential bullying. A teacher is "bad" if they rest a hand on a child's shoulder to comfort a crying child. The safest and least career-threatening path for today's teachers is to not teach the material, and instead concentrate on all the IEP/bullying/allergy/touching/announcements/safety/etc. mandates that could get them fired for noncompliance!

Bureaucracies have micromanaged the classroom to the point where teachers must concentrate on compliance, rather than teaching.

---

[80] Zazzle.com, copyright status unknown

To teachers, a "DoE educator" is someone with no real knowledge of teaching realities who has the authority to impose how to teach. Many have never been in a classroom. Those few senior DoE bureaucrats with teaching experience were last in a classroom years ago – long before the impact of the destructive policies concentrated in the last few years. The bulk of these new educator initiatives are comical in their uselessness, and simply are the result of bureaucrats (or textbook publishers, or PDP content presenters) looking for ways to justify their existence.

Three issues dominate this systemic failure of education caused by career DoE bureaucrats: the PDP system, the Department of Education mandates, and the textbook/content publishers.

The PDP farce – wink, wink, nod, nod

> The Professional Development Program (PDP) has been the basis of some of the worst initiatives in education. All teachers are required to take annual additional training, and be credited with "PDPs" (Professional Development Points) in order to be recertified to teach. In Massachusetts, for example, a teacher recertification every five years requires 150 PDPs during that period. All schools conduct internal PDP training programs periodically, and in addition teachers must find outside sources of training that qualify for PDP credits.

> The problem is that there is a tremendous need for PDPs for teachers (else they lose their license and jobs), but a limited number of useful topics. So a cottage industry has now grown into a major industry to churn out new "content" every few months that could be sold to teachers and schools to meet PDP requirements.

> *The result is exactly what you would expect – the drive in the PDP industry is to create something new and salable – not necessarily anything that helps education.*

> There are always topics required by state DOEs that qualify for PDP credits – such as training for standardized test proctoring, or annual review of restraint training. In addition, most schools carefully choose a new topic relevant to their school for each year's efforts (three to six meetings, half days, etc., for teacher professional development). But these programs typically cover no more than one-fourth to one-third of the PDPs required to renew a teaching license.

> So the PDP industry gets to work and invents new "content" to sell. In recent years, much of this new content has either been "check-the-

box" training that is nothing more than a rehash of old material and will be ignored by the attendees, or it is a new fad-du-jour that someone cooked up to sell a course regardless of educational merit. Teachers routinely sit at these PDP conferences with a "…wink, wink, nod, nod, this is really useful…" view of the meeting. Everyone attending knows it is a farce. The goal is to get through the meeting, get the certificate that awards the mandated PDPs, and then go home and forget all the nonsense you just heard.

No one has an idea for a course we can sell? Anyone? All we have so far is John's "Teaching Calculus with Jellybeans" idea?

Now clearly, not all PDP conferences and classes are bad. But I can only recall a handful in the past decade that had nuggets a good teacher could use. One of the best half-day PDP sessions I ever attended was about ways to discipline with humor and engage today's child centered on an excellent book by Barkley.[81] Another was an excellent course with practical tips on diversified learning strategies.

Most of the other PDP courses were a complete waste of time.

The Power of "I"

> A now-dead fad called "The Power of I" is the poster child for the ills of the PDP system. Thousands of schools across the country jumped on this program a few years ago to fill a couple half-days of PDP training, and yield a few precious PDP credits for their

---
[81] *Wow! Adding Pizzazz to Teaching and Learning*, Barkley

teachers. The program was a huge financial success for its developers. On the surface it was a program designed to help get students to do more homework. In reality, it was a program designed by someone who had absolutely no idea what teachers face with homework, and appears to know absolutely nothing about the psychology and expectations of a child.

"The Power of I" basically said – never give a child a zero for a missed assignment, instead give them an "I" for "Incomplete." By some mysterious process this would incent the child to finish the project at a later date. (Remember, I warned you up front about tone of this chapter, and the disrespect and disdain teachers have for inept bureaucratic educational initiatives.) Somehow in the rush to create saleable PDP content, the creator believed he could convince experienced teachers that this was all needed to get students to do more homework.

Many of us watched with trepidation as several of the newer teachers gave "The Power of I" a try. We watched as the term ended and the homework *still* had not been made up. We watched as the teacher asked in bewilderment what grade should be submitted for the end of the term report card if a student *still* had an "I" for three scores, and *refused to make up the assignments*. It was frustrating and sad to witness the hard lesson the new teacher learned about educational PDP fads, when the students did exactly what the experienced teachers expected. The student preferred the "I" to the zero because it let them safely skip the work, yet kept them out of trouble at home for weeks by hiding the zeroes. They gladly accepted the zero at the end of the term rather than make up the work – knowing they could use the excuse at home that it was too late, and they would just have one "punishment" all at once rather than having had to face the parent for each zero along the way.

Worst of all, by labeling failure with the relatively nice term of "incomplete," we enable the child to duck his/her responsibility. The child <u>knows</u> he/she simply blew off the assignment, but the school tells them it's okay because it is just "incomplete." The school has made it official – skipping assignments is okay.

There are many more like the "Power of I" that could be cited to make the point about useless PDP content. If I had to *try to put numbers on my past ten years of PDP training history, I would estimate the following:*

Useful PDP content:	20%
Rehash of old, known material:	50%
Useless fad content:	30%

Bureaucracy self-justification

It is likely that those outside of the school building could never imagine the burden of endless regulations, forms, paperwork, and mandates placed on schools, *at the expense of education*, by bureaucrats who continually demonstrate very little understanding of the educational environment. As one study summed it up:

[Editor note – the underline is added, not in the original]

"America's schools are being crushed under decades of legislative and union mandates. They can never succeed until we cast off the bureaucracy and unleash individual inspiration and willpower…This is why we must bulldoze school bureaucracy. It is a giant diversion, focused on compliance to please some administrator far away. Every minute spent filling out a form or worrying about compliance interferes with the human interaction that is the essence of effective teaching." [82]

Bureaucracy example: Posting Core Standards:

Several weeks ago, as I write this section in June 2013, yet another example of educational bureaucracy was forced on the classroom. All teachers were required to post a sign in their room, each day, that summarized what state core standards were the basis for today's class. We all were given small whiteboards for that purpose. A typical posting would be of the content, and then the core paragraph number – something like "Normalizing rational expressions, PP12.332.13 and PP5.243.21."

This was a requirement, not a suggestion. A few days after it was announced, one math teacher was criticized in his evaluation for not having a sign posted. Every teacher I know just shook their heads when this was announced – "…SSDD" (same stuff, different day). Now obviously this sign is a small thing, in and of itself. It would not even be worth mentioning

---

[82] The Atlantic, April 2012

if it was an isolated example of useless bureaucracy. But it is not alone. It is just *yet another* senseless mandate that takes *yet another* two-three minutes out of teaching the actual class material.

Bureaucracy at work in the classroom

Ironically, this sign is defended by the bureaucrats as a "good teaching practice." But it is simply a very <u>bad</u> teaching practice to anyone with actual classroom experience. None of us can think of any positive to education that was in this bureaucrat's mind when he or she imposed this inane requirement on every class in every school. Did they think any child would memorize the core standard reference numbers? Did they think a teacher needed to have something on the board to remind them what they were teaching that day? Did they think teachers did not always frame every topic, and every lesson, with its context? Was it a subtle push to get teachers to focus on the core standards?

Framing a lesson plan with its context is a good idea. <u>Micromanaging</u> a teacher – by taking up ever more precious class time in requiring them to create a useless sign before each class – is just another distraction from education. Whatever was intended, it is yet another inane bureaucratic requirement that does not yield any statistically significant positive to education, and steals a couple more minutes from the class time needed for other mandates.

Now this is just one small example. One study listed 75 others, along with a chilling summary of the impact of bureaucracy on education:

"Over the last decade…we have discovered numerous bureaucratic challenges facing urban school district central offices and state education systems that may help to explain why many well-intentioned efforts to improve public schools have not worked.

Bureaucratic systems, policies and practices that have been built up over decades in inner-city school districts have often led to fewer resources that actually reach the classroom, prevented teachers from receiving the support they need to meet individual student needs, and disheartened many people in and around these systems, giving them little faith that conditions will improve.

Policies and procedures – which may be designed to comply to laws and regulations – often don't allow the school system to pursue its core mission: advancing student achievement." [83]

Bureaucracy example: Massachusetts SEI – Secluded English Immersion

The bureaucratic mandates are endless. In March and April; 2013 we invested hundreds of hours preparing curricula for the new core standards. In May 2013 it was a small requirement for the core-content sign (above) in each class. In June it's yet another pass at trying to fix the abject failure of inclusion classes. The bureaucrats churn out endless "initiatives" – and none of them ever work as envisioned by an unqualified "educator" who does not have to live with the consequences.

Yesterday (as I write this section in June 2013) I was at a required teacher assembly to suddenly introduce a massive new Massachusetts mandate that goes into effect this coming fall. There are just three weeks left in the school year to prepare for an ill-designed program that will take effect when school begins next fall, and for which critical components will not be determined or announced until a couple days before the start of school.

This newest bureaucratic nightmare is called SEI – Secluded English Immersion. The basic idea is an honorable one on the surface – to prepare teachers to better handle the increasing number of students with limited understanding of English who are put into inclusion classes. Yet again we have an example of a potentially nice goal that already has been twisted by bureaucratic ineptitude into a program that cannot work or benefit children. It is yet another example of a good

---

[83] *How Bureaucracy stands in the way,* The Broad Foundation

goal with the inevitability of destructive unintended consequences.

SEI, under the banners of "fairness" and "political correctness" and "helping children" is simply very bad educational policy. It is poorly implemented and rolled out, and is <u>certain to hurt the education of the very children it professes to help</u>. It will hurt the ESL students, and it will hurt the non-ESL students in the same class.

The goal is to get teachers better suited to teach children with limited English language abilities, at the same pace and in the same class, with the rest of a fast-moving English-speaking class! Huh? *What possible course content, other than training the teacher to be fluent and bilingual in Spanish, (or French, Italian…) can achieve that goal?* Teachers are already trained in diversified teaching methods. Teachers already are exceptionally careful in the manner they use to engage those who have difficulty with the English Language. Teachers already have years of experience with inclusion of special education and ELL students in a class, and years of experience teaching to a wide range of abilities and effort.

Consider what it would be like if you traveled to France (or Germany, Italy – any country with a language you did not know well) and attended school knowing only the French you learned in a couple terms back in college. Assume the teacher does not know English. What possible chance do you have of learning the same material <u>at the same pace</u> as the rest of the class if you and the teacher have difficulty understanding each other? What possible courses could the teacher take, other than a crash course with Pimsleur or Rosetta Stone to learn English, that could help? *What happens to the education of the rest of the class while the teacher is trying to explain French history to you with broken English?*

Already SEI appears to be the new poster child for inept bureaucratic initiatives.

And as bad as the basic concept is, SEI is also burdened (as are almost all initiatives by these career DoE bureaucrats) by a poorly thought-out rollout, and inept program design. I wish I could take credit for the comment I overheard leaving the meeting. "SEI – must stand for Standard Educational Incompetence." It is a program designed by bureaucrats isolated in their cubicles, with no understanding of the classroom, who simply threw another well-meaning educational grenade over the wall for the teachers to handle.

The preliminary syllabus for the SEI course shows how little thought went into its design. The topics are of almost no practical value for classroom teachers. This is a classic bureaucratic "make-work project" – inventing a lot of plain-vanilla "content" to justify and fill out an ill-conceived new mandate. Here are four examples of content taken from the "model syllabus" for the new SEI course:

> *(4 points) "Write a two-page paper in which you examine you (sic) own social and cultural upbringing. Highlight ways in which your own experience may inform (sic) your practice. Consider ways to build a culturally responsive practice, including the "literacies" (sic) and cultural referents of your students."*

> *(8 points) Visit a site or attend an event in the community of your ELLs (e.g., a religious institution, neighborhood grocery store, athletic or social event) and write about what you observed and learned from this experience. Attention should be paid to any discomfort you experienced and how this visit may inform (sic) your practice.*

> *(4 points) Write a two-page paper about an ELL student who interests and challenges you (from your own experience, from a film clip/video or from a reading), focusing on cultural aspects of the student's experience in an American classroom and ways that you might help bridge these gaps in understanding."*

> *(4 points) Write a paper regarding what is "different" about reading for ELLs."* [84]

Even ignoring the spelling errors and misused words (either the author meant "impact" rather than "inform," or there is very tortured English at work here that none of my professional editors can figure out!) <u>*projects like these are make-work tasks of no practical value*</u> to any classroom teacher. It is hard to envision <u>any</u> classroom teacher, other than a brand

---

[84] Model Sheltered English Immersion (SEI) Course Syllabus, Massachusetts DOE, July 2012

new one just out of college, who has not spent hours thinking about and addressing the capabilities and learning needs of specific students. I can think of no teacher (at least, all those I have met) who has not developed strong methods of listening to students, and methods to deploy differentiated learning to those who have difficulty with the language. Every experienced teacher on the planet has looked at his/her own biases and strengths/weaknesses to see how they impact (inform?) the teacher's effectiveness.

The above assignments are designed by a bureaucrat to fill out a course, not by a teacher trying to explain a concept. The class, as outlined in the "Model Syllabus" is yet another costly bureaucratic waste of time, filled with weak, make-work content that disrupts, rather than helps, the educational process – and the course topics will do absolutely nothing statistically significant to help a teacher overcome a language barrier!

And, by discussing the poor design and inept rollout, it detracts from the larger and far more important question about SEI – why is yet another failed "Inclusion Class" approach being used to weaken the education for everyone in the classroom?

Is it fair to the inclusion students to rush them faster than they can handle to meet the competing mandate to cover the full lesson plan? Is it fair to the education of non-inclusion students in a class to lessen their education in order to stop teaching for mandated support of the inclusion students? How will the entire class actually benefit from the SEI program? SEI simply takes even more time away from the teacher's effort to cover all the mandated core topics. It is yet another example of competing mandates, where one mandate can only be accomplished if we fail to meet another mandate.

The bureaucrats already had two major mandates (core standards and inclusion accommodations – plus lesser administrative and other mandates) competing for the same time that cannot be accomplished in the same period, and already hold the teacher and school responsible for failing to meet those competing mandates. Now the bureaucrats add a third set of major mandates competing for the same 60 minutes that are already double-booked.

Spock and Captain Kirk[85] asked the right question: "Do the needs of the few outweigh the needs of the many?" Bureaucratic educators end up cheating <u>both</u> constituencies by answering "yes" to the Star Trek conundrum.

We have an educational system that fails because it forces all students to be lumped into the same class and taught by the same generalized process. We trumpet the great values of differentiated teaching for diverse student needs, then put all the children in the same blender where, at most, a very watered-down shadow of differentiated instruction can occur. The bureaucrats make everything plain vanilla, when we really need chocolate for some, and raspberry twist for others.

Of course all people are not the same! Even if two people have the same or similar potential, they each have different needs, and different roadmaps for unleashing that potential! But SEI ignores the differences and dilutes the approach for both the ESL and non-ESL students by trying to be all things to all people in the same overcrowded classroom.

---

[85] *Star Trek III, The Search for Spock*, 1984

Meanwhile, the poorly thought-out rollout of the SEI mandate would be a disgrace to any professional manager. Just consider this "process" to get teachers certified in SEI:

- As of 1 September 2013 all teachers who have ESL students must have forty-five hours of SEI training, or their license will not be renewed. By 2016 <u>all</u> teachers must have the SEI course and endorsement or their license will not be renewed.

  "Beginning September 2013, deny advancement or renewal (including extensions) of a core academic license if an educator fails to obtain an SEI endorsement within the time period scheduled for the educator's cohort training, subject to a hardship exception." [86]

- The courses <u>do not yet exist</u>, and in our school only 5-6 teachers (those with the most ESL students in their classes) will be chosen to attend the first classes.

- Anyone not selected as one of the 5-6 in the initial free class must find another for-pay course (<u>none yet exist</u>) on SEI training.

- *Some 40-50 teachers in our school teach classes that include ESL students, not just the 5-6 that will be selected to attend the class*

The Massachusetts DOE bureaucrats have come up with a way so that literally thousands of teachers across the state will lose their teaching license for not taking a course that doesn't exist when given three school weeks of notice! The result will be the obvious one – PDP developers will come up with another crash course that "checks the boxes" but contributes nothing to the education of our children.

---

[86] *Guidelines for Sheltered Immersion Teachers* (SEI), Massachusetts DOE, April 2013

Davey, duck hunting isn't like developing policies at the Department of Education. Here, you need to think first, and actually aim at the target, before shooting.

Brilliant! Now this latest bureaucratic mess is so obviously out-of-control that the procedures will likely change over the summer. Someone will wake up and see there needs to be a phase-in period, and some sensible planning. A "hardship clause" will be added. Yet, an initiative as poorly designed as SEI is common from DOE bureaucrats.

> [Editor's note – shortly before publication of this book, the DOE rushed through a revision adding just such a hardship clause.]

The right answer to the professed SEI goals? One of the few times more expenditures are needed – hire teaching professionals who are fluent in the needed language(s), or invest in language teachers to get the SEI students proficient in English.

Bureaucracy example: Disciplining Students

Bureaucratic rules have as powerful a negative role on non-instructional parts of education as the harm they do to actual teaching. The worst of these indirect impacts is the degree to which discipline has been undermined by bureaucratic mandates. There is little a teacher (or administrator, for that matter) can do today to discipline a child that does not involve very high risk for the teacher.

The poster child for this are the "restraint guidelines" that have been mandated for when a fight occurs at school. I suspect that all parents would hope that should a fight break out, a teacher would quickly step in before anyone gets hurt. It would be expected that in the context of an on-going fight, there would be some degree of firmness and contact by the teacher. *But the new rule is just the opposite – do not step in, even if children are getting hurt, unless the physical damage already is "serious."* Even in non-fight situations, as an example if a child is throwing chairs through windows and hurling desks at the walls, we are not to step in unless the child is doing serious damage to himself or another student.

"A child is not at risk of death if he is angrily punching a wall, so do not step in." [87]

Essentially, this means that the official policy for fights is to wait until blood is flowing (so that a teacher's need to intervene and have some degree of physical contact cannot be questioned) rather than risk the high likelihood of legal action if we rush in to prevent serious harm.

This policy is pure insanity – ignoring the context, and putting children at risk under the banner of political correctness. Bureaucrats treat a teacher trying to stop a fight between children is though he/she is a pedophile, slyly waiting for a fight to break out so that he or she can rush in and have an excuse for touching children. I know something about real pedophiles, having grown up with one, and this is not that! *No – it is just stopping a fight, and should be honored, not condemned, in that context.* And staying away undermines the teachers further by forcing teachers to be seen as uncaring. It takes the horrible risk ("daddy juices" flowing yet again) of having to wait for a "serious" injury to actually occur before you step in.

The risk is huge for a teacher. Two years ago I was on cafeteria duty when a fight broke out between two girls. I was on the far side of the cafeteria and ran over when I saw

---

[87] Restraint Training, May 2013

several teachers near the fight backing away. They were doing the right thing according to what we are told to do in fights. Meanwhile the two girls are scratching, slugging and clawing at each other while 200 kids in the cafeteria whooped and hollered.

I ran over, got between them, and managed to separate them. In the process I took a right to the head from one girl that Sonny Liston would have been proud of. I intervened by getting between them, holding my arms straight out to the side (like a crossing guard stopping pedestrians), and picking one who I knew well to speak to, and try to get her to stop. (She's the one with the great right hook.) The girl behind me kept going, trying to reach over me, and trying to shove me out of the way. It probably took a full minute of "…Toni, you don't want to do this…Toni, she isn't worth this, you don't want to be blamed for this…" before Toni stopped. Meanwhile, the girl behind me kept punching the back of my head, and clawing my shoulders, trying to get past me to continue the fight.

Things finally cooled down a bit with me standing between the two girls, blocking the girl in front of me with my outstretched right arm, and grabbing the girl's belt behind me to hold her back from continuing the fight (and whacking me some more in the process). When they had calmed down (other than screaming out language that described parts of each other that I didn't even know girls had) the other teachers then came over, the deans arrived, and the fight ended with the two girls being escorted to the dean's office.

Sounds good, right? Fight ended, no one seriously hurt, disturbance ended. But hidden in there was the potential end of my career and possible legal charges. Remember the "…holding her belt?" Well, that could have been twisted to be "…his hand was in my pants" or maybe "…he was touching me in an inappropriate area." Both descriptions would have been technically correct. I would have been dead meat had the child, or an observing adult, filed such a complaint. You see – I was violating what we are taught in restraint training – never intervene unless the children are in imminent danger, and if you do, <u>stop the fight without touching anyone</u>.

Huh?

In this case the fight injuries had not yet become "serious" (whatever that means) so I would have been "wrong" to stop the fight, and "wrong" for "touching." Color me fired or in jail.

Bureaucratic rules and regulations like this are absurd. They are all about details and ignore context. There is no part of the daddy in me that could let those two girls continue to hurt each other. I will make the same choice if something like that happens again.

And I will be risking my career and life savings by doing so.

(Aside – experienced teachers would have told me to interfere if it is guys fighting, but run like hell if it is girls. Why? Girls fight far harder and more seriously! When guys fight, it is all bluff and bluster. Inside they are saying "I hope someone ends this before I get hurt." When girls fight, it is to the death. All the girls are thinking is "How can I kill this wench!" Okay, color me politically incorrect, also.)

Rules about handling fights are only one small example of endless bureaucracy on non-instructional matters, like discipline, that hurts education:

> *"Hardly any interaction is free of legal implications. Teachers are instructed never -- never ever -- to put an arm around a crying child: the school might get sued. Misbehavior and disrespect are met with weakness and resignation; teachers are trained to be stoics, tolerating disorder rather than running the risk of a "due process" hearing in which the teacher, not the student, must justify her decision."* [88]

Bureaucracy example: Teaching methods du Jour – course reversals

Improvement good, but change for the sake of change only to justify bureaucratic jobs, is destructive to education. A prime example is defining the "core standards" – those items that should be the basis for what is actually taught.

---

[88] The Atlantic, April 2012

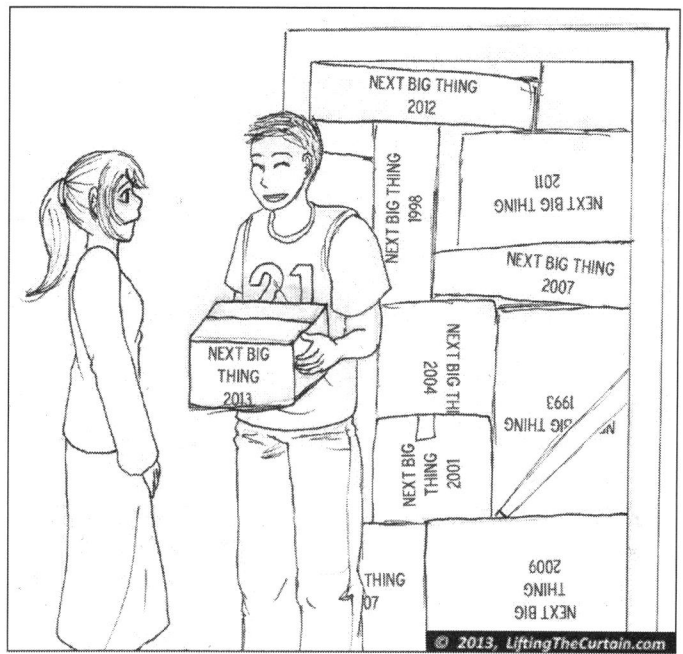

Wow! This is awesome! DoE just sent us the "Next Big Thing" for Education!

Core Standards are very important. They ensure that schools cover the most critical portions of a subject, and that all schools meet the standards. But since about 1960 or so, core standards have gone through a series of revisions, only to be reversed a few years later by yet another "…next big thing."

Each new iteration generates hundreds of hours at each school to rewrite curricula and design new course structures. Teachers go through dozens of hours, each, for new training, PDPs, and assemblies. A few thousand trees, per school, are sacrificed to make paper for stacks of paperwork to cover the changes. Old books are scrapped and new textbooks purchased.

Then the real pain starts. Inevitably the career bureaucrats believe their "next big thing" is so important to the future of humanity that it must be rolled out immediately. So they launch huge changes with just a year or two of advance warning, and with no supporting materials.

Those "educators," back in their comfortable office cubicles far from the realities of education, never realize that a brand new set of core standards for a high school requires that the entering freshmen have had the prerequisite parts of the new core standards in middle school <u>before</u> they became freshmen.

But, of course, they have not. Let me invent a silly example to show how inept such a rollout becomes. Assume a new core standard that children must learn to speak French. They are required to pass a competency in French based upon "French 101" in 6th grade, "French 201" in 8th grade, and "French 301" in 10th grade. Simple idea – and exactly comparable to the new core concepts in Math, English, etc. <u>BUT</u> – in year one of the rollout, the 10th graders will be tested in "French core competency" even though their class never had the 6th and 8th grade prerequisites!

Today (June 2013 as I write this) we are about to launch the newest "next big thing" in a long series of older "next big things" before we get to the following "next big thing" that will be announced in a few years. It happens that I like and support the new 2014 version of core standards (for math). They actually (though no bureaucrat would ever use such non-PC terms) go back to 1940s and 1950s teaching styles of getting children to understand the ideas more than just remember the steps or facts or dates. It is a style of teaching I have always embraced.

But this rollout shares the same terrible flaw of the prior core standard rollouts – middle school curricula assumes elementary schools have been taught all along to the new standards, and high school curricula depends on students entering from middle school with experience and topics from the new core. Obviously, since all occur at once, both middle and high schools start out with a huge problem of students lacking the very prerequisites that the core standards demand for each level.

Even if you like the new standards as I do, they have already taken me out of the classroom for many days of helping to prepare the new curricula. More days for pacing guides, lessons, and new content are needed. Next year we all have a special "math lab" and each teacher will be scrambling to make content for them. Many of our best math teachers are trying their best to do a job they have neither the training nor experience to be expected to do – develop the content that the career bureaucrats mandated, but never bothered to design or develop, and that the bureaucrats have no clue how to structure. Already the new core standards are a time sink, and we have not actually started teaching to them yet.

The next generation of standardized tests, scheduled for 2014 in Massachusetts, will be a *bloodbath* when first rolled out. They are so different conceptually from current testing (concepts versus facts) that children will fail in droves. Massachusetts will likely have to dumb down the scoring even further so that "passing" rates do not plummet. They did this a few years ago when results on one MCAS math test were so bad that the only way to hide the mass failure of their DoE policies from the public was to reduce the number of correct answers needed to pass to 16 out of 64 (just 25% right was "passing" that year), down from the 20 of 64 the prior years. I suspect that when the new tests are rolled out for the new core standards, the passing bar will have to be dropped to 20% for the first years, so that Massachusetts can remain "number one in the nation."

Already, several states (Georgia, Pennsylvania, Oklahoma, and Alabama) have decided to not use the new core standard testing.[89]

Changes to core standards should be like Supreme Court rulings and changes to the Constitution – well thought out and slooooooooow to change. The bureaucrats never worry about details like implementation, rollout, or content – just develop new mandates that justify their position, throw them over the wall like a grenade, then develop more bureaucracy to handle all the problems that quickly surface.

Bureaucracy example – The good, bad, and ugly of new teacher evaluations

Across the nation in the fall of 2013, states are addressing the important need to improve the quality, usefulness, and fairness of teacher evaluations. It is an effort that has a great deal of promise, and eventually could be a significant positive

---

[89] *Georgia the latest state to back out of K-12 PARC tests*, NPR, July 2013

factor in improving education. But once again, bureaucrats attempting to write mandates in areas they are unqualified to address (here it is about advanced human relations policies) has resulted in an initial rollout that is simply a burdensome bureaucratic mess that will not accomplish any of the excellent goals that we all had in mind for fixing evaluations.

> [Editor's note: The look at evaluations is <u>only</u> based upon the initial Massachusetts DoE version – and might not (hopefully!) be relevant to other states.]

There is a lot of good in the new evaluations, but there is also a lot of bad, and some parts that are just plain ugly.

The Good:

- Much better immediacy of feedback
- Evaluations tied to specific, tangible goals
- Involvement of both the teacher and administration in setting goals
- Both announced and unannounced observations
- The system places high emphasis upon raising student expectations
- Realistic categories of performance that tie to potential earned merit pay

The Bad:

- New teachers are held to a much higher standard than experienced teachers. Huh? A new teacher must be terminated after his/her first three years if not <u>fully</u> proficient in all four of the main evaluation groups covering thirty-three different metrics. Meanwhile, an experienced teacher must be proficient in just <u>half</u> of these areas. It is a prime example of a bureaucratic initiative that simply does not make any sense. A rookie leaning the craft is expected to be proficient in 100% of the job requirements or will be immediately terminated and his/her career in teaching over, while an experienced teacher must only know 50% to avoid risking the start of a path to possible dismissal.

- As with so many bureaucratic mandates, there is little or no thought to phasing in the new program. New teachers already in their third year as this mandate rolls out have only one year to become proficient in four major areas covering 33 sub topics – or be fired at the end of the year!

- The system still relies only upon one evaluator with no input by other sources.

The Ugly:

- The new Massachusetts system reflects the complete lack of competency by the authoring career DoE bureaucrats in the area of proven human relations (HR) practices by requiring evaluation in thirty-three different areas. Even a mid-level HR professional knows that an individual cannot be effectively judged based upon metrics in thirty-three different areas. By definition, this means that the evaluation is, on average, looking at factors that comprise just 3% of the individual's work effort. This is akin to the absurdity of evaluating a computer programmer on a metric that evaluated how well aligned were the boxes in his/her flowcharts. Even if we move up a level to look at the sixteen major groupings for the thirty-three, the total runs counter to proven best practices in any HR organization.

- The most discouraging part of the Massachusetts DoE version of the new evaluations is that they were once again created in a bureaucratic bubble – not giving consideration to other competing factors in the system that undermine any chance at success. One simple example is especially disturbing – the excellent idea of emphasizing raising student expectations. The single most important set of factors in a teacher's evaluation is how well they set and raise student expectations – an awesome goal.

   But this is in the same educational system where nearly one half of my students have the expectations-sapping IEP accommodation of allowing unlimited retests, and/or the expectations-destroying accommodation of awarding an "A" for doing just half of the work.

Meanwhile, the evaluations are accomplished in the same environment of cronyism that has undermined so many parts of the current educational system, leading to little initial faith that the evaluations will be fair. Teachers know, from a long and painful history dealing with cronyism and abuse, that the highest evaluations will go to the clique – teachers expect that most principals will take care of their friends, first. It is the nature of bureaucracies.

- There is no effort to incorporate class-level metrics in making the evaluation – a standard-level class in an urban high school is certain to have a much different level of student expectations than an honors class at an affluent high school.

I am hopeful that someday the new evaluations will turn out to be a positive factor in turning around urban high school education. The failings in the initial Massachusetts version and hopefully will be patched in the months ahead. They are the result of bureaucrats with no training, experience, or competency in HR policies trying to mandate an extremely complex HR evaluation plan. It will be up to the schools, once again, to try to fix the mess that was rolled out with flaws no one in DoE was qualified to see, anticipate, and fix before rollout.

But the items under "The Ugly" are critical systemic flaws that require changes well beyond the evaluation structure, itself, for this to work. The causes of systemic failure in education are interrelated – almost always the results in one "fix" are undermined by other areas that remain unfixed.

Fixing the evaluation itself can never have any substantive positive impact until we also fix the other systemic failures.

Bureaucracy example: Boston Public School Truancy

One final example of recent of inane bureaucratic programs (out of so many we could have cited!) is taken from Boston Public Schools. In September 2010 the Boston School

District published a study centering on how to increase the graduation rate of 8th graders they predict will drop out of high school. No one can challenge that this is an admirable and vitally important goal. Yet, once again the bureaucrats seemed to have no sense of cause-and-effect when designing their "solutions."

Their number one finding was that an attendance record of less than 80% (missing at least one day each week) was a good predictor that the student would become a dropout. (Amazing – it took a bureaucrat to realize that children who do not come to school are not likely to graduate!) The recommendation was more funding "…to develop new programs - intentionally designed to meet the needs of particular at-risk populations…"

Now I know the authors of the report are very well-meaning and truly care about what they do. But they seem to have no understanding of cause and effect! They seemed to think truancy was the <u>cause</u> of the dropout rate. They never asked what caused the truancy, and which of those conditions could effectively be addressed by a school. Not once did they appear to ask themselves the key questions. *"If the parents don't care enough to keep their child from skipping school a couple days each week, how does the teacher counter that? What action by a teacher, no matter how well funded, helps teach a child who is not in the classroom?"*

The authors of the report could not see the huge disconnect in their recommendation, so they propose new bureaucratic initiatives destined to fail. The real issue in this specific case is not their plan to <u>pull</u> these delinquent children to school with better classes – it should have been how do we get the parents to <u>push</u> them onto the bus? We can convert the math class to free pizza and beer parties served by the most popular cheerleaders – and Delinquent Danny will still skip his day per week if the parent could care less whether or not he attends. Worse was the drone of Boston morning talk show hosts who jumped on the report citing the dropout rate as "…yet another example of bad teachers…" because 4500 children were seen at risk of not graduating.

Bureaucracy fills every part of the school house, crowding out the actual process of educating our children. Bureaucracy is pervasive and debilitating.

> *"Every minute spent filling out a form or worrying about compliance interferes with the human interaction that is the essence of effective teaching. Law is everywhere in schools. It permeates every nook and cranny. Teachers spend hours every week filling out forms that no one ever reads -- because the laws and regulations that have piled up over the years require them. Principals suffer a similar inversion of authority with teachers, who are armed with hundreds of pages of work rules* [DoE and union] *that prescribe exactly what teachers can be asked to do."* [90]

Educator make-work efforts: Poorly structured textbooks

The problem with "educators" is not just the PDPs and the bureaucrats – it also extends to the textbook publishers. The underlying problem is the same one that causes the PDP system to become dysfunctional – the need to come up with new things to sell regardless of educational value.

New "revisions" of textbooks come out where the only tangible difference is a re-ordering of existing material and a few trivial tweaks. There is nothing new in the "revision," but the hope is to replace the old books with new sales. Often this reordering actually undermines educational effectiveness by placing chapters before other chapters that are prerequisites of the concept. It is akin to (invented example for non-math readers) moving the chapter on exponents before the one on basic addition.

My current textbooks for math are great examples of publications by "educators" who tout their math credentials, but seem to have no understanding of math. (Sorry! Mathspeak follows.) Polynomials are in a chapter *after* factoring, even though factoring requires polynomial division. Volume and surface area are many chapters after basic area and perimeter, though both are natural immediate follow-ups via the linking concept of a prism. The chapters were re-ordered just to create a new "revision" to sell.

These same textbooks severely undercut good education by over-emphasizing technology in order to justify a new "revision." Adding a few pages on using a graphing calculator to do a problem is an easy way to pad the book for a new revision. But over time, after several of these "revisions," the technology starts to crowd out teaching. Students are taught a series of keystrokes to handle topics such as rational expressions or matrices, without ever learning the ideas behind

---

[90] The Atlantic, April 2012

these approaches. The student learns to how to press a key that tells where and asymptote or hole is in a quadratic function, but has no clue what those two things are. A new teacher, following these texts without the experience to know you must <u>first</u> do these operations manually for the student to get the concept, is guaranteeing that the student never masters the topic.

The bottom line: The bottom line is the same as the top line that started this section – career bureaucrats claiming to be educators are killing education. Government bureaucracies are a disaster to education – bureaucrats are not accountable for their actions, ill-qualified for the areas they control, and have little understanding of education. The impact of bureaucrats on education is no different than the excesses of bureaucrats such as in the General Services Administration, the Internal Revenue Service, or Massachusetts Welfare Department – lack of control, lack of accountability, and poor leadership inevitably leads to out-of-control red tape and burdens.

Our children are paying the price for education run by career DoE bureaucrats, not teachers, who have little understanding of what goes on in the classroom.

(Chapter 24)
Systemic Failure #6: Burned out teachers

(Overview: Teachers certainly are part of the problem today, and deserve their #6 ranking on the list of major systemic issues harming education. However, it is not the 5% of all teachers who should be fired for poor teaching that is the problem. The system could and must be fixed to deal with those teachers. The real issue is the overwhelming <u>majority</u> of teachers that has burned out and have given up.

Teachers today are the Vietnam Veterans of the 70s. They have begun to evidence many of the same symptoms of soldiers who came back from DaNang with me in 1968, and were met with insults and spat upon for trying to serve their country. Today I "serve" as a teacher with dozens of teachers who I have watched being forced to morph from being great teachers, to defensive ones just going through the motions.

The problem with teachers is not the 4-5 bad ones in any school, it is the 100s of good ones that the system has forced to become mediocre teachers. It is extremely discouraging, the past couple years, how often you hear a good teacher start to use the deadly phrase:

"I give up. I will just do what they tell me to do..."

I have heard this far too many times over the past two years, even from some of the finest teachers I have been honored to know. What is even worse is what is left off this phrase – the silent:

"...even though I know it's wrong. I can't fight it anymore."

We have created a new generation of teachers who now must focus on compliance, not teaching. The result, once again, is totally predictable – good teachers becoming mediocre teachers, and teachers being seen as the sole problem with education. The problem is *not* that we focus (as we should) on the few extreme cases that make the news, or that we are concerned about the handful of truly bad teachers in any school that we hear about from our children or meet in conferences.

The problem is that this handful of bad teachers has been a national distraction from the real issues besetting education.

---

[91] Copyright 2013 by LiftingTheCurtain.com

Pressure on teachers – a daily fact of life

In the three years of research, surveys, and hundreds of interviews of urban high school teachers and students that went into writing *Lifting The Curtain,* perhaps the saddest finding was that teachers felt 24% of their students did not care what grades they got, and the shocking statistic that 63% of students believe that their parents do not care what grades they got as long as they pass and graduate. Now – truth in advertising – this latter 63% statistic is one I do not personally believe. I am convinced by being in the trenches of teaching, that most parents (75% seems to be a reasonable guesstimate) *do* care, and *do* support their children's education. Of course a teenager tends to see things differently!

But the problem for teachers is the disruption in classrooms, the inordinate time in meetings, and the constant conflict and frustration of the 25% of parents whose actions actively enable their children to fail.

J. B. Banks is an award-winning author, and a veteran substitute teacher in the Chicago school system. Her overview is especially valuable because it is based upon many different schools, based upon being in many different schools, and classes ranging from K to 12, and standard to honors.

(J. B. Banks) Suiting up for another day of teaching

The bell at 8:41 a.m. signifying the beginning of class, and ironically much like a boxing match, the beginning of a heavy weight fight, with you the teacher as the opponent. The prize? Not a belt, nor a purse, or even a title. You fight to make a difference in the lives of kids who have lost direction and hope.

These are kids who come from bad beginnings, broken homes, and bad breaks. By the time many of them reach high school, inner-city gang violence, drugs, fast lane living, and inexplicable tragedies have claimed the lives of both relatives and peers. They have short fuses and even shorter attention spans. On some days, something as simple as the wrong look, the wrong colors, or "perceived disrespect" can ignite a rumble, or compromise your safety.

Although they may not be able to master the lessons of the day, they are masters of strategy. Make no mistake about it – they can size up your weaknesses and vulnerabilities like a pro, and pounce on them to gain a coveted edge. They can smell fear like a dog. It's important to tread carefully.

So every day you suit up. You give yourself a pep talk, prepare yourself mentally, and you get back in the game. On good days, you win a round or two. A student who has struggled with a concept or lesson "gets it" and you get to take credit. Someone gets accepted for an internship for which you wrote a recommendation. Those times you feel blessed for this chosen work.

But more times than not, it's a battle, and you just have to suit up again, secure in the knowledge that when we can help them realize their potential and make them "winners," it's a victory for us all!

Teachers, on average in the survey, had 3.1 very difficult interactions with parents each month, and only 30% of teachers felt they received strong or very strong support from administration in such conflicts. Another shocking statistic from the research: teachers found that 71% of the time they asked for a parent conference about a struggling student, the parent either did not respond at all, or simply refused in an email or phone call with "…don't worry, I'll take care of it."

> *It is difficult for those outside the classroom to even believe the nature of the conflicts every week with this minority of parents, and the terrible impact this has on their child's motivation and expectations. Here are two vignettes by anonymous, a retired high school English teacher from California. Thankfully, 80% of high school parents are great and supportive – but all teachers know the time sink and frustration just a few "Cheer Moms" or "Sports Dads" can cause by confrontations,*

intimidation, and threats of lawsuits. It only takes a handful of "cheer moms" or "sports dads" to undermine a classroom of otherwise great students. These are all-too-common examples. Like most teachers, anonymous prefers to not reveal a name in order to avoid retribution from school administrators for speaking out.

(Anonymous) "Cheer mom" and "sports dad"

"Cheer Mom:" Chatty, flirtatious "Cara" had eked out a C-minus the first semester of Junior English. Her refusal to read *The Grapes of Wrath* earned her an F in the spring. Cheer Mom then called a meeting demanding that Cara be excused from the novel. When asked her objection, she insisted Cara doesn't read big books, not because of limited reading skills but because she's too busy with cheer practice and games to do the readings. She proudly explained that Cara had been cheerleading since 7th grade, she practiced 15 hours a week, and took extra workshops.

We ended up meeting with the vice-principal. Talking to mom was like talking to a wall. She pointedly ignored me and turned her attention to the vice-principal. "Cara liked that man and the mouse book last year. It was just 100 pages, and with her busy schedule she can't be reading a 600 page book!" I was startled when the vice-principal seemed to agree with the mother saying, "She has the right to choose…" until she added, "…and not completing her assignments is choosing failure."

Enabled by her mother, Cara did fail. Maybe she'll have more time to read now that she no longer has the grades for cheer.

"Sports Dad:" Jason's dad accused me of hating athletes, losing his son's work and not helping his son in class. He saw no connection between the 7% Jason had earned and his effort in my class. In meetings with a vice-principal and the student, Dad would get so angry that he would pound the table and occasionally lean across it as if to strike me. During these outbursts, my male v-p would look down at the papers before him as if engrossed by the words on the page and Jason would just grin. Only the fact that I had Jason sign a copy agreeing that he had not turned in his assignments prevented more attacks on me from his dad.

I explained that it was Jason's job to keep his grades up for sports, and that he hadn't turned in any assignments for me to lose. As for in-class help, the only time he raised his hand was to throw papers, pennies or food across the room.

With his father enabling Jason to continue to fail, the gap between his points and the overall points along with M.I.A. assignments continued to grow weekly as he doggedly retained his F. By the end of the year, the file I'd made on this non-working student was extensive but I think someone should have started a file on Jason's dad who seemed quite capable of crossing the line into violence during his tantrums.

Yes – there are "bad" teachers who are part of the problem

> [*Author's note: This section is not about the handful of cases each year, nationwide, of repulsive criminal activity by a teacher. Those exceptions, like any person in any profession accused of pedophilia, drug use with minors, etc., are reprehensible. There is no place for such a person in a school, post office, accounting firm, or any other profession in the country.*]

Bad teachers are real, but are a very minor part of our disgraceful urban educational system. Burned-out teachers, on the other hand, are worthy of their #6 ranking as major contributors to the problems.

Sadly, most outside observers cannot separate the two – bad from burned out. Yet one of the greatest improvements we can do to help our children is to change the conditions that have turned good teachers into the burned-out teachers that occupy today's classrooms. If we can fix the conditions that daily undermine their ability to teach, these teachers will be able to once again focus on encouraging, exciting, and educating our children.

Any look at the teacher role in our declining education performance must break the analysis into three distinct categories:

- (5%) Incompetent teachers – especially the "screamers" and the "nasties" who do not deserve the title of "teacher"
- (20%) Weak teachers that require additional training to become better at their jobs

- (75%) The majority of teachers – good teachers who have developed a classic "bunker mentality" due to the constant drumbeat of inane regulations, inept administrations and cronyism, endless classroom mandates, angry parents, and media blame for any problem with education.

The last category – burned out teachers – has far more negative impact on education than the first two, combined.

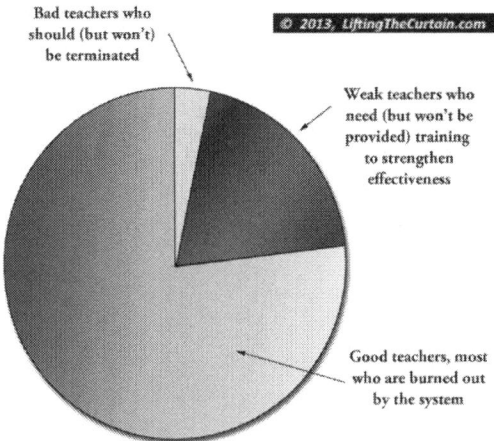

The problem is not a few "bad teachers." It is what the system is doing to the good teachers.

The Screamers and the Nasties (5% of teachers)

In every school, in every state, there are a few teachers who do not deserve the title of teacher. They quickly become known to other teachers and parents, and soon are highly visible. I have no patience with them, and no tolerance for them. Their high visibility has been a distraction from the real issues hurting urban high school education. *It is far easier to focus on 4-5 bad teachers than to look behind the curtain and see what the other 150 good teachers in the same school face every day.* The only good thing about the screamers is that they are a small minority, perhaps five percent of all teachers

Usually these are <u>not</u> the weak teachers who need help in one of the four areas listed in the next section. Instead, these are the ones who project their dislike of children into everything they do.

The classic case for me is a now-retired teacher who was assigned to monitor the front entrance of my school each day when school opened. She would stand at the top of the entry stairs and look for reasons to snarl, yell, and demean children as they entered. A boy wearing his cap as he came up the stairs received a twisted, angry face snarling "…get your hat off now!" Kids chatting would get the same treatment with "…get out of this hallway and stop blocking the stairs." Having your cap on was treated with the same degree of anger as if the child had just set fire to the school.

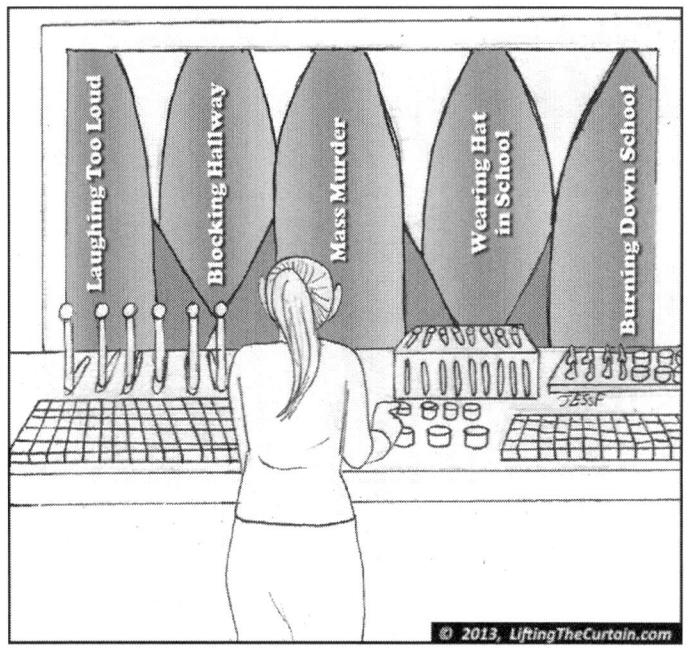

Nuke em! Nuke em all! Muahahahahahaha!
Anything the brats do deserves the maximum punishment!

For this teacher, there was no DEFCON Four. Any issue, no matter how trivial, immediately raised the issue to DEFCON One. She launched her nuclear missiles for any perceived provocation because of her open dislike of children, where both mass murder or wearing a cap were equal offenses worthy of her angriest and most demeaning delivery.

This was how literally hundreds of students started the school day – watching a teacher who "…hates us." It colored their whole school day. She ran her classes the same way. She got away with it because no one would dare challenge a prime member of the "clique" – she was best friends with the superintendent.

Compare that teacher with the teacher who replaced her on entry duty when the first teacher retired. The new teacher, when seeing a student still wearing a cap, would simply smile and point to her head to let the student know he had forgotten to take off his cap. The reaction? Almost all of the kids smiled back, and removed their cap. The intent – removing the cap – was successful without turning it into a confrontation. And every one she caught that way started the school day with a better feeling about being in school.

If education was a commercial business, this would be solved quickly. The "employee" would be warned, efforts to improve it would be put into effect, and if all efforts failed the person would be fired. But in education, unless the person is discovered before tenure is reached, it is nearly impossible to replace such a teacher. The teacher survey, cited earlier, recorded that 96% of teachers felt dismissal of a bad tenured teacher was "difficult or very difficult."

Of even more concern is that those same teachers have little faith that new evaluation procedures being rolled out across the USA will make a difference. "Just wait for the first grievance when someone is fired…" is the usual reply. The only real hope we have for firing the screamers and nasties is that my pessimism turns out to be unwarranted, and the new procedures will actually work.

Weak teachers – stuck in bubble (20% of all teachers)

This is an issue that easily could be remedied overnight. After all, there are weak people in all professions – be it lawyers, accountants, coffee baristas, or teachers. The answer in almost all other professions, except teaching, is training and experience. Management observes such an employee, assesses strengths and weaknesses, and then helps train the employee to become better.

Except, that does not happen in education. Everything in the system fights to prevent it from happening. This could so easily be fixed, yet it is not.

Colleges cannot help here – it takes experience and some gray-haired mentoring to help spot, and correct, in-classroom weaknesses. The best way is to let weaker teachers sit in the back and watch an experienced teacher manage a classroom, and also have the experienced teacher observe the new teacher in classes. Ironically, both will benefit from that process.

Yet weak teachers rarely get effective help. The educational system puts new and weak teachers into a bubble. Union rules typically mean they cannot be observed more than once a year, and that only with prior warning. The new evaluation systems being rolled out this year allow for more observation of teachers. However, these observations are primarily in the context of "judging," not of "helping."

"Mentoring" programs give lip service to helping train a teacher, but since mentoring usually happens *outside* the classroom in one-on-one meetings, the mentor cannot tailor advice to what he/she observed in the classroom. Instead, the mentor can only answer questions that the weak teacher asks, and can only guess where such a teacher might have a weakness. (As well, mentors are one of the "extra-pay" positions handed out by principals and superintendents. Often the mentor was given the paid position as a reward for being one of the clique, and not for mentoring abilities. Teachers with such a "mentor" are very careful to not disclose any weakness that might get back to the principal.) PDP "training" is a farce, and like mentoring, does not benefit from any observation of the teacher in an actual classroom.

When I started teaching, two or three teachers shared a room and could watch each other teach. I remember learning every time I watched other teachers in the same room teach. One was especially good with special education students, and I learned a great deal by watching how he engaged and motivated such students. He liked to watch my approach to discipline using caring and humor. We were lucky, we both shared a passion for children and wore our love of teaching on our sleeves, so it was easy to learn from one another. We did not feel threatened by being "observed."

But today, that cannot happen. We are specifically ordered that we must leave the classroom if another teacher has a class there. At present, there is only one class where I stay in the same room when another teacher has the room. She is relatively new (I taught math to her brother!) and I think she likes having "…the old guy in the back of the class." I do know that a couple times this year, based upon something I saw, I was able to find a quiet non-threatening time to offer a hint or two – just as others did for me years ago.

Weaker teachers especially need help in four areas.

It would be easy to move the weaker teachers into the "good" column if we simply focused our mentoring efforts into four key areas. These four should be the basis for the overwhelming bulk of PDP and training programs. All schools should invest significant recurring efforts into helping all teachers, especially weaker ones, with all four of these topics.

- *Weak teacher need: How to discipline students:*

   Discipline in today's classroom is a challenge that defies even the best teachers. Rules and regulations severely tie teacher's hands, parents challenge almost any effort at discipline, piles of conflicting bureaucratic mandates confuse the issue, and students have reached new levels of resistance to authority. Very few teachers have the patience and self-confidence to handle discipline under these circumstances.

   Yet, there are many teachers who excel at discipline, without ever needing to raise their voices. Always, their approach is based upon genuine care and respect for the students, and a clear effort at consistent fairness. But beyond this, such teachers seem to easily understand the boundaries between "kids being kids" and "unruly students."

   I have a simple rule for classrooms that the children like and respect. When they are working at their desks, they can chat quietly as long as they are working. ("…your pencils have to be moving as fast as your mouths.") But when I am at the board, there must be dead silence and complete attention. *The kids get it.* They don't have to be robots all class. And they end up listening, learning, working their butts off, and being proud of what they do. Oh – and they enjoy coming to class, too.

   However, this "…chat quietly while working but not when I am at the board…" approach is not the "right" way in the view of many teachers. I have often had teachers approach me about passing my classroom and being concerned about all the "noise" (talking) by my students. I always say the same thing. "Next time you have the chance, listen to *what* they are talking about – it's math!" I am always amazed how often that same teacher comes back a few weeks later with something like "I get it! I'm not sure it would work for me, but I get it." Yet, with help and mentoring, anyone can pull this off. The approach just recognizes that things are different today than when we were in school. I realized long ago that I could either try to impose my ideas about silence in class on the children, or I could teach them better by finding a compromise.

One student perfectly summed up the reality with this generation of children:

> *"Teachers should learn how to keep their students interested. You can't learn if you are bored out of your mind."*[92]

There is a lot of humor in the best disciplined classes. I call my students "hideous" and "idiots." They call me "Mr. Hideous" and "ancient" and delight in reminding me that "…you have no chance some grandma will ever give you a date." Yet within the humor and teasing that is characteristic of today's school children, there is love and respect in the taunts that is obvious to anyone watching.

Of course, occasionally there are times I have to tell them "…that crosses a line." The handful of times, over the years, that I had to correct myself in front of a whole class, for something I said that got too close to the "line," was an especially good thing for the class to see. That is how we teach these children about boundaries. Along the way, the children start to learn the difference between fun teasing and unacceptable bullying, and between fun teasing and disrespectful comments. It's a win-win. *And they are engaged because a teacher meets them at their level of humor.*

- *Weak teacher need: How to explain material, rather than just present it*

Many new teachers, and some older teachers, have fallen into the trap of only *showing* students how to do something, rather than *explaining* why you do it that way. You can never be good in math if you just remember some steps. History is useless if you do not understand Santayana's wisdom[93] that "…those who do not understand history are doomed to repeat it." Memorizing the fact that Boo Radley and Tom Robinson were mockingbirds[94] might get you an "A," but *understanding* what Harper Lee was recounting is the heart of gaining insight into the human condition.

---

[92] Tamarijn, Student Survey 2013
[93] *The Life of Reason*, George Santayana
[94] *To Kill a Mockingbird*, Harper Lee

Facts are useless, without knowledge about their context

Yet that is how we usually teach today. Instruction has been dumbed-down to lists. Math is a series of rules. We expect so little of children that we give them just the most basic of by-rote teaching.

I like to explain this idea to others by using math as an example. Math instruction has largely degraded to teaching a student "...the seven steps you follow to do this problem," practicing it for a week, and then taking a test on Friday. The student might well get an "A" (even a monkey can learn to press seven buttons in the right sequence) *but learns nothing*. The seven steps are forgotten by the following week. Next week "... let's learn the six steps of the next problem to be solved." The system is happy – the child passes and will graduate – but we have created a student who is functionally math-illiterate.

At the risk of contradicting myself, because earlier I said frequent core standard changes hurt education, this is a case where the latest "next big thing" might actually become a good thing once we figure out how to implement it. I am not qualified to speak to the approach for other courses, but the new math core is intended to emphasize *understanding* more than *remembering*. It will take time to realize the potential of the new core – the bureaucratic rollout has been so mismanaged that it will take years to fix all the flaws. It will be a bloodbath for the first few years of implementation as children have to learn a whole different approach to school than they have ever experienced before. Many other parts of the system (destructive inclusion classes, expectations-sapping SPED accommodations, etc.) will counter and offset many of the gains hoped for with common core. But if we find the way to launch the new core successfully, despite the inept rollout and the lack of support and materials from the bureaucrats, the new core standards offer wonderful promise for children entering high school 5-6 years from now.

- *Weak teacher need: How to deliver diversified learning to a wide range of interests and abilities in a single large class*

People hear a lot today about class size, yet few understand why that is a very real issue that has a huge impact on educational quality, especially with all the bureaucratic mandates superimposed upon the classroom.

Over the years I have found that the grade average for a class of 20 children will be 10-12 points higher than for a class of 30 covering the same topics, with the same range of student abilities, and taught by the same teacher.

Consider some hard facts:

- Urban high school classes of 25-30 students are common today

- It is not possible to cover all the mandated core topics <u>and</u> provide any meaningful individualized instruction to all students. In a "small" class of just 25 students, if a teacher spends just two minutes of one-on-one with each student, there would be less than 5 minutes available for actual instruction time after attendance and collecting homework.

- In <u>most</u> of today's urban high school classrooms, there will be 10-20 or more students with IEPs, 504s, or ESL/ELL that require the teacher to spend 3-5 minutes each just to meet special education accommodations. This legally mandated special attention uses 30 - 50 minutes of the potential instructional time.

- In almost all classes today there is a wide range in effort, ability, and student needs in a single class. Teachers must be able to deliver a message tailored to a half dozen different learning styles (auditory, one-on-one, visual, analogy-based, etc.).

The significance of the above facts is that all classes, especially inclusion classes, severely limit the amount of general instructional time that is available in the class. I have several large classes with such a wide range of student needs and abilities that on some days I am able to provide as little as 15 minutes of actual instruction from a lesson plan calling for 45 minutes – <u>far short of what is required by the curriculum</u>.

(Note: This technically earns the title of "bad teacher" for me for failing to comply with all mandated requirements.)

Just a handful of inclusion students in a class will severely limit the amount of instruction that can be given to the class. Meanwhile, the core standards and syllabus demand that you cover 40-50 minutes worth of instruction. This is not a commentary on inclusion classes – math is math – <u>the two goals are mutually exclusive, yet the teacher is held accountable for both</u>. It is a lose-lose situation for the teacher and child.

- *Weak teacher need: How to engage students and instill pride*

At the risk of letting my passion for children and teaching show again, *there is absolutely no more important a goal for any teacher than to help children <u>earn</u> reasons for pride in themselves.* And nothing accomplishes that more that helping a child truly understand a subject and achieve his/her potential. The system treats all children as being the same, and as being "dumb." Nothing could be farther than the truth.

I have had the joy of teaching in a classically "disadvantaged" school for years. We draw from urban communities, highly ESL and SPED, where more than half qualify for free or reduced price meals. Most have been treated as though they were dumb for so long that they bought the lie. Multiple choice exams told them they were "wrong" without providing any feedback to see how close they actually were, and how easily they could move up a level. Rules-based teaching prevented them from learning to think.

And yet, these students are every bit as bright as when you and I were in school. *All they needed was someone to believe in them, care for them, and set expectations way <u>above</u> anything they had ever seen in their lives before.* Given so little as that – they thrive!

It is critical to emphasize the idea of <u>earned</u> pride. Children know and dismiss it when "...everyone gets a cupcake" for effort. There is no real pride when a child gets the same "trophy" just for trying or attending, that was given to the top performers. I have failed children by one point who have not earned (or even tried to earn) the passing grade. But I have come to school an hour early every day for weeks, and spent hours of my free time, to positively reinforce and help many other students <u>earn</u> needed points by doing their best to succeed.

No gifts, no do-overs – just earned pride.

Only once in the last ten years have I seen any training on so basic a concept as engaging children and developing <u>earned</u> pride. It is absolutely the best gift a teacher can ever give a child. It will get them to believe in themselves, up their effort to a whole new level, and change their lives.

Today there is a nationwide push, under the mantle of performance-based pay, to allow more observations of teachers. This has the potential to help mitigate the problem. These new plans will allow more frequent (with advance warning) observations, and some degree of unannounced (to-be-negotiated) observations. If the use of the observations is to help develop our teachers, then all will benefit.

Weak teachers need help, but the present system ensures that they cannot get that help.

Good teachers – the silent majority now hiding in the corner (75%)

One of the most intriguing (and absolutely spot-on) studies[95] of what makes great teachers found only two common factors -- a passion to teach, and a knack for engaging children. There was nothing else common to the best teachers they studied. Degrees earned, years of experience, PDPs earned, intelligence, conferences attended, class sizes, or any other standard metric were all found to have little value in predicting great teachers.

Kids immediately respond when teachers have the two characteristics of passion and engaging. It is impossible to overstate this fact. A "mediocre" teacher (in terms of subject knowledge) who has an obvious passion for what he/she does and the ability to excite the children will <u>always</u> do better than a superbly talented teacher who cannot connect with the kids. The reason is not obvious to those outside of the classroom:

The number one function of any teacher is to enable a child to gain <u>earned</u> pride by making the course something worthy of being mastered. Only then can the teacher

---

[95] *The Moral Life of Schools*, Jackson, Boostrom and Hansen

hope to succeed in teaching the material. Only the most self-motivated students are exceptions to this rule.

This is the biggest failure of today's teachers, and one that must be totally laid at our feet. After a decade of being beaten up by parents, career DoE bureaucrats, and legislators, many teachers have simply given up. Even those teachers who once were exceptional at engaging students, no longer have that passion or skill. The fire is gone, and without it they cannot break through to engage the students. The students have lost the number one motivation for them to respond to teaching.

Previously good teachers who give up send entirely a different message to the students. I repeat two student comments that nailed it:

"Teachers don't like to teach and tend to block a lot of things out."[96]

"Fire the teachers that don't want to be here."[97]

The second comment, above, is especially telling. The student didn't say fire the "bad" teachers, or the "mean" teachers. He showed remarkable insight by recognizing teachers just going through the motions.

When a high school teacher projects an image of not caring, two-thirds of the students in an urban school class lose the possibility of mastery for the subject.

The reason for this attitude, which permeates schools today, is the "bunker mentality" of most teachers. For years teachers have been the target of parents, administrators, bureaucrats, legislators, (and news commentators). They have been painted as the problem for all the many problems in education.

A job that once was seen as honorable and good, has now been degraded to be the whipping boy for every educational ill – most of which are completely out of the control of any teacher. They are blamed for conditions they cannot change, and work in an environment of cronyism and poor leadership. All the pride has been sucked out of being a teacher, and the unfairness of most of the charges has created an atmosphere of anger that is unhealthy for all concerned.

---

[96] Mark, Student Survey 2013
[97] Adriel, Student Survey 2013

What we have today is the bunker mentality well known by any war veteran. Yet, ironically, at a time in our history when Americans have finally learned to separate the "soldier" from "…the war they do not like," we have been unable to separate the "teacher" from the "…educational system we do not like." During the Vietnam War we spat on soldiers, blaming 18 or 19-year-old children for a war mandated from Washington. It crushed the spirit of a generation of Vietnam veterans. (Most of us who served in Vietnam are very joyful to see the difference today – when veterans serving in Iraq or Afghanistan can still be honored for their service, even from those who abhor those wars.)

I don't suppose there's any chance they've changed their minds, and are here to help us this time?

Why the reference to Vietnam? It is because the obvious syllogism is the best way I can find to describe what has happened to the attitude of today's teachers over the past decade: *Teacher is to education, as soldier is to Vietnam War.*

We have a generation of Vietnam veterans paying the emotional price for the way they were treated when they returned. The emotional impact of that reception is staggering in the intensity of its impact.

Today we have a new generation of teachers starting to act the exact same way. They withdraw. They go through the motions. They become defensive. They give up. They go out of their way to avoid conflict with administration or parents. They follow the rules, even when the new bureaucratic rules make no sense. Inside there is anger and resentment at what is occurring, but outside is silence. In World War I this was called a "bunker mentality," the withdrawal of veterans hunkered down in the corner of a bunker during days of constant attack.

> *"More than 30 years after the end of the war in Vietnam, the effect of lingering stress on Americans who fought there continues to cause stress among researchers. A new study finds that almost 19 percent of the more than three million U.S. troops who served in Vietnam returned with post-traumatic stress disorder (PTSD). It's a condition that left them with invasive memories, nightmares, loss of concentration, feelings of guilt, irritability and, in some cases, major depression. More than ten years after the war, 10 percent of them still could not leave the war behind."* [98]

This is where most teachers in urban high schools are today. These high schools are failing at an alarming rate due to the many factors outlined in this book, yet the target for blame is laid almost solely, and unfairly, at the feet of teachers.

Being blamed, unfairly, for things out of your control has an impact on everything you do. I still remember vividly a summer day in 1969 or 1970. I had just returned from a tour in Vietnam a months earlier. I was in uniform, driving a car in New Haven, Connecticut. The summer day was beautiful. The Beach Boys were playing on the radio. It felt good to be home. I pulled up at a stop light, and smiled when I saw a beautiful blond in the car next to me, windows open, obviously listening to the same Beach Boys tune. Then she turned and saw me. First she smiled, and then she noticed my uniform. Her face twisted into hate and anger. She saluted me with 20% of her left hand, and spat at my car, before pulling away as the light changed. You see, my uniform instantly labelled me as a baby killer and barbarian. It didn't matter that I was a kid, and was just trying to serve my country. Decades later that girl is still etched in my memories. In five seconds she sucked all the pride out of serving, and made it an ugly thing. Her reaction was common at that time.

Today, we suck the pride out of teaching, and make it an ugly thing. Then we seem surprised at the impact it has on teacher attitudes.

---

[98] *Mental Casualties of Vietnam War Persist*, Harvard Gazette, August 2006

Teachers are to blame for having an attitude of withdrawal, defensiveness, and anger. But, as with the street children in Dickens' London who stole because of famine and disease, we might want to understand why this occurs before we go fire all the teachers.

The result – Cheating, cutting corners, and dumbed-down teaching

The dreadful impact of a host of factors outside the control of teachers is the degree to which we end up dumbing down our teaching. The whole system is so focused on <u>endless rules and mandates requiring that we find a way to pass and graduate children, <i>regardless</i> of effort or ability</u>. We teach by steps rather than by understanding. Parents attack the teacher for bad grades rather than encourage their own children. Bureaucrats impose silliness on the classrooms. Administrators take care of their friends with blatant cronyism rather than help lead us out of the mess.

And Margery Eagan[99] gets on her daily talk show and tells her listeners to "…just shoot all the teachers…" because teachers are ruining the world. (Yes, like the blond in New Haven back in '69, hearing that from someone I respect on so many other topics, does hurt.)

Teachers give up and start to do what they are told to do by the administrators, parents, and bureaucrats – pass the children first, and worry about actually teaching at another time. Classroom instruction is centered on getting children to memorize a series of steps (or dates, words, etc.) for a single week so that the student can spit them back at the end of the week for a test. There is less and less emphasis on getting the children to reason, and to understand the concepts that underlie those steps.

One of the most deadly results of teachers caving in to a bad system is evidenced in the many teacher cheating scandals reported over the past two years. The Washington Post[100] reported that 37 states have had major cheating scandals by teachers and administrators. The Post called the 37 "the tip of the iceberg," yet the Post didn't even have a clue how very much *worse* the actual is, compared to the relatively few that have been reported.

I suspect (with absolutely no possible source of "hard" proof possible) that <u>almost all</u> schools have had administrators or teachers cheat on <u>every</u> standardized test.

---

[99] Boston talk show host, WTKK-FM Boston, show discontinued 2012
[100] *Atlanta Test cheating: Tip of the iceberg?*, Washington Post April 2013

Consider the following interrelated facts:

1. More than 90% of all children who fail standardized tests fail by just one question.

2. Most "average-sized" schools can avoid relegation to a lower state level, and all the risks and sanctions associated by that, by having less than ten (repeat, less than 10!) student standardized test scores go up just that one point from "fail" to "pass."

3. All teachers see the results for prior years, and have a good idea of the students in their class who are likely to fail.

4. *If a teacher or administrator simply changes one bad answer on each of ten student tests within a school, where the students can easily be pre-identified as at risk, the "rewards" to the school are huge.*

Now before anyone misunderstands the conclusion I am about to draw, please understand that I would like any teacher or administrator who cheats, no matter what the motive or incentive, to be fired and banned from teaching for life. What cheaters are doing to harm our children is reprehensible. I have no patience or forgiveness for such cheating.

But, I also know we have to look at the systemic incentives to cheat, just as we must look at the cheaters themselves.

I believe that almost every school in the country (perhaps every school) has at least one incident of teacher/administrator cheating on every standardized test. Yes, that means approaching 100%. Just one weak teacher who is worried about being evaluated based upon low scores the prior year, almost guarantees a multiple-choice answer will be erased and corrected, or a question's topic will be "mentioned" between sessions of a multiple-day test.

As an example, any teacher easily could influence 5-6 points on every Massachusetts MCAS math test if they wanted, potentially even without knowing they are doing it. Multiple choice questions cannot be changed without an "Atlanta-caliber" scandal, but open response answers (half the MCAS math) are far easier to change. MCAS math is a two-day test. Roughly ten questions on day one are open ended – those answers (and all their supporting work) from day one are easily visible in the answer book when the students take day two. So, on the afternoon of day one, or on the morning of day two (before session two of the test begins), a teacher could discuss the day-one open response questions that are still easily accessible in the answer book the student will get back on day two. No test proctor, no matter how vigilant, would ever notice or catch that a student was changing a prior day's answer. And since MCAS test proctors are not allowed to look at the actual test, a teacher might not know that was an MCAS question the students were discussing – just that they wanted to review a topic between test sessions.

Atlanta was the anomaly, along with 37 others, of school-wide cheating on a major scale. Small-scale cheating, enough to change just a handful of failures to passing and "save" the school (or the teacher/administrator job), occurs every day.

Don't shoot the messenger. It is what it is.

Once again, we can fix this. Easily. The answer to raising standardized test scores is not what we have tried to date. It is not cheating, not test-taking strategies, not special test preparation classes, and not dumbed-down tests. It is simply letting the teachers teach the original material better.

The bottom line: We have created a system where children can get an "Easy A" without having to actually understand anything, or remember anything past next Friday. We have teachers going through the motions – defensive and angry after being blamed for everything wrong in education.

If we cannot reverse this, and get teachers back to using their passion for teaching and engaging students, then two thirds of the children in urban schools will fail high school – failing despite an "all A" report card.

(Chapter 25)
Systemic Failure #7: The Untouchables – Parents, and Teacher Unions

So far this book has antagonized Departments of Education, career bureaucrats, principals, superintendents, PDP content developers, the clique, textbook publishers, special education paraprofessionals, and those few teachers in the "screamers and nasties" category. We might as well go for the full house, and speak about parents and teacher unions.

The problem with discussing the contribution of these two groups to systemic failures in education is that they are untouchable in any practical manner. It is hard to see what can be done to directly (there are indirect options) influence the numerical minority of urban high school parents whose actions (or inaction) hurt the education of their own children. And the difficulties with changing union approaches to education are well known, and are a topic that could fill three more books.

Parents – Missing in Action

> There are tons of great parents out there. Even in the weakest classes in the most disadvantaged urban high schools, three-quarters of the parents are fully supportive and encourage their children. I have had the pleasure of working with many who are the reason for their child's success, and the best ally a teacher could ever have. After being in a classroom enough years, teachers develop an uncanny sense of being able to spot children whose parents clearly have had a great role on their lives. No, it is not manners, nor language, nor "respect" that gives these children away as having great parents. It is the child's expectations and work ethic. I can spot from across the room, through a child's eyes, parents I would instantly respect and like if they were my neighbors.
>
> > *But not all parents are in that class. Carol L. very accurately describes a growing numerical minority of urban high school parents that have become no-show parents in their children's education. It is one of the most frustrating and discouraging facts for teachers that the parents of the students who most need help are the ones that are least involved in their child's education. Carol L. is a retired high school English teacher in Pennsylvania.*

> **(Carol L.) A minority of parents – not there when we need them most**
>
> Teaching high school English for thirty-two years before retiring provides strong insights regarding education. First I must be clear: I loved the craft of teaching. I looked forward to interaction with the students, I relished their triumph when they met with success, and, most important, I discovered that while kids might never verbalize it, they wanted structure and discipline. The problem I found most discouraging rested squarely with the minority of parents who ignored the latter. I believe, unfortunately, the number of parents falling into that category today has increased dramatically.
>
> Too often teachers must deal with the ever-present reminder that society as a whole, and parents in particular, believe they are experts in the education process, simply because they spent thirteen years in the system. Add to that mistaken perception the fact that so many parents live their lives vicariously through their kids. Finally factor in the sense of entitlement that is growing exponentially, and the stage is set. Rather than working with the teacher to help the child, the parent aligns himself with the child against the teacher.
>
> When all parents finally accept the idea that teachers and parents should and must work together, and that kids are just that – adolescents who rarely think beyond the ringing of the next bell – then the vital structure and discipline so necessary for truly successful students will fall into place.

Many teachers dread parent-teacher night, because of what they expect to occur from some parents. I still remember very clearly the one time in school I got closest to taking an action that would have had me fired or arrested. I had a student who was really struggling at the start of the year. "Myrtle" failed term one, and there was every indication she would fail the year. Yet, it was clear this was a bright student who simply had lost all confidence in her abilities. I worked with her closely, teamed her in each class with another student who could help, and slowly we found the gaps in her approach and reversed them. In term two she passed, just barely with a D-minus as I recall. By term three, Myrtle was approaching a B and visibly growing in confidence and enthusiasm. So I asked her parents to come in to parent-teacher night so that they could hear about her performance, share the pride in what their daughter had accomplished, and so we could plan some follow-up tutoring or extra help to help her continue that path.

On parent-teacher night, Myrtle's mother did attend. She was one of the last to arrive, and staggered through the door with disheveled clothes and the obvious smell of alcohol on her breath. She looked at me as she approached the table and called out, *"Okay, what has the little shit done now?"* I am still not sure today how I avoided a reaction that would have had me thrown out of school (or jailed) for what I wanted to say to that "parent." All the "daddy juices" in me recoiled at a parent viewing their own child that way. Somehow I kept it civil, but I ended the evening with an even deeper appreciation of what Myrtle had accomplished, despite being thought of that way at home.

Is Myrtle's mom typical? Thankfully, of course not. This is the extreme case where the lack of caring was also matched by an extreme personality archetype that is easy to spot and ridicule. *But if you ask "…are parents who care so little (like this one, but without the alcohol) common?" the answer is a very disturbing "absolutely yes."* For the students in these urban communities that I serve, I believe that up to one quarter of all parents are just a small cut above Myrtle's mom – a more polished version of parents who simply don't care.

Don't shoot the messenger. Once again, it is what it is.

For those outside the classroom, it is impossible to overstate how important parents are to a child's success. A study by the UK's Royal Economic Society has the most dramatic and powerful research finding I have ever seen published, estimating that <u>parents were five times more important than a teacher</u> to a student's success.

> *"A study by the Royal Economic Society, to be presented this week, finds that parental effect on test results is five times that of teachers' influence. This comes in the wake of warnings by Sir Michael Wilshaw last week that teachers were unable to properly do their own jobs because parents were expecting them to cover their own parenting skill shortfalls and to become surrogate family for the students."* [101]

The above paragraph is the most accurate and spot-on assessment I have ever seen, outside of the teacher lounge, of the view all teachers have of trying to educate a child without parental support. I wish we could tattoo it on the left arms of all those parents of struggling

---

[101] *Parents, Not Teachers, Key to Education*, UK Royal Economic Society, March 2012

students who never responded to parent-teacher conference requests. (The tattoo on the right arm would be that all children must be able to fail before they will be able to succeed.) It is a losing battle. The last line of that assessment is especially powerful – speaking to the change from co-responsibility for a child's education (teacher, parent, and child) to sole responsibility of the teacher.

Shifting view of expectations for our children, and who we hold accountable for student performance and effort.

A 1994 Educating for Diversity study provides important insights into reasons other than "not caring" for lack of parental participation, but also comes to the same conclusion about the powerful impact a parent has on a child's education.

> "The institutional perspective holds that children who do not succeed in school have parents who do not get involved in school activities or support school goals at home. Recent research emphasizes the importance of parent involvement in promoting school success." [102]

A Center for Public Education[103] report lists the impact of good parenting on education, including better test scores, improved attendance, and better social skills. Meanwhile, Henderson and Berla had the following impressive list[104] of benefits of good parenting:

- "Children tend to achieve more, regardless of ethnic or racial background, socioeconomic status, or parents' education level.
- Children generally achieve better grades, test scores, and attendance.

---

[102] *Why some parents don't come to school*, Educating for Diversity, May 1994
[103] *How parental involvement affects student performance*, Center for Public Education, Aug 2011
[104] *The Benefits of Parent Involvement*, Education.com, original publication date unclear

- *Children consistently complete their homework.*
- *Children have better self-esteem, are more self-disciplined, and show higher aspirations and motivation toward school.*
- *Children's positive attitude about school often results in improved behavior in school and less suspension for disciplinary reasons.*
- *Fewer children are being placed in special education and remedial classes.*
- *Children from diverse cultural backgrounds tend to do better when parents and professionals work together to bridge the gap between the culture at home and the culture in school.*
- *Junior high and high school students whose parents remain involved usually make better transitions and are less likely to drop out of school."*

Despite the importance of parents, a large minority of parents in urban schools appear to take little or no interest in their children's education. Whether it is the 4500 children in Boston Public Schools that BPS predicts are at risk of not graduating due to truancy, or the US Census report that 40% of parents admit they do not attend parent-teacher or similar conferences, or the student survey that 70% of the parents don't care, or the parent at my parent-teacher night who asked "...what has the little shit done now?" – the result is the same. The children suffer.

And even some who do show up – with the misguided thought that they are "helping" their child by getting IEP provisions that lessen the burdens on graduating – only hurt their child in the long run.

And there is absolutely nothing a teacher can do about it.

The parent issue is unsolvable. We cannot force parents to care or attend. Many, as in the Educating for Diversity study, have reasons other than "not caring" for their lack of attendance. Regardless of reason, the negative impact is staggering. It is so endemic and frustrating that as silly a "solution" as trying to arrest parents of truant children has been considered. (Detroit schools[105] actually looked at making it a misdemeanor crime, three days jail, if a parent missed a parent-teacher conference!)

However, there are two indirect actions that we must take that will help overcome the negative impact of no-show parents – revamping special education accommodations, and allowing children to fail. Both are part of the solutions offered in the final chapter of this book.

---

[105] *No-show parents could face jail time*, CNN, July 2010

Unions – too busy being PACs to care about education

Any responsible analysis of the role of teacher unions on education would fill a half dozen more books like this one. Most of the issues are well known and actively covered – from both sides – in the national media.

Most teachers now find that unions are becoming less and less relevant, and less and less useful, to their members. Instead, all the negative impacts that teachers see unions have on education are becoming more important to teachers than the few remaining positives.

> [Author's note: There might be a very encouraging change occurring in the Massachusetts Teacher Union (MTA) since the following passage was written for the 1st edition of *Lifting the Curtain*. In the spring of 2014, new MTA leadership seems to have made a strong change in direction. There is a clear focus on education again (at least as shown in the emails) and an apparent genuine concern for listening to teacher concerns. Even during the 2014 elections there was far less PAC activity than before. Too early to tell, but a *very* encouraging sign!]

I am a member of the Massachusetts Teacher Union (MTA). I get inundated with emails from them – almost every email for political action requests. Vote for candidate X, call your congressman for bill Y, attend fundraiser Z, read a whitepaper on why we need more money for schools. Oh, and every few months, I get an email with something actually about education. I tabulated 10 months of emails from the MTA back, and found 81% were dedicated to PAC issues. The remaining 19% had a plain-vanilla educational topic that sounded as though it was the result of someone asking "…please see if you can find something about schools to send out. We're overdue."

The midyear summary in 2013 by the Massachusetts Teachers Association (MTA) cited their number one accomplishment for the year as electing their favored candidates. The same email dismissed the crucial topic of new teacher evaluation methods as "…something we will be interested in watching…."

Our local union leadership finds that the MTA is useless on most of the issues for which we need help. We are now actively investigating whether affiliation with a non-NEA union would help us try to fix education – the one remaining area where a teacher's union could help us. New legislation has significantly eroded any role unions have in determining member health care, so the number one past usefulness of teacher unions is gone. Teachers cannot strike, so the number two reason for a union does not exist. I was part of a teacher "job action" where our only recourse to challenge a major issue was to come to school early and assemble outside the front door so we could be "seen" by parents who dropped off their children, in hopes the parents would put pressure on the school committee. We were not allowed to have signs or handouts. We were not allowed to send anything out to the parents.

Sixty teachers standing in the snow drinking coffee – what an exercise in union futility.

Even in negotiations, members of the "clique" often become officers in the union to ensure that their friends in administration are well aware of any union plans and negotiating positions. In Massachusetts, teachers recently went through a very significant change in healthcare benefits coverage that involved many months of negotiations. In several of the schools I researched, teachers specifically pointed out instances where having a member of the clique on the union leadership committee meant that the administration was "…remarkably aware and prepared" for union efforts, and very effectively outmaneuvered or blindsided the union negotiators. All it needed was a member of the clique who was more interested in being rewarded with a paid position as basketball coach or senior class advisor than in the duties and trust of their union officer position.

So what is left? We have our union dues doing little more than support a political action committee that represents candidates and views not shared by a significant part (perhaps a majority) of current teachers. We pay for membership that can (and will) do little for any meaningful teacher issue. And the unions block many of the changes outlined in this book that most teachers beg the system to make. One teacher said it well:

"Why not just quit the union? I'd get an $800 raise instead of funding a bunch of election candidates I'd never vote for?"

Many teachers share that view. For many teachers the only strong reason to remain in a union is their deep distrust of administrations, and the need to have a collective reply to excessive abuse and cronyism. It is no surprise, therefore, that teacher union membership nationwide is dropping precipitously. Some unions have dissolved. Other teacher unions, like ours, are actively investigating whether affiliation with a national union other than NEA might be more beneficial.

The decline is accelerating:

> *"Things are looking grim for teachers unions. The National Education Association (NEA) membership has declined by more than 100,000 since 2010, and the union's own projections indicate that within two more years it could have lost a total of 308,000 full-time teachers and other workers. This would represent a 16% drop in membership from 2010."*[106]

It does not have to be this way! Teachers would sign up in droves to a union dedicated to helping fix education for our children. But our only choice at present is a national and state union that is focused solely on "more money" as the answer to everything: getting more money from union member dues…using more money for lavish union leader salaries and perks…spending more money on bankrolling political candidates…demanding more money from taxpayers for programs that have not worked, and will not work.

Instead, give us a union that fights to get summer school expanded to be a meaningful replacement for a failed year. Support us in eliminating the destructive and expectations-sapping SPED accommodation of "unlimited retests." Promote limited liability so that a teacher trying to break up a fight is not treated like a pedophile when he/she incidentally touches a child while trying to prevent serious injuries. Actively lobby to allow children to fail so that they (and their parents) will immediately hit the "reset button" and start to succeed. Help fight for ways to help new and struggling teachers improve.

Stop being a fulltime PAC, and notice that the word "education" is in your name.

Sadly, the unions are a no-show for helping solve the systemic problems in education, and are rapidly being pushed to the sidelines as a NOP (pronounced "no op") – the computer term for an instruction that does nothing except occupy a place in the program.

---

[106] *NEA membership decline heralds loss of power and influence*, Education News, July 2012

(Chapter 26)
Systemic Failure #8: Rewards unrelated to performance

The final systemic failure in education is that the vital cause-and-effect relationship between an employee's rewards, and their performance, does not exist for teachers. Worse, the only significant differentiators in pay between two teachers in the same position is that one might be receiving special assignments (coaching, club leaders, class advisors, paid conference attendance, etc.) because of blatant cronyism in administration's assignment of those duties.

There is little challenge to the concept in commercial businesses that there must be a strong tie between rewards and performance in order to incent excellence. But this has long been an issue in education. Having a teacher and administrator pay structure unrelated to performance actually made some sense back in the first half of the 1900s, but little has changed since then even though the conditions that warranted them have changed.

> *"Teacher compensation has long been based solely on individual development criteria such as length of service and level of education attained. These criteria were initially aimed at preventing pay inequity between men and women prevalent until the 1940s. These criteria also helped to protect teachers against subjective administrators, and to give incentives to younger teachers to stay in the classroom (Firestone 1995). Recently, this traditional compensation system has been criticized as there are weak relationships among teacher skills, teacher development, student performance, and teacher compensation."*[107]

We are at an important transition point for education with the rollout in all geographies of a new performance evaluation system that offers much promise if it allows pay based upon merit, is not based only upon years as a teacher, and is not based upon whether or not you are a member of the clique.

The bottom line is that teacher motivation for excellence <u>today</u> must come from within the teacher – it has nothing to do with rewards in the current system.

Crony Perks

The fact that the <u>only</u> source of variable pay for teachers is not tied to performance or qualifications, but rather is based largely upon

---
[107] *What do we know about teacher pay-for-performance.* KSBE, November 2010

cronyism, undermines any possibility that the rewards play a part in teacher performance. Only two things matter in determining the salary of a teacher – how long have you been teaching, and does the principal (or in schools like mine, the superintendent) like you. Earlier in this book ("Systemic Failure #2) the degree of cronyism in selection of teachers to get the annual paid positions was detailed. Several summary points are repeated from that discussion:

- 60% of teachers surveyed found strong cronyism and unfairness in the award of positions.

- 81% of teachers in an Education News survey <u>expected</u> "abuse" by administrations

- Principals (or superintendents) have virtually unchecked and unchallenged authority to make appointments, with no accountability for their choices, and no requirement to justify any appointments.

- A typical school principal (or superintendent) hands out 30-50 paid positions each year, with combined annual extra pay of $250,000 to $400,000.

- Typical extra-pay appoints are worth $2,000 to $7,500 per year in additional pay

- In many geographies this extra pay counts towards pension calculations

- The "clique" is especially focused on channeling extra-pay appointments to their members in the final three years before retirement because of the huge impact that can have on their retirement pay.

A high priority must be placed upon having such appointments start being based upon qualifications, not cronyism. It is needed for fairness, integrity, and restoring faith in all those administrators (60% to 81% seen by teachers as abusing their powers, depending upon survey cited) who have lost the confidence of their teachers.

Evaluations

The role of evaluations might finally be changing. It is too soon to tell, but evaluations that might actually mean something are starting to appear in school districts. Up to now, it is unclear than any of the millions of teacher evaluations done each year have any value to anyone other than "checking the box." They do not influence pay, only <u>very</u> rarely can result in a teacher being fired, are accomplished under carefully controlled conditions that do not reflect the teacher's usual approach, and do not result in training actions for weaker teachers. They are little more than an annual paperwork exercise that gets filed away and forgotten.

In many schools, the annual evaluation is based upon a single "observation" where the teacher must be warned well in advance so that he/she has plenty of time to prepare a "special" instruction plan, and time to prepare and warn the students in the class.

Even Simon Legree[108] can look like a saint for one hour a year, given enough advance warning.

Worse, under many union contracts, principals and administrators are forbidden to do any spontaneous observations of teachers. There is an unwritten rule in every school that "…what happens in the classroom stays in the classroom."

The result is that to date, it is nearly impossible to fire a bad tenured teacher other than for non-instructional reasons (stealing, substance abuse, sexual misconduct, etc.). If a teacher cracks a coarse joke, he/she can be fired for offending a student or parent. But if that same teacher (using math as the stalking horse) cannot add two plus two and get it consistently right, he/she still can teach addition to our children forever.

The new evaluation systems being rolled out in many districts have the potential to help here. They tend to increase the number of formal (pre-warned) evaluations, and also add some degree of unannounced observations. Most teachers hope they will be used to identify and <u>help</u> the weaker teachers, and to fire the 5% we all know who are just down the hall from us. But we all doubt that will happen. One teacher put it especially well: "A bad evaluation is all well and good, but just wait for the first grievance when they try to use it to fire someone."

---

[108] *Uncle Tom's Cabin*, Harriett Stowe, (a cruel slave owner)

Merit Pay

One thing is sadly unclear at this point – will the new evaluation system have any positive impact on merit pay? If the same crony-focused principal does an evaluation that determines who gets merit pay, it will just be "same stuff, different day." The jury is still out on this one.

Oh, I almost forgot in all the fun of our weekly Principal's BFF golf match -- I am selecting the three of you for the top award in the new merit pay system.

The real problem with teacher merit pay is that merit cannot be quantified with any clear statistical measure, and relies almost entirely on the subjective assessment of the person doing the evaluation. Thus, having faith in the fairness and integrity of both the evaluator and the process is crucial. That faith simply does not exist in schools today.

This is a case where the NEA took enough of a break from being a fulltime PAC to actually look at an educational issue, and got it right:

> *"Also, in the past, they [the top teachers] have been identified through fuzzy criteria."*
>
> *Timothy Dedman, policy analyst in the teacher quality department of the National Education Association (NEA), said that unless certain criteria are met, the NEA opposes merit pay. "We're afraid it could be used to discriminate," Dedman said. "Administrators could look at*

incidents that had nothing to do with performance [in determining salary increases]." [109]

The above is NEAspeak for "…merit pay means no crony left behind."

Merit pay tied to standard test results – a horrible idea that sounds great on the surface

One recurring idea is to partially tie performance to standardized test scores. That is a very attractive concept, on the surface, and appears to take a lot of the subjectivity and fairness issues off the table. But, in truth, the unintended consequences of such a plan would be as dysfunctional as so many other failed bureaucratic DoE initiatives described throughout this book. Why criticize a "pay-based-upon-standardized-test-results" approach? Simple – *test results depend upon what classes the principal assigns (standard, CP, honors…) – the same principal who bases all other assignments on cronyism!*

A simple fact: if a teacher gets all honors classes, the "passing rate" is going to be significantly higher than if that same teacher was assigned to standard classes. It is not even close. If merit pay is tied to state test results, a teacher must be out of his mind, and also be willing to work for a lot less, to volunteer to teach urban standard-level classes. The "luck of the draw" on what classes you got would have a huge impact upon your "merit" pay, and would swamp any consideration of how good or bad you were as a teacher.

But it is far from "luck" that determines choice assignments in schools, such as teaching CP and Honors classes. The same system of cronyism that assigns coaches and club heads at $4,000 per position is the one that determines who gets the fun (CP and Honors) classes, and who gets the grind (standard) classes. Once again, the systemic failure of the current system ensures unfairness, and that "merit Pay" is really is just another perk handed out by the principal to his/her cronies.

Consider math (again, going with the one subject I have some qualifications to discuss). In my school I have always requested, and was assigned, standard-level classes with mostly struggling students. I would like to believe that the assignment was based on my passion for getting the weaker students to earn success and really start to

---

[109] *Pay for Performance: What are the Issues*, Education World, date unclear (June 2013?)

understand math. But the real reason was that even my standard classes have always outperformed the school's CP and honors classes on standardized state tests, and so that helped us keep from slipping down a level based upon test scores. When my "standard" and CP students were passing MCAS (the Massachusetts standardized test) at a 99% passing rate, compared to 88% for the school as a whole, it was a no-brainer for the school – any increase in MCAS passing rates kept us away from dreaded Level Two or Level Three. The school was happy assigning me to weaker classes, and I was equally happy to work with the children I most love to help.

But now, look at this in the context of merit pay tied to MCAS scores. No teacher in their right mind would want to teach standard classes if CP or Honors classes are available. (Okay, no one ever accused me of being in my right mind.) The diversity of students in large standard classes, often the dysfunctional inclusion classes, makes it nearly impossible to keep up with the state DOE curriculum standards. The special education, no-show parent, inclusion, and student attitude issues described earlier are all centered in these standard classes. Student results will be much less than for a CP or honors class, so the chance for merit pay based upon such scores is highly unlikely – *regardless of your qualifications as a teacher.*

The bottom line: With the rest of the unresolved systemic failures in education, merit pay is an idea that is dead on arrival, and will not work. There is far too much distrust in the current system, and far too many examples of abuse and excesses, for merit pay to work. But there is a second message here that lies beneath the surface – fixing the other systemic failures that destroy trust and integrity in the system will allow merit pay to work. It's a package deal to fix education – no single Band-Aid will work.

Practical Solutions

(Chapter 27)
The solution – Surprise! There is one, and it is not more money!

When I started researching this book three years ago, I was afraid that the problems facing education were not solvable. So many of them are based upon things we cannot effectively control or change – bureaucracy, legislators, parents – that I feared the problems were due to a social movement that has no possibility of reversal. The view from the teacher's union was always the same simplistic answer – more money, lots more money. But I know that was a failed approach for two reasons. First, most of the answers I *did* see involved no need for more funds, and often meant <u>less</u> funding. Second, it only takes a brief look at my tax bills to know that more taxes cannot be justified as simple answers to problems that are far from simple. "More money" simply lets unqualified career DoE bureaucrats guard their positions while doing little for the systemic issues in urban high school education.

Finding answers looked bad. Then it got worse.

Every time I found a "solution" to one issue, I found something else in the system that would cancel it out. As an example, even a "perfect" merit pay answer would fail if the same principals and their cronies were in charge of the evaluations. I knew we had to allow children to fail before they could start succeeding, but also know DoEs would punish teachers for each failure. I knew we had to raise the expectations of children, even when some parents would not even get them on the bus to go to school, and when SPED accommodations sapped any expectations by allowing endless retests, and A's for doing just half of the work. I wasted a lot of time trying to figure out solutions for things that cannot be changed in any practical, achievable way – legislators, bureaucrats, the growing minority of no-show parents, and unions.

Finally, I realized that there really <u>was</u> a set of changes that could work. They met the test of being both practical and achievable. It only came together when I made a list of the overriding principles that must guide making education changes. These are the "givens" that are critical to understand when assessing the individual recommendations.

If a reader finds an error with these fundamentals, then the recommendations which follow will fall apart.

The fundamental pillars of change for education:

- **We cannot depend upon any change in major social structures – unions, legislators, bureaucracy, and no-show parents.** It is pure silliness to expect initiatives – such as term limits, reduced bureaucracies, or Detroit's inane proposal to jail no-show parents – to be enacted in our lifetimes. And it is our children's lifetimes we are betting. Should these change in the future, it will be even better. But any recommendations that depend upon parents, bureaucrats or legislators changing, are a waste of planning effort.

- **We must fix trust and integrity issues within the school walls.** Without faith in the integrity of the way schools are managed, teachers are evaluated, and extra-pay jobs appointed, then we have no chance of successfully making many of the initiatives work. A teacher who has faith in the system will crawl through ground glass to help a struggling student excel – it's in our blood. But without that faith, it is hard to maintain the spirit and energy it takes today to focus on engaging the children through all the anger about the unfairness and cronyism in the system. This "faith in the system" issue has *huge* indirect impact on teacher attitudes and their effectiveness in the classroom.

- **We must let children fail.** All else falls apart without this. It will be a bloodbath in most urban schools for just <u>one</u> term of the first school year when this goes into effect, but it is the only way for a self-correction in student and parent attitudes.

- **Teacher union issues are self-correcting**. The path the teacher unions are on has made them less and less relevant to the teachers, and less and less effective in helping or hurting education. Unless unions choose on their own to become less of a PAC and more of an active participant in helping fix education, they will slowly melt away. *The only positive reason to remain in a teacher's union in 2015 is to provide a weak counter to the abuse of cronyism by administrators.*

- **No Band-Aid works – we need to do all of these!** "Answers" to education for the past twenty years have been Band-Aids that gave zero attention to the long-term, unintended consequences of their enactment, and gave zero attention to how one "solution" might impact another. The recommendations must all (repeat – all!) be enacted, or we will make no real progress.

- **This really can be fixed, and would dramatically improve education nationwide within just <u>one</u> year of enactment.** It just takes courage!

- **Expect strong opposition from bureaucrats, legislators, many principals, and some parents** – the vested interests will fight these changes. Education, as it is today, is their cash cow – they highly profit from the current disarray. Cronyistic principals will not give up easily their ability to benefit themselves and their friends. Career DoE bureaucrats guard their lifetime jobs, and are used to being unchallenged as to whether their "education initiatives" have had any value at all. Many legislators cannot see behind the curtain to understand that well-meaning programs (inclusion, special education accommodations, and punishing schools if children fail) have actually been a disaster for education. And, a numerical minority of parents will still fight to get their child a free ride through high school.

Here are the specific recommendations, <u>not</u> in any priority order. It must be emphasized that they all work together – deleting any one of them will harm the effectiveness of several others.

- Teacher Training Committee
- Four-week Summer School
- Principal Qualifications
- School Appointments Board
- Elimination of Inclusion Classes
- Make-up days for absences or truancy
- Merit Pay Board
- Special Education Accommodations
- Student Failing Grades
- Focused PDPs
- Limited "in-context" liability for teachers

Teacher Training Committee

Overview: A committee to effectively help weaker teachers without posing a risk to the teacher being helped

Benefit: Strengthen the performance of weak teachers.

Opposition: Colleges, PDP developers, bureaucrats

Cost: Trivial – approximately the combined annual cost of an extra-pay position for a soccer coach.

Savings: Significantly reduced PDP expenditures and outside reimbursed training courses

Discussion: Every school should name a teacher training committee of 4-5 senior, well-qualified teachers. Members would be named only by the teachers (perhaps recommendations or applications, and a vote), would *not* report findings to administration, and would receive only a nominal stipend (perhaps $1,000 per year and/or comp time and/or PDP credits). The committee members would observe teachers in classes, with emphasis on those who would appear to most benefit from improving teaching methodologies based upon recommendations from department heads and other teachers. Observations would be both announced and unannounced. The teacher being observed would not be required to accept or enact any recommended changes, and no file copy of the recommendations would be retained other than by the teacher being helped.

An indirect benefit of this approach would be minimizing the need (and cost) for PDP-based training or outside training courses.

Four-week Summer School

Overview: Convert summer school from a farce to a meaningful vehicle to replace a year's failure.

Benefit: Create a summer school that is a worthy replacement for a failed year. Improve student performance significantly.

Opposition: Students, a small minority of parents.

Cost: Trivial, to none. Summer school is paid for by students and the increased tuition fee will cover the increased expenses

Savings: None

Discussion: Summer school would be expanded to a four-week session, with each day being 8:00 to 2:00 with a half hour for lunch. A maximum of two absences would be allowed, whether excused or unexcused. There would be no make-up possibility for missed work (a zero stays a zero). The passing grade for the course, to get credit for the prior failed year, would be a 75. If more than two days were missed, even for medical or other "good" reasons, the child would automatically fail the course (unless the local summer school had a (legitimate) "Saturday Make-up Day" option).

Principal Qualifications

Overview: Develop guidelines and certification requirements designed to incent persons with prior leadership and management experience to apply for principal and superintendent positions, and to favor hiring principals from outside the hiring school.

Benefit: Develop and hire principals with the leadership, training, and experience sufficient to lead today's highly complex school environments

Opposition: Some Principal candidates, the clique.

Cost: None

Savings: Huge indirect savings from improved management of schools

Discussion: All future principal hiring decisions must give preference to candidates from outside of the hiring school, or who have not worked in the hiring school in the past five years. Non-education leadership and management skills (business and/or military) would be weighted co-equally with past education experience. Course requirements for online certification programs must be expanded to include reputable business management courses comparable to a strong MBA program.

School Appointments Board

Overview: For the first year at a new school (three years if they were promoted from within the hiring school), new principals would not have sole authority for appointing special assignments (coaches, clubs, etc.). A screening board, chaired by the principal, would evaluate and select candidates by an open discussion and vote. After the initial year (or three years for internal hires) the board would become advisory with sole final authority reverting to the principal.

Benefit: Eliminate cronyism, and increase the qualifications of persons appointed to special extra-pay positions within a school. Rebuild trust in the system.

Opposition: Principals, the clique.

Cost: Trivial – approximately the combined annual cost of an extra-pay position for a soccer coach.

Savings: None

Discussion: Sole and unchallenged responsibility for appointments would no longer be help only by a new principal (or superintendent). Every school would name a board responsible for screening and selecting candidates for all of the extra-pay positions in a school. The board would be chaired by the principal, and include two other administrators selected each year by the school committee, the athletic director, and a teacher chosen by the teachers (union appointment or a full teacher vote). The teacher member would receive a nominal stipend (perhaps $1,000 per year and/or comp time and/or PDP credits).

The meeting would be closed to attendance other than the board. The board could invite a candidate or others with good insights for a specific position, to attend for that one discussion. All appointments would be based upon an open discussion and an open vote of all members. The board would only be required to report the final "winner," and would not be required to report the vote, nature of the discussion, etc.

After the first year (three years for a principal who had worked in the hiring school during any of the prior five years) the board recommendations would be advisory, and the sole authority to enact or change the board's recommendations would revert to the principal.

Elimination of Inclusion Classes

Overview: Dramatically improve diversified education by centering each class on being able to go at a pace an depth that challenges all members of that class.

Benefit: Ensure that abilities-leveled groups get the optimum education possible from qualified teachers. Eliminate dumbed-down education for all members of an inclusion class when differentiated learning cannot meet the needs of a wide range of abilities. Provide more challenging education for highest-ability members of a prior inclusion class. Improve the attention and educational quality for the struggling students

Opposition: Bureaucrats, legislators, some parents

Cost: Significant – some increase in the number of classrooms needed. Some increase in salaries to hire fully-qualified teachers to replace unqualified "co-teachers" and paraprofessionals for the subject matter.

Savings: None

Discussion: All classes would be ability-leveled (within reason) so that a teacher can optimize instruction to the particular ability level of the students. Previous inclusion classes with a co-teacher would be split into two classes with those same two teachers. Co-teachers without sufficient subject matter knowledge and qualifications would be replaced by fully qualified teachers. No student who was in a separate class due to ESL, SPED, or other issues, would be "included" into a regular class until the sending teacher, the parents, and SPED/ESL attest that the student is ready to keep pace with the receiving class.

Make-up days for truancy or excused absences

Overview: Ensure that all make-up time for an absence is used to accomplish a meaningful educational goal.

Benefit: Ensure children meet education requirements. Eliminate "make-work" approaches to give children credit for missed days without educational effort. Incent school attendance and reduce truancy.

Opposition: Students, parents

Cost: Monthly "study hall" or "detention" monitor for Saturday classes.

Savings: None

Discussion: Every student must meet the state minimum standard for days attending school. A maximum of fifteen missed school days, for any reason (excused or unexcused), would be allowed. Days for unexcused absences could not be made up. Excused absences could be made up in "official" after school extra help sessions, and in Saturday sessions held monthly from 9:00 to 2:00. In those Saturday sessions the student would have to work on a meaningful assignment(s) given by their teachers. The assignments would be graded. No credit for make-up days would ever be granted for just "…being in the building" without also being in a structured learning environment.

Merit Pay Board

Overview: A merit pay board would be responsible for preparing the initial set of merit pay recommendations based upon multiple sources of input. A Principal would have final authority to override the board recommendations.

Benefit: Eliminate cronyism, restore trust in the system, and increase the fairness of personnel evaluations.

Opposition: Principals, the clique.

Cost: Trivial – approximately the combined annual cost of an extra-pay position for a soccer coach.

Savings: None

Discussion: While the principal should make the final determination, merit pay cannot succeed, and trust rebuilt, if the determination of rewards is in the hands of a single principal and a single evaluation. Every school would name a board responsible for categorizing teacher evaluations for the purpose of merit pay, and making specific recommendations to the principal. The board would consist of two administrators, four department heads, and one teacher assigned by the local union (or vote of the school teachers if no union exists). The teacher member would receive a nominal stipend (perhaps $1,000 per year and/or comp time and/or PDP credits).

The goal of the board would be to categorize each person eligible for merit pay into one of three categories: The top 20% of persons (A), the bottom 10% of persons (C), and the middle 70% (B).

Determination would be made in May, and go into effect the following start of school year.

Consideration must be given to at least the following:

- A department head ranking for each department that gives the department head's A-B-C ranking of all his/her teachers. (At least one "A" and one "C" for any department of six or more teachers.)

- Personnel evaluations for the current and prior years

- A mandated survey of students during April of each year asking to "…list the five best teachers" in the school. (This recognizes and incents the student's co-responsibility for educational success.)

- A mandated survey of parents during April of each year asking to "…list the five best teachers" in the school. (This recognizes and incents the parent's co-responsibility for educational success.)

- Non-paid contributions to the school by the person, above and beyond job requirements

- Student performance on standardized tests that must include an allowance for the level of class (standard, CP, Honors, AP…).

- A group discussion about the individuals, as needed

The meeting would be closed to attendance other than the board and any candidates or "witnesses" that were invited by the board. The final determination of the A-B-C categories would be based upon an open discussion and an open vote. The final list would be delivered to the principal for his/her final review, with the principal authorized to make any unilateral changes to the list he/she determines are necessary. Any changes must be reported back to the Merit Pay Board.

Those in category A would receive merit pay bonuses for the following school year, on top of regular contractual salary. Category B would see no change to their contractual salaries. Those in category C would be subject to the requirements of the school's formal evaluation system for "weak" employees – including such possibilities as required training or termination. A teacher in category A or B for the current year could not be terminated other than for non-instructional issues (drugs, inappropriate activities, etc.)

Neither the board nor the principal would be required to make public the final categories, and would not be required to report the vote, nature of the discussion, etc. Results would only be used to determine merit pay categories.

Special Education Accommodations and Goals

Overview: Eliminate accommodations that undermine special education for those who really need the strong benefits of SPED. Restore the original superb goals of special education. Eliminate accommodations that destroy a teacher's ability to engage students and set high expectations.

Benefit: Improve educational results for all special education students. Enhance attitudes and expectations of students and their parents. Eliminate the high degree of abuse in the current system

Opposition: Students, a minority of parents, bureaucrats, legislators, some special education professionals

Cost: None

Savings: None

Discussion: Immediately eliminate the use of accommodations such as "…can retake any failed test" and "…gets an 'A' for doing 50% of the expected work." Delete all such provisions from existing IEPs and 504s. A retest would still be allowed if the teacher or head of special education felt that other IEP accommodations were not provided (extra time, use of calculators or outlines, small group or private settings, etc.).

A special education student with demonstrated need for accommodations should be in a class environment focused on challenging him/her to the limit of abilities, and teaching the student workarounds for his/her condition.

The goal of every IEP or 504 should become helping the student learn how to deal with his/her difficulty so that by no later than the start of senior year the plan is terminated. This will not always be possible, but we are cheating our children if we keep them dependent upon this "extra help" forever.

Prevent reclassification of a school based upon aggregate data

Overview: Eliminate school and teacher sanctions that are based solely or mainly upon aggregate student failure rates, or standardized test scores, without looking at underlying conditions. Allow children to fail so that we can help them succeed.

Benefit: Within two academic terms achieve a very substantial improvement in student effort, parent support, retained learning, and educational performance.

Opposition: A minority of parents, students (at first), bureaucrats.

Cost: Unknown

Savings: None

Discussion: Schools must not be allowed to be categorized solely based upon a statistical measure such as failures, standardized test scores, or graduation rates. It is perfectly sensible to use such results as an index for identifying schools to be visited for evaluation. However, such statistics must never be the reason, in and of themselves, for the final conclusion.

It is bureaucratic ineptitude of the highest magnitude to think a single statistical measure can provide an accurate picture of what is happening in a school.

If a school triggers an evaluation based upon failure rates or low test scores, a site evaluation by qualified DOE and teacher personnel is certainly warranted. The evaluation team must include as many working teachers with classroom knowledge (from distant schools, akin to occasional "jury duty") as it does career DoE bureaucrats. The site evaluation might end up determining that the school was at fault, and it should be "…moved down a level." But before such a finding is made, the full evaluation must include:

A review of all specific students who failed, to categorize them by:

- Attendance rates and truancy
- Homework grades
- Disciplinary records
- Extra help sessions attended
- Parental involvement in conferences
- An analysis of failures that <u>cannot</u> be tied to truancy, discipline, etc.
- A classroom observation (unannounced) for any teacher with a "high" (criteria TBD) incidence of failures that cannot be tied to truancy, discipline, etc.
- A review of teacher evaluations for any teacher with a "high" (criteria TBD) incidence of failures that cannot be tied to truancy, discipline, etc.
- A review of the socioeconomic basis of the enrolled students to determine external factors influencing performance. Comparisons of a extreme-case urban school (high free lunch, ESL, etc.) to an extreme-case affluent suburban school is unreasonable and ignores statistical reality.

After a <u>full</u> site evaluation, a school can only be sanctioned if the analysis of all these factors proves that the school is deficient in its educational methods.

Focused PDPs

Overview: Replace the out-of-control and costly PDP system with focused PDPs that help teachers in critical areas.

Benefit: Eliminate dozens of wasted hours per teacher in courses with little or no value. Reduce costs significantly. Increase training in areas most needed by weaker teachers. Grant significant ability and autonomy for local schools to tailor training to their specific needs.

Opposition: Bureaucrats, colleges, and PDP development companies.

Cost: None

Savings: Very significant

Discussion: Immediately reduce PDP requirements to focus on the areas of highest needs.

- Not more than ten hours per year of state-mandated training. Bureaucrats must prioritize or alternate the needs, rather than "…just add more."
- Ten hours per year of training determined by the school to meet their specific needs
- Any teacher in Merit Pay Category "C" must take an additional 10 hours per year of instruction, as directed by the school, in one or more of the four core areas:
    - Discipline
    - Explaining versus presenting material
    - Diversified learning
    - Engaging students and instilling pride

Limited "in-context" liability for teachers and schools

Overview: Shelter teachers and schools from liability for incidental actions that are, in context, reasonable, proper, and good for the students. This specifically applies to incidental "touching" or "force" used to break up a fight, and to actions such as touching an arm or shoulder to comfort a distressed child.

Benefit: Allow teachers to stop fights before a student is hurt when the context for any teacher action is stopping an existing fight. Allow teachers to innocently comfort a distressed student when the context for any teacher actions is genuine concern for a child. Allow teachers to better engage positively with students. Eliminate frivolous hearings and liability for teachers taking actions that, in context are reasonable, proper, and in the best interests of our children.

Opposition: Bureaucrats and some parents.

Cost: None

Savings: Very significant – school legal expenses and meeting time

Discussion: Teachers and schools need to be sheltered from liability for actions that, <u>in context</u>, are both reasonable and proper. These are actions that allow teachers to relate, protect, and engage our children. *<u>None</u> of these limits are intended to apply to inappropriate acts such as punishing a child or contact meant to be of a sexual nature.*

Examples of actions that must be allowed and protected include:

- (Distressed child) Comforting a distressed child must allow for responsible touching of hands or shoulders in the context of holding a hand or hugging shoulders.
- (Students fighting) A teacher must be encouraged to break up a fight between children. Brief incidental contact with genitalia or breasts in the middle of such a fight must be accepted as likely to be forced by the act of "joining the fray." A degree of "force" must be expected and allowed, though violence of any kind is not.

The key here is the idea of looking at something "<u>in context</u>." If the only incident for a teacher accused of "inappropriate touching" is one time over the past six years she stepped in the middle of a fight and incidentally brushed a child's breast, that must never be allowed to be treated at the same level as an action of sexual misconduct!

The above plans are presented as outlines for good reason – the idea is to present the foundation of a complete solution, and let others with far more ability and experience work out the details. If we have the courage to take on the bureaucrats and the clique, these changes all <u>will</u> work.

(Chapter 28)
Concluding Remarks

I became a teacher because children are the passion of my life. I know they are capable of so very much more that we give them the chance to achieve. We cheat them every day when we expect less from them, and dumb down our teaching efforts to meet the needs of some career DoE bureaucrat miles from any school, who claims to be an "educator," yet has no concept of what goes on in an actual classroom and is not held accountable for bad policies.

Are some teachers a problem in the system? Absolutely. But the problem is not the 5% who should not be teachers, just as 5% of bartenders, accountants, software developers, and plumbers should be fired. The real teacher part of the problem is the <u>majority</u> of teachers that the system and bureaucrats have driven to the point of frustration, anger, defensiveness, and a classic "bunker mentality."

But even the negative impact of burned-out teachers is <u>trivial</u> compared to the unintended impact of well-meaning laws, unqualified and cronyistic principals, inclusion classes, a special education system that has been hijacked by parents, and the policies of inept career DoE bureaucrats. We have created an environment that rewards lack of effort by children, and allows parents to find ways to get their child through high school without learning.

The problem is the <u>system</u> – driven by unqualified career bureaucrats, inept principals, no-show parents, and burned-out teachers who have given up.

Teachers get the brunt of the criticism because they are the most visible target. They are the "cash cow" for commentators – an easy and lightning-rod topic for exciting an audience. It was exactly because of hearing such views, even from a commentator I highly respected, that I decided to write this book. It was only a passing joke, but a comment that the solution to education problems was "…just shoot all the teachers" struck home. My hope was that if I could lift the curtain a bit, one of the Margery Eagans[110] of the world might see what the system so carefully hides, and conclude "…hmmmmm, maybe there is a little more to the story than just bad teachers." If just a few of the best and brightest start looking behind the curtain, then real progress will start to become possible.

---

[110] Boston newspaper reporter and radio talk show host

Yes, there are some bad teachers in the system, and <u>all</u> teachers (including me) need an attitude adjustment after all the frustration and anger from years dealing with a failing system. Yet teachers are actually a very small contributor to the rapid decline in the quality of education. These same teachers, especially all those good ones who have been burned out by the endless bureaucracy, are the very ones who can help turn education around. We just need to let our teachers do something they used to be allowed to do twenty years ago – focus on teaching our children to excel.

Perhaps the answer to all the world's ills is not to "…just shoot all the teachers." Perhaps it is as simple as fixing education by allowing good teachers to teach again.

Made in the USA
Middletown, DE
15 February 2015